Library 2035

Library 2035
Imagining the Next Generation of Libraries

Edited by Sandra Hirsh

ROWMAN & LITTLEFIELD
Lanham • Boulder • New York • London

Published by Rowman & Littlefield
An imprint of The Rowman & Littlefield Publishing Group, Inc.
4501 Forbes Boulevard, Suite 200, Lanham, Maryland 20706
www.rowman.com

86-90 Paul Street, London EC2A 4NE

Selection and editorial matter © The Rowman & Littlefield Publishing Group, Inc., 2024
Copyright in individual chapters is held by the respective chapter authors.

All rights reserved. No part of this book may be reproduced in any form or by any electronic or mechanical means, including information storage and retrieval systems, without written permission from the publisher, except by a reviewer who may quote passages in a review.

British Library Cataloguing in Publication Information Available

Library of Congress Cataloging-in-Publication Data Available

ISBN: 978-1-5381-8039-6 (cloth)
ISBN: 978-1-5381-8040-2 (pbk.)
ISBN: 978-1-5381-8041-9 (electronic)

To those who have inspired me and helped me achieve my dreams . . .

my grandparents, Helen and Lewis Goldstein;
my mom, Gail Schlachter;
my husband, Jay Hirsh;

my colleagues, mentors, and collaborators:
Eugenie Prime, Christine Anderson,
Linda Main, and Elaine Hall;

and to all current and future library leaders;
who are and will continue to transform the libraries of the future
and better the world for all of us.

Contents

Introduction Sandra Hirsh		1
	PART I: LANDSCAPE	**5**
Chapter 1	The Janus Library Joseph Janes	7
Chapter 2	Predictions about Future Technology in Libraries and Epistemic Collapse: Laws and Models Jason Griffey	13
Chapter 3	Sustainable Libraries in 2035: Refuge. Resistance. Resilience. Regeneration. Rebekkah Smith Aldrich	21
Chapter 4	Teetering on the Edge of Trust Cliff Erin Berman	29
Chapter 5	Stories: At the Heart of It All Chris Brown	35
	PART II: COMMUNITY	**41**
Chapter 6	There Is No Future of Libraries. There Are Many. R. David Lankes	43

Chapter 7	The Future of Libraries: A User- and Community-Centered Perspective *Anthony Chow*	49
Chapter 8	The Library as Community Enthusiast, Champion, and Advocate *Patty Wong*	57
Chapter 9	We Are Not Alone: Libraries Making a Stronger Impact in a Global Community *Lynn Silipigni Connaway*	63

PART III: EQUITY AND INCLUSION — 69

Chapter 10	Equity Is a Necessary Foundation *Nicole A. Cooke*	71
Chapter 11	Libraries, Trust, and the Cultural Booty Call *Veronda J. Pitchford*	79
Chapter 12	The Library in 2035 Will Be *Universal* *Annie Norman*	87
Chapter 13	Open, Inclusive, and Diverse: The Academic Library of 2035 *Alexia Hudson-Ward*	93
Chapter 14	The Future of School Libraries: It's About Equity *Joyce Kasman Valenza and Debra Kachel*	99

PART IV: ORGANIZATIONS — 107

Chapter 15	The Future of Libraries: Adapting Our Mission and Our Buildings to Demographic Growth and Change *Kelvin Watson*	109

Chapter 16 Collaborative Collections and Content Considerations in Research and Academic Libraries: Possible Pathways by 2035   115
Raymond Pun and Tarida Anantachai

Chapter 17 Survive or Thrive: Can Community College Libraries Surmount the Challenges They Face?   121
Peter Hepburn

Chapter 18 New Jersey School Libraries 2035   129
Ewa Dziedzic-Elliott

PART V: LIBRARY WORKERS   137

Chapter 19 The Library CEO: Money in the Bank, People on the Bus   139
K. Matthew Dames and Tony Zanders

Chapter 20 Wellness for Librarians: Innovative Solutions to Foster Transformation   147
Loida Garcia-Febo

Chapter 21 Future Library Job Descriptions 2035   155
Stacey A. Aldrich and Jarrid P. Keller

PART VI: VISION   161

Chapter 22 Come Back Yesterday: Paradoxes of Library Progress   163
Joel A. Nichols

Chapter 23 Changing Our How, More Than Seeing Clearly Our What   169
Miguel Figueroa and Lessa Kanani'opua Pelayo-Lozada

Chapter 24 Immersive and Virtual Technologies: The Future of Libraries   175
Susan W. Alman

Chapter 25 The Way Forward for Libraries 183
Sandra Hirsh

Bibliography 191
About the Editor 217
About the Contributing Authors 219

Library 2035 Webcast Series

Sandra Hirsh, editor, has hosted webcast interviews with contributing authors to discuss their chapters and their vision for the library of 2035. The webcast accompanies this book and can be accessed at: https://sites.google.com/sjsu.edu/library2035/home.

Introduction

Sandra Hirsh

I am honored to present *Library 2035: Imagining the Next Generation of Libraries*. As a follow-up to *Library 2020: Today's Leading Visionaries Describe Tomorrow's Library*, edited by Joseph Janes, this book aims to forecast the landscape, services, community, profession, and future of libraries over the next decade. While it is a forecast, it offers the reader a reflection of where libraries are today and insight into how technology, society, and even the environment (e.g., climate change, politics, economics) will influence the priorities and sustainability of libraries of the future.

Why 2035? By looking a decade in advance, we are encouraged to see the possibilities that are not only just ahead of us (in the next five years), but also on the horizon. Consider for a moment how quickly things changed for libraries between 2020 and 2023. Now triple that. What will libraries look like a decade from now? What services will they offer? What will patrons be asking of libraries, and how will libraries remain resilient and relevant to the communities they serve? How will libraries respond to continued globalization, artificial intelligence (AI), and other technologies not yet imagined? These questions and more are explored throughout this book.

There were many milestones and advances predicted by the authors of *Library 2020*. The popularity and demand for digital collections increased as expected, as did concerns over the digital divide of all communities being able to access those collections. Correlating to the era of digital collections was how content was accessed—with Google and other search engines becoming the default platform for many information seekers. *Library 2020* authors further addressed the increasing need for librarians to help guide information users on how to responsibly search, access, and interpret that information—much of this happening via chat or text messaging. Speaking of access, personal devices were accurately forecasted to be the preferred method for information-seeking and communicating, increasing the need for library outreach to incorporate social media into their engagement strategies. With more and more collections going digital, fewer patrons would be coming to the library in 2020 for materials; however, programming (makerspaces, story times, workshops, etc.) would increase in demand, and the concept of "library as place" was born, reinvigorating the design of library spaces as well as programming. Other key topics within the library space in 2020 included equity, diversity, inclusion (EDI), and access; the increased dependence on partnerships and collaborations; and the need for ongoing advocacy to sustain the library's presence and relevancy in the communities they served.

While the *Library 2020* authors accurately identified many of the trends that would impact libraries and librarians, one thing in particular could not have been predicted: the COVID-19 pandemic and the global disruption of how societies learned, worked, engaged, and communicated. Also unpredicted were the critical issues that came simultaneously to the forefront of all societies, such as social unrest surrounding issues of racism against blacks and Asians, economic stressors due to worldwide unemployment and the halt of the global commerce infrastructure, and the 2020 elections followed by political upheaval and an attack on the U.S. Capitol. These factors have influenced libraries since 2020 and set a new course for libraries and librarians. Furthermore, and even more recently (as I write this in 2023), libraries have seen a dramatic increase in book bans and materials challenges that appear to have undone much of the progress made over the past decades for freedom of access. If I were to coin a single term for what happened to libraries in 2020, I'd call it *transformative*: transformative in response, transformative in service, transformative in innovation, and transformative to how libraries fulfill their core mission.

When I was approached about writing *Library 2035*, I was honored to be considered. I thought, "What a dynamic opportunity to bring together industry thought leaders from this point of our collective history, past and present, and predict what the library of 2035 will be." What was important to me was bringing together key thought leaders within the library field and offering a broad range of perspectives and experiences representing all types of libraries, specifically public, academic, and school libraries. The twenty-nine contributing authors were selected based on my respect and admiration for their work as well as for their leadership and impact on the field of librarianship. While the authors were able to select the topic of their choice for this project, I encouraged them to reflect upon the future of libraries, including the challenges, opportunities, threats, modes of service, etc., that they believed would impact our collective future the most. With that in mind, the authors approached their chapters by answering the following: "The library in 2035 [will be/must be/must not be/will not be/can't be . . .]." I am honored and grateful for all the authors who contributed to this project, including Joseph Janes, the editor of *Library 2020*.

What has resulted in *Library 2035* is a dynamic collaboration of diverse ideas and visions, hopes and concerns, threats and opportunities, and predictions for libraries in 2035. While many of the topics presented in this book build on some of those predicted for 2020, such as EDI and the importance of collaboration and partnerships, the urgency of some of these issues is more important than ever. For example, the issues concerning EDI, as well as access and belonging, are perhaps more on the forefront than ever before. Climate change is another factor that will alter societies' livelihoods and will impact space design, programming, and services of all libraries. The rapidity of technological innovation only seems to speed up year over year. Take a moment to consider the technologies that were on the horizon just three years ago, such as AI and ChatGPT; these topics are mentioned in the majority of the enclosed chapters, and these technologies may forever change our outlooks and predictions for the future. *Library 2035: Imagining the Next Generation of Libraries* is reflective, yes, but it should also serve as a guide to think of what is possible.

To all the contributing authors, thank you! *Library 2035* would not have come to fruition without your expertise, perspectives, and insights. I also want to thank my publisher, Charles Harmon, for all of his support and for considering me for this project. A huge and heartfelt thank-you goes to my colleague, Elaine Hall, who has helped me prepare several books (including this one!), presentations, and research projects for more than a decade! She started as my research assistant when she was at the School of Information at San José State University, and we have worked together synergistically ever since. I would also like to thank my husband, Jay; my daughter Hayley and her husband, Chris; and my daughter Leah, for their love and support. They enrich my life and always make me feel more hopeful and excited about the future.

I
Landscape

Part I: Landscape invites you to envision the environmental factors influencing the library of 2035, including the threats and opportunities that exist, and some of the foundational elements needed to uphold the library's role in connecting with its communities in ways that offer hope, value, trust, and resiliency. The authors of chapters 1 through 5 share their vision for how the library of 2035 will perform in this landscape, specifically noting that these libraries will:

- need to take care in crossing the street *(Janes)*.
- be organized and interacted with by the public very differently than libraries were in 2023 *(Griffey)*.
- be a place of refuge, resistance, resilience, and regeneration *(Smith Aldrich)*.
- have to make a choice between becoming a privacy safe haven for all or fully stepping into the world of surveillance capitalism *(Berman)*.
- use storytelling to advocate and promote the library as an essential community entity *(Brown)*.

When considering the library of 2035, we often begin with envisioning the "place" of the library; however, how relevant is that to the library of the future? Libraries are in constant transition. While this is a good thing, libraries must also be mindful of how the library is perceived from the community's perspective. As Janes notes in chapter 1, relevancy is determined by how well the library meets the needs, views, experiences, and expectations of the users who access the library environment. The library of 2035 will need to align its services to match these expectations; not doing so may be detrimental to the library's existence.

OpenAI and generated media are creating both opportunities and challenges for how libraries will procure, manage, and provide access to information in the future. In chapter 2, Griffey highlights how the library of 2035 will continue performing its role in recording and archiving our historical past while also helping society create and access customized user-created and user-manipulated media such as books/stories, video/movies, and music. These developments are making it challenging for libraries to manage the explosion of generated content today, alluding to the increased complexity libraries will face in managing content and collections in libraries in 2035. It's almost unimaginable.

When thinking about the resiliency of libraries in this landscape, we must identify both the opportunities and the threats that are present. Smith Aldrich in chapter 3 emphasizes the myriad of external forces that threaten the future for libraries, such as climate change, natural disasters, and economic stressors; however, she notes the important role libraries are playing as community connectors and first responders that can bring hope and resiliency to the communities they serve. Berman, in chapter 4, highlights the challenge libraries face in terms of balancing the need to provide access to information and, at the same time, protect the privacy of users in their use of that information. In particular, she discusses the importance of ensuring the trust relationship between libraries and their users doesn't break to sustain this resiliency.

The beauty of any landscape is the stories it holds and creates. Brown, in chapter 5, highlights the important role of these stories—and the power of storytelling—to advocate for the value of libraries, as well as the unique and diverse characteristics of the community it serves.

Archived webcasts of author interviews are available at: https://sites.google.com/sjsu.edu/library2035/home

1
The Janus Library

Joseph Janes

The library of 2035 should take care in crossing the street.

I'm looking at a picture from a summer class I taught at the University of Toronto called "Rethinking the Library." Here is a brief excerpt from the syllabus to give you an idea of what we were up to:

> Libraries aren't what they used to be—thank goodness. As with most institutions, they grow, change and evolve as times and surrounding contexts change. This is what makes them vital, strong and ever responsive to the needs of their communities and clienteles.
>
> And yet—in recent times the very concept of the "library" has been thrown into doubt. In times of dramatic and profound change, the concept of the library could use a fresh look and, perhaps, some renovation. In this course, we will explore what "the library" has been, what it is, and what it should become.

One of the class exercises was intended to help students think through two important and connected aspects of libraries. First, I drew a big, amorphous shape on the board (which affectionately became known as "the blob") and asked them to brainstorm and fill the inside with the functions and features typical of libraries. No great surprises emerged here: space, presence, clientele, community, place, collections, materials, staff, resources, help, support, organization, and service.

I then turned their attention to the outside of "the blob"—and asked them what institutions, organizations, or phenomena were close to what libraries did or represented, or which shared features or functions with them. Who, in other words, were our neighbors and competitors? After more brainstorming, ringing the blob were, again, many familiar names: museums, archives, community networks and centers, social service agencies, daycare centers, bookstores, and schools, as well as Google, Wikipedia, Amazon, YouTube, and BitTorrent.[1] The point behind this exercise was to get students to identify and think through the things that made libraries and their work unique, and how they were similar to, and differed from, some of those neighbors and competitors, as a foundation for thinking forward to what libraries could and should be.

Looking at it now, it's clear that this picture—which I'll spare you—is from many years ago (and not only because it shows a younger and thinner me posing somewhat uncomfortably in front of the blob). Snuggling up next to Netflix, we find Blockbuster; across the way is MySpace; and waaay up in the corner lurks Second Life, none of which had the staying power of their cousins listed above. The obvious and trite observation is that Technology Changes All The Time and that libraries have to be aware of and responsive to that. True, and . . . I suspect if we were to repeat this exercise today, there would be a different set of technological neighbors and a sharper and more nuanced focus on communities and connectedness, cultural competence, equity, and social justice.

Which is exactly the point. Note that Blockbuster, MySpace, and Second Life withered while Netflix, Facebook, and other augmented reality systems thrived, and not purely for technological reasons. All organizations, including libraries, exist in multiple overlapping and occasionally contradictory contexts: technological certainly, along with societal, legal, economic, political, cultural, linguistic ones, and more. These contexts impact what any particular library is and does, as well as the overall notion of "libraries" in general.

Further, these contexts are rarely static, and that dynamic has prompted changes and innovations in libraries over the decades, as have developments from within our own domain. Limiting ourselves largely to the North American context over the last century and a half, let's consider the following:

- The public library movement, accelerated and greatly enhanced by Andrew Carnegie's building program, gave rise to the idea that the local public library is expected or assumed in large sections of the country. Indeed, approximately 80 percent of public libraries in the United States are considered either small or rural, or both. Notably, Carnegie's largesse was limited to building and fixtures, leaving the development of collections and staffing to the hosting community.
- The Williamson Report,[2] commissioned by Carnegie in 1923, laid out perceived shortcomings in the preparation and education of library staff leading to a broad migration from baccalaureate- to master's-level degree programs in librarianship over the next decades.
- The development, also in the late nineteenth and early twentieth centuries, of the service function in academic libraries, expanded and augmented them from repositories that were largely used by faculty for research to

more fully featured institutions serving students and other members of the institution and in many cases beyond.
- The standardization of cataloging, again in the late nineteenth century, laid the foundation for libraries to share data and systems. Cataloging evolved from institution-specific and idiosyncratic methods to what became the nearly universal Dewey and Library of Congress systems, followed by catalog card distribution systems and then networks (including OCLC and the rise of copy cataloging).
- The development of periodical indexing and, later, electronic databases, and eventually, full-text retrieval massively increased and accelerated availability and access of serial and scholarly literature.
- And, yes, lots of technology changes have occurred over time. Consider the technological evolution starting all the way back with typewriters, through filing systems, early adoption of mainframe computer technologies (notably in cataloging and circulation), personal computers, compact discs, networking, the internet, the Web, integrated library systems, standardization, and mass digitization efforts. We all know the pace and scope of those changes will likely only accelerate in days to come.

Against that backdrop, after all those innovations and transitions, if you walk into most public or academic libraries today, they would be familiar and recognizable from what you might have seen twenty-five, fifty, or even one hundred years ago, at least in some ways. To be sure, there would be differences—more spaces dedicated for seating, study, collaboration, and research; less space for stacks and materials; a different mix of materials; a greater prevalence and influence of technology; quite possibly the lack of a distinctive reference desk in favor of a more generalized service point; and certainly a broader and more representative staff and clientele.

Thus, there's a level of predictability, expectation, and comfort with libraries as they've been typically known—a sense of continuity, that a new-to-you library resembles the one you knew as a child, as a student, or in another setting. This is all to the good; libraries aren't necessarily the only institutions or organizations we could say the same of. It also similarly bespeaks a sense of continuity within the library field and profession, which is rightly often concerned with long timescales in terms of collections, preservation, and durability, though as with many phenomena, too much of that can be too much.

While libraries in general remain somewhat familiar, the library of today cannot *only* be the library of yesterday, or, worse still, the day before yesterday. Nor, I would posit, can it necessarily *only* be the library of the day after tomorrow. Libraries must grow, change, and evolve. That said, there are equivalent, if distinct, perils in *too much too fast*, and *not enough* or *not fast enough*, running Scylla-and-Charybdis risks of obsolescence or irrelevancy. Moreover, there is the additional, orthogonal challenge of being aligned with what any particular community or clientele wants and needs, as well as having a purpose, mission, and operation that fits those wants and needs, that is right, workable, acceptable, and palatable to them. It is further important to recognize that, given the complexity and breadth of many communities, there is no single "right," but there are many potential "wrongs," which can lead to disassociation and disaffection.

Many discussions and conversations about the future of libraries involve some question like: "What is a library for?" This is fine if often unhelpfully generic. For the vast majority of library users, I suspect the more pointed and relevant questions include:

- "What is *this* library for?"
- "What is *our* library for?"
- "What is *my* library for?"

Each person has their own view of this, shaped by their prior experiences with libraries (if any), generalized or societal expectations, and the overall tenor of the area and community, among other factors. As "the library" conforms, or fails to, with each individual's vision, so will their opinion and acceptance of the library rise or fall. Their opinion of the library will, in turn, contribute to the clientele's collective perception, level of use, and support.

Our responsibility, as librarians, is to explore and understand those individual and collective visions and aspirations for our libraries and then overlay that on the grubby realities of money, staffing, space, time, laws, technology, bathroom maintenance, politics, and so on. These visions and aspirations need to be filtered through our professional experience, expertise, and judgment concerning collections, services, and resources to come up with an operating strategy that can actually work. This is all necessary so librarians can do the best job we can to meet those needs and expectations in the real world, which is increasingly and rapidly changing in myriad, and often conflicting, ways. How hard can that be?

We should also acknowledge that we have our own perceptions, wants, desires, and expectations of libraries, particularly the ones in which we work, which can at times overshadow or obscure those of our clients. This is natural and understandable, likely the case for many professions and institutions, and occasionally deeply problematic in obvious ways.

> Our responsibility, as librarians, is to explore and understand those individual and collective visions and aspirations for our libraries and then overlay that on the grubby realities of money, staffing, space, time, laws, technology, bathroom maintenance, politics, and so on.

So, you might be asking, where does "Janus" come in? (No, it's not a narcissistic typo.) Many people know that Janus was a Roman deity, the source of the name of January; he may have been the god of beginnings, though there is a consensus that he was the spirit of archways, doors, and gates, and he was typically depicted with two faces, one looking forward and one back.

As a metaphor for thinking about libraries and their future, Janus is doubly helpful in reminding us of the importance of balancing yesterday and tomorrow. Looking back only to the familiar, the traditional, and the comfortable might be easy, though it's clearly insufficient and myopic. However, it's equally insufficient to look exclusively forward without regard for what people are likely to expect; the library needs to foster a sense of continuity to help ensure people don't find themselves bewildered and dismissed by the library and its mission.

The Janus metaphor is also apt for an institution that so often provides gates and doorways, figuratively and occasionally literally, for people and communities of all kinds, new worlds, new ideas, new visions, and new versions of themselves. We can even stretch that metaphor juuuust a bit further, to extend to the renewal of libraries' visions and versions of themselves as well.

CONCLUSION

No library is ever finished. (Arguably, that extends even to the ones that close, as their influence and impact stays with the people they touched.) Libraries are eternally in transition, reflecting, being shaped by, and indeed also in turn shaping their environments. Libraries and librarians have always been adaptable—usually at moderate timescales, occasionally much more rapidly. Who would have imagined, in late 2019, that services like curbside materials pickup, remote story hours, lending mobile hotspots, and emergency full-text online book lending would have to be spun up on the spot? And yet it was, to the great relief of many of our users and communities. And who would have imagined, within a year or two, some of those same users and communities would be attacking—in multiple senses of the word—libraries, staff, and boards, for collections and services they'd been providing uncontroversially for years, leading to a coordinated and shocking rise in challenges to materials? And yet they did.

The path ahead is not always clearly marked, but it is always important to keep moving, keep progressing, keep developing new ideas and new approaches. As we forge ahead, each in our own settings, toward 2035, remember the advice you probably got from your mom, as I did: "Look twice before crossing the street—and then go."

NOTES

1. "BitTorrent," (2023), https://www.bittorrent.com/.
2. Charles C. Williamson et al., "Training for Library Service; a Report Prepared for the Carnegie Corporation of New York," Ann Arbor, Michigan: University Microfilms, 1923.

2

Predictions about Future Technology in Libraries and Epistemic Collapse

LAWS AND MODELS

Jason Griffey

The library of 2035 will be organized and interacted with by the public very differently than libraries were in 2023 (when this chapter was written).

The difference will be largely due to the explosion of machine learning tools involved in creating, discovering, evaluating, and manipulating text, images, audio, and other forms of information. As I'm writing this, machine learning systems have recently become the subject of popular public conversation due to the emergence of ChatGPT.[1] However, this emergence is not surprising to anyone who has been paying attention to the rapid rise of what are popularly called Generative Large Language Model (GLLM)[2] systems.

The last year has seen an explosion of public-facing machine learning systems that have one core thing in common: they appear to produce new things previously seen as solely within the domain of humans. For example, machine learning systems like . . .

- DALL-E,[3] Stable Diffusion,[4] and Midjourney[5] can produce entirely novel visual media from textual prompts;
- Microsoft's VALL-E[6] and Google's AudioLM[7] can produce novel audio media;
- OpenAI's GPT models, such as ChatGPT, can produce novel textual media; and
- OpenAI's Codex[8] and Salesforce's CodeT5[9] can produce novel computer code.

It is difficult to overstate the speed with which these technologies are progressing. To use just one example from the above, OpenAI's first GPT model was described in a white paper on June 11, 2018. GPT-2 was announced in February 2019, and the real turning point was GPT-3 in May 2020, when significant breakthroughs were achieved in text completion. The most popular service built using GPT-3, ChatGPT, is one of the fastest-growing technology services ever. It launched in November 2022 and reached one hundred million active users in only two months; by way of comparison, it took Apple four years to sell one hundred million iPhones, and Facebook just over four years to reach one hundred million users. In March 2023, OpenAI announced the release of GPT-4, offering another enormous leap in complexity and ability. Within five years, we have gone from the idea of a generative pretrained transformer to one that can pass the bar exam in the top 10 percent of test-takers.

The techniques used by OpenAI to generate these technological leaps are not secrets. Their exact methodology might be slightly different from one company to another, but all machine learning systems rely on three central things: raw computing power, data, and training. Increase any of these, and the system will get better (as judged by its users): faster and more flexible in its answers, accurate, believable, and capable. Moreover, as systems begin to feed one another (e.g., ChatGPT reinforcing Codex[10]), the degree to which all of them will get better and faster is going to be extraordinary.

LAWS PREDICTING THE FUTURE OF COMPUTER POWER

We can predict the degree to which computing power will grow, at least within a minimal margin of error, thanks to the combination of Moore's Law[11] and Koomey's Law[12] of computing. Moore's Law is the more familiar of the two and states that computing power doubles roughly every eighteen months while at the same time halving in price to produce. Koomey's Law is the corollary to Moore's Law, except regarding electrical consumption per unit of computing. Koomey's Law says that for a stable amount of computing effort, the energy required to do that computing will half, again, roughly every eighteen months. Both of these laws have slowed somewhat in the last decade for computing power overall. However, the computing power specifically designed for machine learning has increased at a much faster rate than even Moore's Law would predict. In 2019, Stanford University reported that starting in 2012, machine learning computing power was approaching a doubling rate of closer to 3.4 months.[13]

Computing power can grow in other ways relative to the difficulty of machine learning models; the models themselves could be written in a more efficient language that requires less computing power to achieve the same ends, or breakthroughs could be made in how models are trained that reduce the power consumption. Nevertheless, even without those potential efficiencies, the moment you are reading this is the most expensive, slowest, and least-efficient that computing will ever be. Computing power only ever gets better, faster, cheaper, and more energy-efficient over time. This type of progress is radically unintuitive to the human condition and counter to many of our expectations. These ever-increasing improvements, combined with our general inability to fully understand exponential growth, make machine learning and artificial intelligence (AI) particularly challenging for humans to understand.

THE CATEGORY COLLAPSE

What does all this mean for the library in 2035? How does this continued growth of GLLM systems affect the work of creating, organizing, discovering, and preserving information? To put it bluntly, it explodes our foundational understanding of data, information, media, and creation to the degree where we may be passing a fundamental boundary in the true sense of a paradigm shift. One of the core indications of a paradigm shift, outlined by Thomas Kuhn's[14] foundational work in the philosophy of science, is that when you have a field amid such a shift, individuals on both sides of the epistemological divide will use the same word, but that word will mean entirely, radically different things to each. For example, before Darwin, the word *evolution* was used to describe the growth and spread of life on earth. However, Darwin's use of the word belied a fundamental difference in meaning, grounding, and predictive power than did the pre-Darwinian meaning of the word. There is a risk, I feel, that the future of the library is going to involve exactly this sort of epistemological rift when discussing words like *book*, *movie*, or *metadata*.

In his keynote address to the NISO Plus 2023 conference, Dr. David Weinberger hinted at one piece of this category collapse. His talk, titled "Unanticipated Metadata in the Age of the Net & the Age of AI,"[15] discussed how the idea of metadata is reduced to an epistemological perspective rather than a content type when AI is used as the inquiry tool for a corpus. It has always been the case that metadata is, in some sense, dependent on perspective; when you want the date of publication but only have the title, the former is the data and the latter is the metadata, but reverse the query and so, too, does what is considered metadata. With machine learning systems, however, we have a combination of factors that will complicate matters. In a machine learning system, not only is the entirety of the content of a piece of media part of the "index," but the syntactical relationships—both within a specific work and its relationships to other works in the same data model represented as vectors in Nth dimensional space—can be a part of the decision to return a specific answer.

In the case of machine learning driven discovery, it is impossible to see inside the black box of how the output was chosen or constructed. You can see the training data, and you can see the training methodology/algorithms, but there is no way to understand the totality of the weighting and vectors that make up the connections inside the model. Either everything is metadata, or nothing is, for an large language model (LLM) system.

NEW OPPORTUNITIES THROUGH GENERATED MEDIA

In 2035, there will also be a related collapse of what is understood as media. Today, we have the initial building blocks of a world of entirely generated media. In this near future, nothing is "fixed," and the things most people read, watch, listen to, or interact/play with are generated by machine learning systems. What does it mean to be a "novel" when the reader can access a GLLM or similar system, and type something like: "I want to read a fantasy novel, but with an Agatha Christie style plot, with no fighting. And make it romantic";[16] and the result is a bespoke piece of fiction created on the spot for them, of whatever length they desire. While major intellectual property holders like Disney will definitely try to prevent people from creating stories using trademarked and copyrighted characters, they will be approximately as successful as they currently are in preventing piracy of their movies.

What does "publishing" even mean in a world like this? What is a "book"? We will be living inside Borges's *Library of Babel*,[17] or perhaps a bit more hopefully, inside of Neil Gaiman's *Library of Dream*, where every story that was never written is to be found. As described in Volume 4 of his work *The Sandman*, *Season of Mists*:

> "So this is your library, huh, Lucien? It's a big place. What's so special about it, then?"
> "Oh, it's a very unusual library, Matthew. Somewhere in here is every story that has ever been dreamed."
> "They're just books."
> "Oh yes. But unusual books. You'll find none of them on Earth. In this section, for example, are novels their authors never wrote, or never finished, except in dreams."[18]

Anyone will be able to snap their fingers and generate the exact type of story they would like to read, featuring beloved characters, and in exactly the style they like. Or perhaps someone will choose to generate a never-ending text, that auto-generates as one reads, with new characters introduced and new plots unfolding forever.

This sort of generated media is not just limited to text, of course. Since these tools will be equally capable, in time, of generating audio, images, and video in real time and on demand, this same magic will be available for audiobooks, comics, or video. You will be able to choose the style of film you would like, even the actors that appear in it, and have it generated for you. Would you like to star in a sci-fi adventure movie in the style of *Star Wars*? Add your image to the request, give the system three seconds of your voice, and you will be right in the action alongside your favorite stars. Want to hear a brand new U2 song that has never existed until the moment you ask for it? Not a problem for a system trained using their catalog. Wonder what the Beatles' twentieth album would have sounded like, or what sort of album they might have put out at the height of the grunge movement? Type a few commands, and you will have it. Curious about what Mozart would have written for the electric guitar? Also not a problem.

We have a somewhat troubled early attempt at this sort of thing with a project called *Nothing, Forever*,[19] a procedurally generated 24/7 sitcom based on the American television show *Seinfeld*. This show is entirely computer-generated; the script, the voices, and the extremely simple animation all are the product of a machine learning system. It takes very little imagination to see how the continued march of machine learning (ML) will make a difference in how this sort of show moves into the future.

CONCLUSION

So, what will the library look like in this generative world in 2035? I do not think the library will ever cease being a connection to the past—in other words, an archive of human story and history. But will it become the place people go to generate new works? Will "publishing" evolve into a sort of gatekeeping around the use of intellectual property from the past? Will licensing deals for the rights to generate, for example, new Marvel stories be the future of collection development? There will continue to be a market for human-written stories, in the same way there is a market for other bespoke, luxury goods, but that publishing landscape harkens back to the earliest days of publishing being the domain of the wealthy.

The changes in our way of understanding the creation, discovery, evaluation, and manipulation of text, images, audio, and other forms of information will be changed by 2035 to a degree that will likely be unrecognizable to those of us who are not native to it. The roles libraries play in collecting, describing, organizing, preserving, and sharing information each have the potential to be affected by generative media, and those effects are all in the direction of making it impossible for libraries to complete those functions.

How would a library collect these individualized, generated works? Even in situations where a generated novel is shared rather than created and consumed by only the individual, the possibility of these being shared via traditional publishing models that feed into traditional collection development isn't very likely. If a library manages to find a way to collect these, it's difficult to imagine them being physical volumes, which then brings in all the difficulties that are already in place

> The changes in our way of understanding the creation, discovery, evaluation, and manipulation of text, images, audio, and other forms of information will be changed by 2035 to a degree that will likely be unrecognizable to those of us who are not native to it.

for local collections of electronic works and the corresponding preservation issues. Description alone would be a nightmare of specificity and variability if generative works really do take off, just based on volume of works. Right now the model of *many identical copies, one description* works well, but imagine a million different works, each generated by an individual child for their summer reading project. In that instance, you've got a million unique novels, and library models simply do not scale in that way.

The havoc this could wreak on society is hard to imagine. We have seen the challenges inherent with having individualized social media experiences, where algorithmic timelines have reduced the once-shared experience of news and facts to division and argument about the most basic realities of the world. The impossibility for libraries to collect media for study, evaluation, and understanding by future generations has the potential to disrupt the future by making it impossible to understand the past.

I hope that libraries can continue to claim their space in the world in this new generative media landscape. However, regardless of how they do it, it will not be business-as-usual. If we see an explosion of customized, bespoke books, music, and video that are tailored to the wishes of the individual consumer, libraries are going to have an extremely difficult time pivoting to remain centered in their traditional (and needed) roles.

NOTES

1. Wikipedia, "ChatGpt," accessed October 18, 2023, https://en.wikipedia.org/wiki/ChatGPT.
2. Sean Michael Kerner, "large language models (llms)," WhatIs.com, accessed October 20, 2023, https://www.techtarget.com/whatis/definition/large-language-model-LLM.
3. Wikipedia, "DALL-E," accessed October 18, 2023, https://en.wikipedia.org/w/index.php?title=DALL-E&oldid=1150373107.
4. Wikipedia, "Stable Diffusion," accessed October 18, 2023, https://en.wikipedia.org/w/index.php?title=Stable_Diffusion&oldid=1150723699.
5. Wikipedia, "Midjourney," accessed October 20, 2023, https://en.wikipedia.org/w/index.php?title=Midjourney&oldid=1150344616.
6. "VALLE-E," accessed October 20, 2023, https://vall-e.pro/.
7. Github, "Audio LM: A Language Modeling Approach to Audio Generation," accessed October 20, 2023, https://google-research.github.io/seanet/audiolm/examples/.
8. Wikipedia, "OpenAI_Codex," accessed October 20, 2023, https://en.wikipedia.org/w/index.php?title=OpenAI_Codex&oldid=1149385669.
9. Github, "CodeT5," accessed October 20, 2023, https://github.com/salesforce/CodeT5.
10. OpenAI, "OpeanAI Codex," accessed October 20, 2023, https://openai.com/blog/openai-codex.
11. Carla Tardi, "What Is Moore's Law and Is It Still True?" Investopedia (March 22, 2023), https://www.investopedia.com/terms/m/mooreslaw.asp.
12. Wikipedia, "What is Koomey's law," accessed January 12, 2024, https://en.wikipedia.org/wiki/Koomey%27s_law.

13. Stanford University, "The 2019 AI Index Report," Human Centered Artificial Intelligence, accessed July 27, 2023, https://hai.stanford.edu/sites/default/files/ai_index_2019_report.pdf.
14. Stanford Encyclopedia of Philosophy, "Thomas Kuhn," accessed January 12, 2024, https://plato.stanford.edu/entries/thomas-kuhn/.
15. NISO, "Unanticipated Metadata in the Age of the Net and the Age of AI," (March 2023), https://www.niso.org/niso-io/2023/03/unanticipated-metadata-age-net-age-ai.
16. I used this exact prompt to see what sort of short story might be written using today's tools. Those results are here: https://docs.google.com/document/d/1CdGlvAc_ABnQxK8bEVHUZpg9bXFxrvm9G8gpWedAl1g/edit?usp=sharing.
17. Jorge Luis Borges, *The Library of Babel* (Boston: David R. Godine, 2000).
18. Neil Gaiman, *The Sandman Vol. 4: Season of Mists* (Vertigo, 2011).
19. Wikipedia, "Nothing, Forever," accessed January 12, 2024, https://en.wikipedia.org/wiki/Nothing,_Forever.

3

Sustainable Libraries in 2035

REFUGE. RESISTANCE. RESILIENCE. REGENERATION.

Rebekkah Smith Aldrich

The library of 2035 will be a place of refuge, resistance, resilience, and regeneration.

Libraries are, always have been, and will continue to be beacons of hope in our communities. The fundamental role of libraries will hold into the future. We will be faithful to our core values by contributing to participatory democracy, supporting lifelong learning, and strengthening social cohesion. We will foster literacies that enable our communities to develop more profound empathy, respect, and understanding for one another. The core of who we are and why we do what we do will not change. However, how we work and solidify our role in our communities will shift.

The intensity of all climate predictions greatly depends on the actions we take between now and 2033. Climate scientists have given us just one more decade of effort on climate change mitigation (reduction of greenhouse gas emissions) to avoid the deadliest of predictions.[1] By 2035, we will experience climate change's effects in new, uncomfortable, and possibly deadly ways. Depending on the area of the world in which you live, this may look different on the outside, but what will need to happen "on the inside" will be a common experience for all libraries.

SUSTAINABLE LIBRARIES: EXTERNAL FORCES

Climate scientists predict that, even if we do everything "right" to combat climate change today, we will still suffer from the increasingly severe effects of climate change for the remainder of our generation.[2] The earth will continue to warm, driven by increased human emissions of heat-trapping greenhouse gasses, and the effects will be profound. For example:

- Sea levels will rise.
- Hurricanes will become stronger and more intense.
- Wildfire season will last longer.
- Precipitation patterns will continue to take communities by surprise, with some regions experiencing increased precipitation and flooding and other regions experiencing more extreme drought.
- There will be more heat waves, and more that last for an extended period of time.

By 2035, we will see more evidence of the Great Displacement.[3] For example:

- Climate refugees will seek safer, more stable environments in which to live as they flee regions beset by patterns of flooding, heat waves, and routine wildfires.
- Food scarcity issues will continue to worsen, impacting the cost of growing fruits, vegetables, and grains. Less biodiversity will also threaten the food supply chain, as well as the development of medicines. Both issues will contribute to political and societal unrest.
- Corporate manipulation of markets and politics will continue to disenfranchise the most vulnerable in our communities, creating artificial reliance on products and services that are detrimental to the human condition.
- We will continue to fight for the right to repair our stuff,[4] the right to privacy,[5] and the right to food security and sovereignty.[6]

The systemic causes of climate change can be overwhelming. We are contending with the fact that our economic system, built on premises such as self-interest and unchecked growth, has accelerated the negative impacts of climate change. This scenario is entangled with the reality that systemic racism, marginalization of low-income communities, and a growing lack of social cohesion are exacerbating climate change's impact and producing barriers to helping one another.

We live in the most nonsynchronous time ever. Technology, mass production, educational options, geography, and corporatized news media have all collaborated to allow folks living through the same period of history, on the same timeline, and in the same country, to exist in a peak number of alternate realities.

Our everyday experiences vary from family to family, and person to person. Who our ancestors were; where we live; the degree to which we consume streaming media and news outlets of our own curation; and how we shop for the lifestyle we desire—all continue to water down a sense of community and collaboration, which has greatly led to the factionalization of our society.

A shrinking number of the younger generations is following established patterns to adulthood. The growth in education options may lead to different decisions about what success will look like as an adult. Having children is not a foregone conclusion. Going to college is not the surest path to success. This generation is forged in perseverance in the face of mass shootings, a pandemic, artificial intelligence, political upheaval, and book bans. Their attitudes about the future, the pace at which they expect change to happen, and their willingness to fight for what they believe in will significantly shape our future.

Finding the future in today's noisy environment is difficult but not impossible. The future is already all around us, mixed in with the past and present. How this is experienced moving forward will be greatly shaped by the choices of library leaders at all levels of our institutions.

INSIDE SUSTAINABLE LIBRARIES

Sustainable libraries in the future will have four attributes:

1. *Strong and authentic institutions that live their values out loud.*
   Libraries that thrive will adopt internal policies, procedures, and practices that reflect the core values of librarianship, for example:
   - Treating library workers with respect and dignity.
   - Reducing barriers to library services and ensuring library patrons are treated with respect and dignity.
   - Operating library facilities with human health as a prime directive.
   - Expending library funds in a manner consistent with the triple bottom-line definition of *sustainability*[7] by seeking balance among environmental stewardship, social equity, and economic feasibility.

2. *Catalysts for civic participation and social cohesion in communities.*
   Libraries will focus energy and efforts to accelerate participatory democracy in communities and in more expanded governmental units to empower formerly marginalized voices to be a part of conversations that shape policy and decision-making. Our collections, programs, and partnerships will be designed to ensure neighbors have deep respect, empathy, and understanding for one another so that they support the needs and aspirations of all in our communities and combat social isolation and factionalization. For example, libraries will provide a range of programs to address this need, such as:
   - Events and programs that are designed to specifically bring people in communities together—to learn, repair items, celebrate local

successes, and solve problems together—that otherwise would not have the opportunity to interact with one another.
- Library programs and collection curation that celebrate different cultures and life experiences as well as the place we all locally call "home."
- Libraries of Things that lend items to support those who organize and create community (e.g., folding tables and chairs, water coolers, coffee carafes, and pop-up tents).
- Civics labs for people to learn how to research topics, run for election, and influence legislation. Spaces where the right to read and the First Amendment will be inviolate.

3. *Deliberate climate mitigation action to reduce greenhouse gas emissions.*
Libraries will be living laboratories that utilize facility operational choices to educate and inspire their communities to think differently about how we power, heat, and cool our built environment; transport ourselves and goods around the globe; and manage resources and dispose of them at the end of their useful life. For example:

- New library facilities will be net zero energy and net zero water focused. They will not rely on fossil fuels to power themselves. Instead, they will produce enough energy, on-site from renewable sources, to power library operations. In addition, they will use less water and minimize wastewater discharge from a building and create on-site filtration systems through landscaping.
- Existing library facilities will be retrofitted with electrified heating and cooling systems and solar installations to offset increasing percentages of the electricity needed to power library operations.
- Libraries will be a predictable place to connect with electric vehicle (EV) charging infrastructure.
- Some libraries will host microgrids, powering neighborhoods and providing redundancies to existing electrical grids.
- Library grounds will be teaching spaces to celebrate native plants, offering edible landscaping, space to grow food for neighbors, pollinator gardens, and housing bee colonies.
- Libraries with outdoor space will prioritize green space and shade-creating trees.
- Library interiors will feature living plants, low-VOC fixtures and furnishings, and locally sourced materials that cut down on transportation needs to deliver.

4. *Active participation in climate adaptation action to strengthen community resilience.*
Libraries will be part of their community's disaster preparedness, emergency management, and disruption-recovery strategies.

SHORT TERM:
- Libraries will have clear, practiced, and up-to-date emergency action and disaster preparedness plans so that, in the event of a disaster, the library as an institution can recover in the shortest possible cycle to ensure essential services can be restored for the community.
- Libraries will have whole-building generators that serve as cooling, warming, air quality, and recovery centers for their communities.
- Library workers will be provided with the emergency preparedness skills and know-how needed to ensure they, and their families, are safe and cared for in the face of disruptive disasters.
- Libraries will be at the table for planning discussions with emergency management agencies to ensure the assets libraries offer are considered in emergency management strategies.
- Libraries will participate in or host routine efforts to help community members prepare for severe weather events and extended power outages.

LONG TERM:
- Libraries will specialize in combating infodemics,[8] misinformation, and disinformation attempts.
- Libraries will be the advocates for, and guardians of, the knowledge commons and will fight for policies that "ensure all publicly funded research becomes public knowledge by contractually requiring it to be licensed in the knowledge commons."[9]
- Libraries will prioritize accessibility, digital equity, inclusion, and literacy.
- The Library of Things will be developed to provide more access to gardening, food preservation, and disaster recovery items. This will include hand tools to facilitate growing food, canning and preserving supplies, mobile solar panels, walkie-talkie units, and satellite phones.
- Partnerships developed by libraries will place a high premium on participating in collective impact[10] efforts that have broad, positive outcomes for the community.
- Libraries will be go-to partners in citizen science efforts.
- Libraries will develop specialized services to aid climate refugees to flee an area or find their way around a community they have relocated to.

> Most of all, [libraries] will enable neighbors to come together, learn together, and grow their empathy, respect, and understanding for one another.

- Library programs will focus on homesteading, repair, coding, and disaster preparedness and recovery—but most of all, they will enable neighbors to come together, learn together, and grow their empathy, respect, and understanding for one another.
- New library facilities will be designed with resilience and regeneration in mind. These facilities will utilize passive design to cut down on the reliance on electricity to heat, cool, and light the library. In addition, libraries will embrace the opportunities renewable energy provides and will design energy systems that can help power or create energy redundancies for a neighborhood, not just its own facility needs.

CONCLUSION

Kate Marvel of the National Aeronautics and Space Administration (NASA), one of the co-authors of the forthcoming fifth National Climate Assessment,[11] was recently quoted as saying: "The world will be what we make it." The overarching theme of the future of libraries is hope. Libraries have always been hopeful places, providing windows to the past, mirrors of the present, and portals to the future.

Our daily challenge will be to understand and contend with the weight of the future while being purposefully present without succumbing to exhaustion, depression, or hopelessness in the face of the aggressions and aggrievements of the day. On some days, to believe in the goodness of our neighbors, to focus on the shared values that define us, and to respect the hopes and aspirations of the younger generations will take grit and determination. On other days, the goodness of folks will shine through and remind us why we chose this profession.

We must believe, and count on, the goodness of others, including ourselves. Libraries matter. They transform lives, and the library workers who commit themselves to carrying out the work of libraries are at the heart of this transformational purpose.

But we must also be realists. The world can be a harsh and unforgiving place. So, while this chapter has focused on an idealized state for libraries in the future, we must never lose sight of the power of story. What we put on our shelves, provide access to through our e-collections, and produce through programming must be focused on telling the stories of the human condition. So even if your library facility is not as sustainable as it could be, we are sustaining the human spirit through kindness, understanding, respect, and empathy. That will be the greatest achievement of our profession with the most lasting of impacts in the year 2035.

But, hey, while you are at it, and since you are making these choices anyway, why not choose to model other ideal choices that treat not just humans, but our planet, with dignity and respect. For inspiration today to shape the library of tomorrow, check out the Sustainable Libraries Initiative.[12] This collaborative project has been working for a decade to help libraries lead by example into the future using the four characteristics described above. These are real libraries, practicing these attributes in real time and reporting back so other libraries can iterate and go further, faster—which is what our future is calling for.

NOTES

1. Ippc, "AR6 Synthesis Report: Climate Change 2023," accessed August 6, 2023, https://www.ipcc.ch/report/sixth-assessment-report-cycle/.
2. Global Climate Change, "The Effects of Climate Change," updated July 26, 2023, https://climate.nasa.gov/effects/.
3. Jake Bittle, *The Great Displacement: Climate Change and the Next American Migration*, Simon & Schuster, 2003.
4. The Repair Association, "The Repair Association: Moving the Repair Industry Forward," accessed October 18, 2023, https://www.repair.org/.
5. Legal Information Institute, "right to privacy," Cornell Law School, accessed October 18, 2023, https://www.law.cornell.edu/wex/right_to_privacy.
6. Food Secure Canada, "Our Work," accessed October 18, 2023, https://foodsecurecanada.org/our-work/.
7. American Library Association, "Resolution for the Adoption of Sustainability as a Core Value of Librarianship," accessed August 6, 2023, https://www.ala.org/aboutala/sites/ala.org.aboutala/files/content/governance/council/council_documents/2019_ms_council_docs/ALA%20CD%2037%20RESOLUTION%20FOR%20THE%20ADOPTION%20OF%20SUSTAINABILITY%20AS%20A%20CORE%20VALUE%20OF%20LIBRARIANSHIP_Final1182019.pdf.
8. World Health Organization, "Infodemic," accessed October 18, 2023, https://www.who.int/health-topics/infodemic.
9. Monika Antonelli, Rene Tanner, Rebekkah Smith Aldrich, and Adrian K. Ho, "Libraries in the Doughnut Economy," Rollins College (2022), https://scholarship.rollins.edu/cgi/viewcontent.cgi?article=1372&context=as_facpub.
10. See https://www.ala.org/tools/future/trends/collectiveimpact.
11. David Wallace-Wells, "Beyond Catastrophe: A New Climate Reality Is Coming into View," *New York Times* magazine (October 26, 2022), https://www.nytimes.com/interactive/2022/10/26/magazine/climate-change-warming-world.html.
12. Sustainable Libraries Initiative, "Home," accessed October 18, 2023, https://sustainablelibrariesinitiative.org/.

4

Teetering on the Edge of Trust Cliff

Erin Berman

Library stands at the edge of Trust Cliff. The tips of her boots graze the rocky outcropping, sending a scattering of pebbles to the depths below. She inhales deeply, chest expanding, eyes closed. A heavy exhale slips through her lips. Does she take that step forward into uncharted water, forever changing? Or does she step back into her warm coat of ethics? Standing firmly at this edge is where Library finds herself in the year 2023.

This Trust Cliff is found in Privacy Canyon. While Library was born long ago, it was just one hundred years ago when Library found Privacy Canyon as she was exploring Intellectual Freedom Valley. Library had begun to stake claim in Intellectual Freedom Valley, calling it home. Privacy Canyon was beautiful, and Library knew that the Valley would not exist without the Canyon's presence.

As the decades passed, Library had to fight off those who would destroy the Valley. They created laws that violated the rights of the people who visited. Library built new paths to grant visitors access to everything they needed while visiting the Valley, protected by the Canyon's high walls. People from all over the world came to visit Library, who had built her home there. However, over the years, people noticed that Library was only to be found closer and closer to the edge of Trust Cliff.

See, Library had found a new friend, Technology (also known as "Tech"). Tech was a fantastic friend! They could create pathways for access that had never been there before. Now people could visit from all over the world, without leaving their homes. Library's biggest dream was to provide everyone free access to information. Tech explained to Library that the only thing they needed was a little bit of information about the visitors. Library felt this was a fair trade and opened her record books for Tech. As she did this, she took one step closer to the edge of Trust Cliff.

As the years passed, Tech and Library became inseparable. The two were so close that visitors could not tell them apart. Tech kept bringing new tools to Library. Sometimes Library was as excited as Tech, but other times she was hesitant. Some tools could track everything a visitor did in the Valley without their knowledge. Tech would then combine that data with data gathered from other sources, spitting out an analysis and promising that the Valley would be better than ever. Some tools automatically told parents what their children were doing in the Valley. Library was starting to feel uncomfortable with some of the things Tech showed up with. When she pushed back or rejected a tool, Tech sometimes got angry. Tech told Library they knew what was best for the Valley.

Then one day, Library looked down and she was standing on the edge of Trust Cliff. She had a decision to make about the future of the Valley and its Privacy Canyon. She did not want to end the relationship with Tech; it was impossible to do so anyway. The world was changing so fast. Could she get Tech to adapt to her or was it time to go full into their way of operating?

The library of 2035 will have to make a choice between becoming a privacy safe haven for all or fully stepping into the world of surveillance capitalism.

In this chapter, we will explore Library's two paths. What does Intellectual Freedom Valley look like in the year 2035 if Library takes that step off Trust Cliff? How might Library's Valley be different if she steps away from the edge?

STEPPING OFF TRUST CLIFF

Imagine if in 2023 libraries realized that their ties to privacy were antiquated. The foundation of privacy had been so eroded by the practices of big tech that few library users expected privacy anywhere they went. Users demanded that their library provide them with an Amazon- or Google-like search experience. They were irritated when library workers could not give them a list of all the materials they had checked out over the past year. Library workers were frustrated when they could not gather instant analytical reports on how people used the library and interacted with the community. With all the tension boiling to the surface, a resolution to remove privacy from the Code of Ethics, Library Bill of Rights, and Core Values was brought to the American Library Association's (ALA) Council.

Most library privacy advocates demanded that ALA strengthen its privacy rhetoric and policy. Some understood that the battle was lost. They already knew that libraries of all types were ignoring their privacy mandate. The inclusion of privacy as a core value seemed misplaced, a lie to users about what they could expect from libraries. Even those who believed in privacy as a foundational principle of librarianship knew it was time to remove it from policy if libraries no longer supported it.

Over the next twelve years, the world at large will continue to see the crumbling of privacy laws in this scenario. Every time the United States tries to pass a federal law, lobbyists will decry how it will break the internet and the services people have come to love. Some privacy advocates will try to update their state library privacy and confidentiality laws instead. Most of these laws existed before the digital age and no longer covered the vast majority of library use records. However, the political divide in the country will continue to widen. There will be no taste for strengthening privacy protections, especially in states where parents insist on being notified about their child's library use. As libraries strengthen their integration with technology, outdated state laws will hold little power in protecting users' privacy rights.

Once library privacy and confidentiality laws lose their bite, law enforcement will take notice. Law enforcement has known the power of accessing library records for over a century. Initially, libraries freely gave over records to assist law enforcement's efforts. In 1906, New York librarians helped Russian agents arrest a suspected anarchist immigrant who had taken flagged books.[1] Then in the 1970s, libraries gave users' names and reading habits to the Federal Bureau of Investigation as part of their Library Awareness Program.[2] It was not until the *New York Times* exposed the program in 1987 that states began passing library privacy and confidentiality laws.[3] However, these laws will be eviscerated by 2035, meaning law enforcement could return to using libraries as a prime source of information.

In 2035, public libraries will regularly have law enforcement asking staff at the reference desk to give them details about someone's library use. Towns close to the border of Mexico will have law enforcement ask to see records of who attended citizenship classes. This will become so common that most libraries will stop hosting these programs, which could lead to national news stories that celebrate law enforcement's use of library records (e.g., the arrest of suspected Antifa members after discovering searches in library databases on how to build bombs). The libraries of 2035 that step off Trust Cliff will no longer provide an anonymous place to search for information.

The repercussions of this lack of anonymity reach beyond law enforcement requests. With unfettered access to digital analytics tools, libraries will use them en masse. School, public, and academic libraries will track all user interactions with library services through these third-party vendor products. The analytics tools use complicated algorithms that put users into various categories, allowing for personalized marketing. In 2035, the largest of these analytics vendors will likely have a major breach. For example, imagine if a member of the Proud Boys[4] hacked the company, doxxing the personally identifiable information of all users who have attended drag queen story times in a major U.S. city. One of these families could be stalked and killed in a live stream. The libraries of 2035 that stepped off Trust Cliff will no longer be a safe place for LGBTQIA+ users.

A teen could experience this lack of protection when they check out a book, such as a highly acclaimed title about a transgender kid navigating their day-to-day life, from their school library. In 2035, all school libraries will automatically send check-out notices to parents. When this teenager gets home, their parents could confront them with the email sent by the school library. This could have devastating consequences, with the parents demanding their child pack their bag and leave the home, never to return.

Imagine another situation; a sixteen-year-old female checks out a book on abortion from the public library. Her check-out history is stored in a data-sharing platform the public library and school are using to measure student success. The school could choose to flag certain titles and themes and send a message to parents when their children access these resources. When she comes home, her parents might be very upset, and even possibly beat her and call her a slut. The libraries of 2035 that step off Trust Cliff will no longer give minors a place to safely explore their identities or answer questions about their bodies.

Public and school libraries will not be the only institutions facing the ramifications of their step off Trust Cliff. Imagine how academic libraries could see a decline in their usage after a news story like the following breaks in 2035: A professor used the details found in a student's library record to blackmail the student into a sexual relationship. For years, this student was held hostage by their professor before finding the strength to come forward. The libraries of 2035 that step off the Trust Cliff will no longer provide students with the freedom to research without fear of reprisal.

As libraries step away from their privacy ethic, they will find themselves less relevant. People will no longer trust libraries. The thing that once set them apart from those big tech companies, the ability to access information freely and confidentially, will no longer be true. Over the years, libraries may attempt to scramble back up Trust Cliff. However, they will find that once they step over the ledge, there is no getting back up.

TAKING A STEP BACK FROM THE EDGE

Library peered down over the edge of Trust Cliff. A rush of vertigo swept over her, and she stepped back. What was she doing? How had she made it this far into the Valley? Why was she teetering on the edge? What might happen if Library decided to fully embrace privacy as a core value? Where might she find herself in a decade?

In this scenario, libraries of 2035 will reaffirm their place as one of the most trusted institutions. As surveillance capitalism continues to penetrate all other aspects of society, libraries will become a Faraday cage: the only place people can seek information anonymously. The first step back from Trust Cliff will happen when a mighty few push for sweeping changes to the state library use of privacy and confidentiality laws.

Imagine if, in 2023, a group of library workers begins devising a plan to update the outdated state library record laws. Most of these laws do not protect digital records. The laws also allow libraries to create their own internal surveillance systems without gaining user consent. With this push to update to the modern age, new laws are updated state by state. Grasping onto the momentum, advocates push for updates to the Family Educational Rights and Privacy Act.[5] These changes now mark school library records as confidential. Caregivers no longer have carte blanche access to their children's library use data.

These new laws drive vendors to redesign their products with privacy first and in partnership with libraries. A thriving community of practice blossoms where library workers and vendors come together to discuss privacy issues and challenges. Vendors begin telling libraries that they will not create products that violate the core ethics of privacy in librarianship.

One of the biggest changes comes from how library analytics products are designed. With the new laws in place, libraries, as well as colleges and universities, are required to gain user consent before tracking and monitoring their library use. Many students opt out of this tracking. Before long, schools decide that libraries no longer have to prove their worth through learning analytics products. Students want their privacy to be respected and to understand how and why their data is used.

Knowing that the library is a safe place to seek information, there will be an uptick in usage. People will seek out the library to find reproductive health information, become a citizen, and escape domestic violence without the fear of reprisal. If the process of updating state laws began in 2023, by 2035 library users at all types of libraries would have autonomy, privacy, and control over their data.

CONCLUSION

Libraries need to make a choice. While many of the scenarios in stepping off Trust Cliff seem far-fetched, nearly all of them could occur today. There is still time to alter the path and to take a step back. Now is the time to fight for updated privacy laws. Now is the time to push back on vendor products that violate privacy. Now is the time to stand up for our users from less-privileged situations who desperately need libraries to be a privacy safe haven.

> Now is the time to fight for updated privacy laws. Now is the time to push back on vendor products that violate privacy. Now is the time to stand up for our users from less-privileged situations who desperately need libraries to be a privacy safe haven.

The library of 2035 is ours to strengthen or lose. If we want to hold tight to our ethical commitment and truly value the privacy of our users, then we must take action now. Library is standing on the edge of Trust Cliff. What will you do over the next decade to prevent Library from falling over the ledge?

NOTES

1. *The New York Times*, "RUSSION SPIES ON WATCH IN NEW YORK LIBRARIES; They Follow All Who Call for Books on Anarchy. FACT COMES OUT IN COURT Secret Service Agents Never Relax Their Vigilance in Reading Hours, Says Astor Library's Chief" (June 23, 1906), https://www.nytimes.com/1906/06/23/archives/russian-spies-on-watch-in-new-york-libraries-they-follow-all-who.html.
2. Wikipedia, "Library Awareness Program," accessed October 18, 2023, https://en.wikipedia.org/wiki/Library_Awareness_Program.
3. Today in Civil Liberties History, "*The New York Times* Exposes FBI Library Awareness Program" (September 18, 1987), http://todayinclh.com/?event=new-york-times-exposes-fbi-library-awareness-program.
4. Wikipedia, "Proud Boys," accessed October 18, 2023, https://en.wikipedia.org/wiki/Proud_Boys.
5. U.S. Department of Education, "Family Educational Rights and Privacy Act (FERPA), accessed January 30, 2024, https://www2.ed.gov/policy/gen/guid/fpco/ferpa/index.html.

5
Stories

AT THE HEART OF IT ALL

Chris Brown

The library of 2035 will use storytelling to advocate and promote the library as an essential community entity.

As librarians, we understand and respect the power of a good story. A favorite story may have even been the catalyst for launching us into this career. Now we work in buildings filled to the brim with stories. Some come in book form, and others are told through the movies, recordings, and music in our collections. Our programs also center around stories—and not just story hours for children, but talks, presentations, classes, and much more. Moreover, what about the communities we serve? Communities have shared stories, and each individual in the community has their own unique story. Whether we realize it or not, the library itself also has a story to share. A library's mission, staff, resources, and community of service make up this story. Our history is also part of the story, and perhaps even more importantly, so is our future.

In this chapter, I propose that we harness the power of storytelling to promote the importance of public libraries and to ensure we are meeting the needs of communities now and in generations to come. As library commissioner of the City of Chicago, I have been privileged to witness firsthand the impact of storytelling on the individuals and communities served by the Chicago Public Library (CPL). I have also seen the effectiveness of storytelling in advocating for ourselves. Perhaps our experiments will spark conversations within your organization and inspire ideas for advocating your library's value now while building a sustainable foundation for the vision of your library in 2035.

WHAT IS A STORY ANYWAY, AND HOW IS IT POWERFUL?

According to *Merriam-Webster*, a *story* is merely "an account of incidents or events."[1] In an interview with the *Harvard Business Review*, screenwriter and lecturer Robert McKee offered a more compelling definition: "a story expresses how and why life changes."[2] Whether fiction or nonfiction, a good story is relatable and memorable. It stimulates the imagination and fosters empathy. It forges a connection between the storyteller and the audience, building a relationship based on trust and familiarity. In short, it is personal and effective.

Think about it. If someone was trying to convince you to try an orange for the first time, what would resonate more: statistics on citrus consumption or a personal story about the experience of peeling and eating an orange? As the authors of a scholarly article about using storytelling in science communication put it, "compared to evidence-based argumentation, narratives do tend to be more engaging, more comprehensible, more believable, and more persuasive."[3]

JUMPING INTO THE STORY

The power of a particular story is amplified if a reader (or listener) can put themselves into the narrative. With their diverse collections, libraries are exceptionally well-positioned to offer such an experience. We have something for everyone.

As a kid growing up in Los Angeles County, California, public libraries were not part of my life. I may have occasionally ventured into my school library to pick up required reading, but I did not see my local public library as relevant to me. I did not know that a library might contain stories that reflected my experiences. It was not until I became a literature major in college that I began seeking out stories, especially ones connected to my Jewish, Filipino, and Irish-German background.

A few years later—already in the library field—I found a book that changed my life: Dawn Mabalon's *Little Manila Is in the Heart*.[4] This carefully researched social history tells the story of the Filipino community in Stockton, California, from its origins in the early 1900s through its eventual disappearance in the 1960s due to redevelopment and gentrification. My interest in the book was personal: my family traces its roots to Little Manila,[5] and, in fact, my great-grandparents appear in the book. It was so meaningful to gain context and understanding of the community's struggles and resilience. And I learned for the first time that my great-grandmother gave up a full-ride scholarship to Stanford University to marry a farm-labor contractor and support her family. Reading about my people made me feel seen and heard.

EXTENDING THE EXPERIENCE

I want to help others find the stories that make *them* feel seen and heard. My colleagues already do so much to ensure that our collections and programs represent a diversity of perspectives. I think libraries can do even more. Libraries are uniquely positioned to help build a more inclusive and equitable world, a place where everyone's stories are valued and celebrated.

For example, libraries can reach a broader audience through virtual storytelling. During the COVID-19 shutdown, the CPL partnered with the Chicago Public Library Foundation[6] and Foote, Cone and Belding (FCB)[7] advertising agency to create Live From the Library (LFTL).[8] LFTL brought children's story time online, hosted by celebrity guests like Barack and Michelle Obama, Oprah Winfrey, John C. Riley, and Kristen Bell.[9] Broadcasted on Facebook, LFTL provided a fun and engaging storytelling platform for children during a time of crisis. Additionally, CPL children's service staff followed each session with early literacy practices for parents. These recorded broadcasts showcased the versatility and ingenuity of CPL in its commitment to building community. LFTL was a smash hit, garnering an international audience of more than two million viewers.

DEVELOPING IN-HOUSE SKILLS

The success of LFTL showed that the public is hungry for good storytelling in any form. How can we springboard our in-house knowledge and expertise to meet this demand? Children's librarians are well-known for their captivating story time performances. What other storytelling opportunities could they bring to our communities? Could they teach storytelling and techniques for audience engagement to the rest of our staff?

We must also consider incorporating storytelling skills into library and information science (LIS) programs. It is exciting to see that some programs have already started offering courses dedicated to storytelling, but usually the curriculum only includes one course on the subject.[10] We should strive to make storytelling a core competency of our field. By doing so, we can equip future librarians and information professionals with the skills necessary to connect with their communities.

> We should strive to make storytelling a core competency of our field. By doing so, we can equip future librarians and information professionals with the skills necessary to connect with their communities.

STORYTELLING ON OUR OWN BEHALF

A decade ago, the Pew Research Center published a report showing that public libraries in the United States were viewed positively.[11] In fact, a staggering 95 percent of Americans believed that public libraries play a big role in ensuring everyone has an equal opportunity for success; a similar percentage said libraries are essential because they foster literacy and a love of learning.

And yet, the same report showed that only 23 percent understood the extensive range of services and programs offered by their local library—despite efforts by the library field and such partners such as the Aspen Institute[12] and the California State Library[13] to showcase the value of public libraries through positioning papers and reports.

Once again, consider the delivery. An academic-style white paper filled with statistics and broad, abstract statements does not win hearts and minds. How can libraries tell their own stories in a more compelling way? As a start, libraries need to gather baseline data about how they fulfill marketing functions. How many marketing staff do we have, and what specific roles do they play? Is there the right mix of executive, mid-level, and entry-level positions to develop capacity?

And just as importantly, consider how outside partners and allies might help tell our stories. In Chicago, we have cultivated a remarkable ecosystem of library support. The Chicago Public Library Board includes civic and philanthropic leaders like former Johnson Publishing Company CEO Linda Johnson Rice,[14] Poetry Foundation CEO Michelle Boone,[15] and Library Foundation Chairperson Bob Wislow.[16] We recently celebrated CPL's 150th anniversary with an event that included a proclamation from the city council.[17] Many of the alderpersons present at the event shared personal stories about the libraries in their wards.

In other words, the messenger matters. In yet another example, the library and its foundation recently partnered with the City Club of Chicago to host a panel discussion entitled "Defending Democracy: The Role of Libraries and Civic Leaders in the Fight Against Book Bans and Censorship." This event brought together influential leaders from the public, private, and nonprofit sectors.[18] Opening remarks were by Illinois secretary of state and state librarian Alexi Giannoulias, who had recently introduced legislation to financially deter libraries from banning books.[19] The panel itself was moderated by Sylvia Ewing, a renowned journalist and television host, and also included Tracie Hall, executive director of the American Library Association; John Bracken, executive director of the Digital Public Library of America; and myself.

Bringing together influential and trusted leaders to share their perspectives on the importance of libraries is a playbook I wish I had discovered earlier in my career. Building these relationships is not something that happens overnight. It requires strategic efforts, such as inviting leaders onto library-related boards and then involving them in a high-profile moment that elevates the brand.

CONCLUSION

The value of public libraries in America cannot be overemphasized, but most Americans are still unaware of the extensive range of services and programs offered by their local library. As we look ahead at the library of 2035, we need to prioritize storytelling on several fronts. We need to develop the storytelling tools that help us engage effectively with our communities and expand our reach. To do so involves taking stock of our existing assets and determining what we need to build capacity. Meanwhile, we need to strengthen our foundation of support: to build fruitful partnerships with outside organizations and to seek community, political, and business leaders who are willing to act as our advocates. These supporters will help us tell our own stories, promoting our remarkable resources and programs as essential to a stronger, more engaged society.

NOTES

1. Merriam-Webster, "Story," accessed May 1, 2023, https://www.merriam-webster.com/dictionary/story.
2. Chip Heath and Dan Heath, "Storytelling That Moves People," *Harvard Business Review* 81, no. 6 (June 2003): 51-55.
3. Liz Neeley et al., "Linking Scholarship and Practice: Narrative and Identity in Science," *Frontiers in Communication* 5 (2020): n. pag. doi:10.3389/fcomm.2020.00043.
4. Dawn Mabalon, *Little Manila Is in the Heart*. Duke University Press, 2013.
5. Wikipedia, "Little Manila," accessed October 18, 2023, https://en.wikipedia.org/wiki/Little_Manila.
6. *Chicago Sun Times*, "Obama's, Oprah on growing list of top names reading children's books for Chicago Public Library," May 13, 2020, https://chicago.suntimes.com/2020/5/13/21257776/obamas-oprah-growing-list-top-names-reading-childrens-books-chicago-public-library.
7. FCB 150, "Who We Are," accessed October 18, 2023, https://www.fcb.com/.
8. Chicago Public Library Foundation, "Coming to You Live from the Library!" accessed October 18, 2023, https://cplfoundation.org/coming-to-you-live-from-the-library/.
9. "Obama's, Oprah on growing list of top names reading children's books for Chicago Public Library," *Chicago Sun-Times*, May 13, 2020, https://chicago.suntimes.com/2020/5/13/21257776/obamas-oprah-growing-list-top-names-reading-childrens-books-chicago-public-library.
10. University of Illinois at Urbana-Champaign School of Information Sciences, "IS 410: Introduction to Data Science," accessed April 23, 2023, https://ischool.illinois.edu/degrees-programs/courses/is410; University of North Carolina at Chapel Hill School of Information and Library Science, "Courses," accessed April 23, 2023, https://sils.unc.edu/courses#558; University of Washington, "LIS 561: Database Management," accessed April 23, 2023, https://myplan.uw.edu/course/#/courses/LIS561.
11. Pew Research, "How Americans value public libraries in their communities," December 11, 2013, https://www.pewresearch.org/internet/2013/12/11/libraries-in-communities/.
12. Aspen Institute, "Rising to the Challenge: Re-Envisioning Public Libraries," 2017, https://www.aspeninstitute.org/wp-content/uploads/2014/10/Aspen-LibrariesReport-2017-FINAL.pdf.
13. California State Library, "The Value of California's Public Libraries," August 2021, https://www.library.ca.gov/wp-content/uploads/2021/09/Value-of-Libraries.pdf.

14. BlackPast, "Linda Johnson Rice (1958-)," accessed April 23, 2023, https://www.blackpast.org/african-american-history/linda-johnson-rice-1958/.
15. Andrea Chang, "Poetry Foundation Selects Michelle T. Boone as Its President," *New York Times*, April 29, 2021, https://www.nytimes.com/2021/04/29/arts/michelle-t-boone-president-poetry-foundation.html.
16. Parkside Realty, "Bob Wislow," accessed on April 23, 2023, https://www.parkside-realty.com/bob-wislow.
17. Chicago City Council. April 19, 2023, https://youtu.be/1jqbZPkN0Lc?t=1510.
18. City Club of Chicago, "Defending Democracy: The Role of Libraries and Civic Leaders in the Fight Against Disinformation," Published on November 15, 2021. Video, 1:01:08., accessed April 23, 2023, https://www.cityclub-chicago.org/video/3572/defending-democracy-the-role-of-libraries-and-civic-leaders-in-the-fight-against.
19. Jeremy Gorner, "Illinois House OKs Measure to Allow the State to Deny Grants to Libraries That Ban Books," *Chicago Tribune*, March 22, 2023, https://www.everand.com/article/633178336/Illinois-House-O-Ks-Measure-To-Allow-The-State-To-Deny-Grants-To-Libraries-That-Ban-Books."

II
Community

Part II: Community is based on the premise that the library is, and always has been, built upon community. The community served by libraries today will not be the same community served by the library of 2035. Recent events, such as the pandemic, economic instability, war, and ongoing social distress, have demonstrated how both connected and diverse our communities are. The authors of chapters 6 through 9 share their vision for how the library of 2035 will support and contribute to their communities, specifically noting that these libraries will:

- be as unique, innovative, and representative as the communities they serve (*Lankes*).
- be supercharged to help more people in a customized, tailored, and relevant way (*Chow*).
- continue to be vital to community engagement and success, but the depth of that participation will depend upon the library's ability to adapt and respond effectively (*Wong*).
- be dependent upon relationship building and adaptability (*Connaway*).

In chapter 6, Lankes emphasizes that there is no single future for the library; that is, because there is no single community served by the library. The needs, desires, diversity, and personalities of each community will define the resources, services, and programming of each individual library. Similarly, Chow outlines in chapter 7 how, while the library's "why" has not changed much over time, the library's "how" will continue to evolve and change. He highlights how libraries need to pay attention not only to technological change, but also to the health and wellness of the community the library serves. He discusses the importance of making data-driven decisions in determining the services most desired and needed by their communities. Wong echoes similar themes in chapter 8, noting the library of 2035 will not look the same, nor serve the same community, as they do today. She advocates that library workers at every level center their efforts and work on one thing—the patron—and to do so no matter their demographic profile.

In chapter 9, Connaway asserts that we need to recognize we are now living in and serving a global society. The success of the library of 2035 will be dependent upon addressing the digital divide, focusing on participatory learning, and placing a high priority on building strong relationships, collaborations, and partnerships.

Archived webcasts of author interviews are available at: https://sites.google.com/sjsu.edu/library2035/home

6

There Is No Future of Libraries. There Are Many.

R. David Lankes

The library of 2035 will be as unique, innovative, and representative as the communities they serve.

The fracturing of librarianship is inevitable. It will happen because of large societal forces colliding with trends within the field itself. What is more, far from being the death knell of libraries, the landscape today offers an opportunity to move past a nearly century-long fascination with efficiency and standardization to a landscape of hyperlocal services, new definitions of professionalism, and an increased importance of librarianship. Essentially, there is no single future for libraries, but there are as many futures as communities served. Moreover, I think we should fight for this new, complex future.

The future is a river, with its current pushed forward by the actions of the past. In the present, we seek to control its course, but we cannot fully predict the downstream effects. Therefore, any glance forward is really a picture of today. So let me start with what factors today, influenced by the past, will fragment the discipline and impact the library of 2035.

FRAGMENTATION FACTORS: CENSORSHIP AND DISTRUST

When I talk of fragmentation, the forces I am talking about are global, presenting themselves from outside the profession. The clearest example is the rise of materials challenges and the ideological attempts to control what stories we pass from one generation to another and what is now considered acceptable.[1] These forces of censorship are intermingled with valid concerns about parental rights and local community control. They also come at a time when we see books being challenged; in the past, the majority power structures prevented challenging books from being published in the first place, and too many librarians misconstrued the dominant narrative with objectivity.

The challenges come at a time when the intellectual freedom narrative within the field of librarianship is changing from one of *neutrality* to one of *professionalism*. In essence, librarians are not neutral because that is impossible, but they are professionally trained to represent the whole community.[2]

Even this understanding of the impossibility of objectivity is a response to science and scholars shifting from positivistic belief in a rational and deterministic universe, to a complex view of patterns, chaos, and agency. Critical librarianship continues a trend in knowing the world from critical theory, postmodernism, and complexity theory.

Today we are seeing the collision of distrust in science, government institutions, and the emerging narratives of "truth" roiling the political sphere. The first force that will fracture librarianship is the act of local, regional, and national governments enforcing ideological beliefs about the work of librarians. To be a librarian in Texas, Illinois, South Korea, or China will be different because of laws around obscenity, parental control, and, ultimately, about making librarians directly liable in law. What today starts as banning drag queen story hour or teaching critical race theory will evolve into narratives of history and the removal of societal guardrails of intellectual freedom (such as tenure and nonprofit status). If we do nothing, we will be limited, silenced, and isolated into policy silos.

EXTERNAL FORCES: MEDIA CONSOLIDATION AND INCREASED COSTS OF HIGHER EDUCATION

Another example of external forces fracturing the field is media consolidation. In the United States and across the globe, the number of organizations, primarily for-profit companies, that control the creation and distribution of creative content is shrinking. As a result, fewer companies control more content and own the channels that distribute the content.

In 1983, 90 percent of U.S. media was controlled by fifty companies. By 2011, 90 percent was controlled by just six companies: General Electric, News Corp, Disney, Viacom, Time Warner, and CBS. In 2019 it was down to four: Comcast, Disney, ViacomCBS, and AT&T (formerly Time Warner). These organizations have regularly bypassed libraries and all concerns of archiving content.[3]

Furthermore, these media organizations have amassed great wealth and used it to extend copyright protections. They have also used their money to supercharge take-down notifications using artificial intelligence (AI) to force the removal of content on platforms like YouTube and Facebook—forcing individuals to defend fair use.[4] If we do nothing, our shelves will be wiped clean as digital streaming builds a walled-garden of content for those who can afford it, drawing a thick line between libraries with large budgets and those with small resources. Another risk is forcing a line between libraries primarily divided by content purchasers (e.g., public and school libraries) and those that have fought for open access in scholarly literature (i.e., academic libraries).

In fact, the growing cost of higher education is another factor that will drive library fragmentation. This fragmentation will take place not just between academic libraries in the Ivy League and those in community colleges and financially unstable small liberal arts schools, but also in the larger society. In his book *After the Ivory Tower Falls: How College Broke the American Dream and Blew Up Our Politics—and How to Fix It*,[5] William Bunch makes a compelling argument that the reduction in public funding for higher education in the United States, the corresponding rise in tuition, the need for federal research dollars, and new corporate management trends can account for most of the political polarization in the United States. Put very simply, the post–World War II GI Bill created the narrative of colleges being meritocracies when they were virtually free.

Now that colleges are increasingly unaffordable for whole socioeconomic strata of societies, those without a college education risk being presented as without merit. Therefore, those "being left behind" seek redress in the political sphere. Those without access to higher education begin to doubt the merit of expertise. Science, expertise defined by degrees, and even research skills become elitist institutional mechanisms to preserve power. At the same time, web search and generative AI allow anyone to do their own "research." If we do nothing, libraries of all types will be associated with an elitist definition of knowledge and attacked with other elite concepts in the "culture wars."

Additional external forces include technological shifts and the rise of AI, public health policies, and climate crisis. We can never escape the bitter race battles fought over the redistribution of power underlying many of these issues.

THE RISK OF DOING NOTHING

If we do nothing, collections will become increasingly restricted by partisan policy or become inaccessible, resulting in a shift in focus from collections to services. We will see more libraries and states move to their own library preparation over formal graduate programs to ensure access (due to unaffordable tuition) and ideological consistency (due to the need to foster self-censorship from liability). We will see travel and membership in professional associations banned by local policy. We will see some libraries able to provide outstanding service and other libraries relegated to little more than limited reading rooms based on their zip codes or the size of their endowments.

This depiction of the future is foreseen by a straight, white, middle-aged male library professor living in Texas. It is driven by the fatigue of fighting for libraries in technological advances, pandemics, and economic downturns. It is the result of a series of crises in the faith that librarians can make the world a better place. It is driven by a past and present looking to an information field shaped by conflict and war. It is a future of an optimistic pragmatist that has often been driven to pure pragmatism.

HAVING FAITH: LIBRARIANS BRIDGING THE FUTURES

Two things give me faith that we can avoid a horrible, fragmented future for libraries in 2035. First, we have been here before. Thousands were jailed for speaking against the U.S. government in World War I under the Sedition Act[6] (supported by the Supreme Court). Antisemitism kept the horrors of the Holocaust from the public in World War II,[7] the same antisemitism that blocked large-scale Jewish immigration from Axis countries.[8] From McCarthyism to Jim Crow to the Patriot Act,[9] the United States has swerved close to authoritarianism and managed to swing back to an expanding democratic opportunity (with a long way to go, to be sure).

Yet it took the work of people, including many a great librarian, to bring us back from the edge. It took looking into the darkness, addressing the issues, and understanding that the future is an act of creation. There will always be a predicted future (things we see happening on their own), and there is always a desired future (what we would like to happen). The distance between the *predicted* and the *preferred* may be a small—or it may be a huge—chasm. The trick is to determine what changes need to be made to bridge the gap and how to either use or blunt the forces pushing the current forward.

The way we avoid a future of isolated libraries pushed by bad policy and a lack of resources is to let libraries fracture, but have librarians come together. Traditional divisions within libraries make little sense. A small public library has more in common with a four-person staff of a community college than either has in common with a very large urban city library or an ARL (Association of Research Libraries) academic library. Even in rural communities, some libraries serve a growing population headed toward urbanization, while other libraries are serving a population falling precipitously. The point is—despite their disparities—all libraries share a mission in learning and helping a community (e.g., a city or a campus community) find meaning and make better decisions.

The communities we serve are diverse in terms of race, income, religion, and politics. The idea that one set of standards in the form of classification or best practices can cover the range is untenable. Much of the drive for standards and toolkits can trace its origin to the late 1800s and early 1900s, when the major force shaping society was industrialization. The Dewey Decimal System was as much a response to the first assembly lines as it was a colonialist belief in universal cultural truths.

We need to see libraries looking at and matching the communities they serve rather than comparing themselves to other libraries. Texas libraries should look like, well, Texas. To be *very* clear, Texas libraries should look like *all* of Texas, not just those Texan parents who feel they can dictate what is acceptable for all. Similarly, South Korean libraries should look like their university/town/

school.[10] Some public libraries will have makerspaces, other libraries will have the ability to earn academic degrees, and some will offer both. The fact that the City Library San Matteo degli Armeni,[11] a public library housed in ancient Roman ruins, consists of a modest interior space surrounded by gardens does not mean that every library needs to find itself within the remains of ancient buildings. As institutions, libraries should, once and for all, break away from the idea that there is a sort of prototypical library in the clouds to which they should aspire, or worse, adhere.

By aligning and building trust with local communities, libraries are better positioned to push against ideological divides. By building hyperlocal identities co-owned by communities (e.g., universities, municipalities, schools, law firms), librarians can work to ingrain the values of the discipline into the community itself. Then librarians can begin to knit together a cohesive social fabric.

CONCLUSION

This is the key to a bright future for libraries in 2035: librarians. Librarians by education, name, or spirit must not simply reflect or defer to loud members of a community, but they should be a strong voice for serving the whole community. Specifically, librarians should be a strong and trusted voice for learning, openness, diversity, intellectual honesty, intellectual freedom, and safety. Librarians should come together, not to standardize practice, but to reify values and seek out great new ideas to adapt (not simply adopt) into their local settings. Associations will continue their transformations into peer-learning and advocacy networks focused on individuals, not institutions. Librarians will share across borders and institutions. They will embed themselves in the work of communities as librarians, regardless of whether the word *library* remains in the organization's name. And institutions that do identify as "library" will shed nostalgic stereotypes for the role of trusted partner and true anchor institutions.

> Librarians by education, name, or spirit must not simply reflect or defer to loud members of a community, but they should be a strong voice for serving the whole community.

Imagine a future not of one body seeking to correct the course of a nation, but thousands of voices, backed by thousands of communities, steering the course of the river that is the future. That is the future I have faith in.

NOTES

1. A. Alter and E. Harris, "Attempts to Ban Books Are Accelerating and Becoming More Divisive," *New York Times*, September 16, 2022, https://www.nytimes.com/2022/09/16/books/book-bans.html.

2. *American Libraries*, "Are Libraries Neutral? Highlights from the Midwinter President's Program," 2018, https://americanlibrariesmagazine.org/2018/06/01/are-libraries-neutral.
3. R. David Lankes, *Forged in War: How a Century of War Created Today's Information Society* (Lanham: Rowman & Littlefield, 2021).
4. Maayan Perel and Niva Elkin-Koren, "Accountability in Algorithmic Copyright Enforcement," *Stanford Technology Law Review* 19 (2016): 473, https://law.stanford.edu/wp-content/uploads/2016/10/Accountability-in-Algorithmic-Copyright-Enforcement.pdf.
5. William Bunch, *After the Ivory Tower Falls: How College Broke the American Dream and Blew Up Our Politics—and How to Fix It*, First ed. (New York, NY: William Morrow, an imprint of HarperCollins, 2022).
6. History, Art & Archives, "Sedition Act of 1798," accessed January 30, 2024, https://history.house.gov/Historical-Highlights/1700s/The-Sedition-Act-of-1798/.
7. Laurel Leff, *Buried by the Times: The Holocaust and America's Most Important Newspaper* (Cambridge: Cambridge University Press, 2006).
8. Andrew Buncombe, "Allied Forces Knew About Holocaust Two Years Before Discovery of Concentration Camps, Secret Documents Reveal," *Independent*, April 18, 2017, https://www.independent.co.uk/news/world/world-history/holocaust-allied-forces-knew-before-concentration-camp-discovery-us-uk-soviets-secret-documents-a7688036.html.
9. Barbara M. Jones, "Librarians Shushed No More: The USA PATRIOT Act, the 'Connecticut Four,' and Professional Ethics," IFLA, 2009, https://www.ifla.org/past-wlic/2009/117-jones-en.pdf.
10. R. D. Lankes, "Exploring the Innovative Community Libraries of Korea," *Publishers Weekly*, January 12, 2023, https://www.publishersweekly.com/pw/by-topic/industry-news/libraries/article/91274-exploring-the-innovative-community-libraries-of-korea.html.
11. San Matteo degli Armeni Library, https://turismo.comune.perugia.it/poi/san-matteo-degli-armeni-library.

7

The Future of Libraries

A USER- AND COMMUNITY-CENTERED PERSPECTIVE

Anthony Chow

The library of 2035 will be supercharged to help more people in a customized, tailored, and relevant way.

In my twenty-three-year career in the library and information science (LIS) field, I have witnessed all types of people use libraries across different periods of their lives; it is a deeply personal relationship. Often taken for granted, libraries must remain responsive and move fast, or they risk being forgotten and replaced with more modern, easier, and convenient digital alternatives.

The Information Age presents us with many choices, and libraries have continued to play the same role since antiquity—a place that organizes, ensures the quality and integrity of, and provides access to information to all people free of charge. Advances in technology and the field have significantly increased how this happens. As the scholarly hub of any community or organization, libraries in 2035 will continue to offer knowledge, services, programming, and resources from which all community members will greatly benefit.

LIBRARIES OF THE FUTURE: INSIGHT WITH HELP FROM ARTIFICIAL INTELLIGENCE (AI)

OpenAI[1] has only been in existence since 2015. ChatGPT,[2] publicly released on November 30, 2022,[3] immediately transformed how we write and draft initial ideas. ChatGPT also raises concerns around plagiarism, misinformation, and degradation of human-driven evaluation of how we define a "quality" resource.

In preparation for this chapter, I asked ChatGPT: "What is the future of libraries?" as it pertained to public, academic, and school environments. A summary of its responses,[4] as well as my reflection, are listed below.

> **Textbox 7.1**
> **ChatGPT Response: "What is the future of libraries?" (All Libraries)**
> Libraries will increasingly be digital and accessible remotely; continue to adapt and offer new services to meet the changing needs of their patrons; offer spaces for people to meet, work, and collaborate; and increase programming, including workforce development. The future will be driven by technology and changing societal needs and trends.

I agree with all the AI-driven recommendations for libraries, but I also immediately see the lack of human nuances behind its recommendations—or what we refer to as "coloring between the lines," informed by a lifetime of experience. Additional trends I see as important for all libraries include the following:

- Libraries will redesign and transform physical spaces to accommodate digital spaces and hubs of learning and inquiry as well as spaces for reading, working, innovating, and collaborating.
- Libraries will reallocate funds to acquire more digital hardware, software, subscriptions, training, consultants, and specialists.
- Libraries will advocate and educate decision-makers, as these transformations will require additional funding, such as retrofitting the physical facilities of the past to meet the demands of the digital future.
- Libraries will increase their aesthetics and curb appeal as their facilities become modernized inside and out.

> **Textbox 7.2**
> **ChatGPT Response: "What is the future of libraries?" (Public Libraries)**
> Libraries will continue to meet the needs of their communities while adapting to changing technology and societal trends. Four major areas of focus: 1) digital resources; 2) community engagement; 3) inclusivity and accessibility; 4) collaboration with other organizations.

While I agree with these trends identified by ChatGPT, there will also be increases in data and the use of data, digital literacy and information security, technology petting zoos and devices for checkout, virtual reality, mixed reality, augmented reality, outreach, and community-situated physical and digital services.

Textbox 7.3

ChatGPT Response: "What is the future of libraries?" (Academic Libraries)

Libraries will continue to support the research, teaching, and learning needs while adapting to technological changes in scholarly communication and education. Four primary focuses: 1) increased focus on digital resources; 2) collaborative spaces and services; 3) open access and scholarly communication; 4) integration with teaching and learning.

In addition to these trends identified by ChatGPT, libraries will also help their users be more discerning and information literate through increased digital and information literacy support; this is especially important given the risks that AI-assisted resources present (e.g., by introducing misinformation). Academic libraries will also continue to focus on instruction, teaching, and training through improved instructional design and more eLearning offerings. Finally, robots and AI-assisted support for faculty and students are also likely to serve as supplements and assistants/co-workers with librarians of the future.[5] This technology already exists; for example, Pepper, the semi-humanoid robot created by Softbank Robotics, can read emotions, hold an independent conversation, do internet or catalog searches, and bring a patron to a resource—all on its own.[6]

Textbox 7.4

ChatGPT Response: "What is the future of libraries?" (School Libraries)

Libraries will change as education becomes more personalized and technology-driven to better meet the needs of teachers and students. Three focuses: 1) centers for digital learning; 2) places for collaboration and project-based learning; 3) teaching digital literacy and information literacy skills.

In addition to these trends identified by ChatGPT, there will also be more print books for the underprivileged, relevant books and resources for immigrants and diverse cultures,[7] and instructional technology and digital teaching and learning for teachers.

The Future of Libraries

PEOPLE AND DATA: GOALS, RELEVANCE, USE, AND CONTINUOUS IMPROVEMENT

Powering these new library trends is our enhanced ability to identify, communicate, gather, and analyze data about the people we serve to create more customized library resources, services, and programming. With communities across the globe becoming more diverse, libraries must consider the diverse needs, wants, and preferences of their own community and how best to serve them. The library of the future will reflect the individual information demands and behaviors of society and its local communities.

The more real-time data we have, the more information we will have to make informed decisions about patron needs, preferences, what's successful, and what needs improvement. Librarians need to know the demographics of the people they serve within narrowly defined boundaries that can be drawn around any library branch. With this data, they can analyze the usage trends and hold an ongoing dialogue with their "representative" users on what is important to them in their daily lives and what services, resources, and programming they would like the library to provide. Using this information, librarians can establish short- and long-term goals designed to anticipate their user needs and preferences.

This process involves measuring use and satisfaction quantitatively (e.g., number of users, circulation, attendance, and satisfaction ratings) and qualitatively (e.g., focus groups, interviews, and qualitative comments) and can help libraries determine whether they are, in fact, meeting the needs of their users. Identifying and continuously refining short- and long-term goals is an ongoing improvement process that defines the modern library. Technology innovation and digital usage continue to increase access to real-time data that then can be used to make informed future decisions *and* provide progress updates at any moment. Building such a system, while a lot of work and much allocation of resources, can exponentially increase the library's chances for success into 2035 and beyond.

CHALLENGES, THREATS, AND OPPORTUNITIES

A metaphor I like to use when facing challenges, barriers, pain, and uncertainty as we tackle future goals is hiking to a mountaintop. The path to the most breathtaking views is usually defined by steep inclines, windy switchbacks, and much discomfort. The key is to put one foot forward and push through the challenges to the top of the mountain; the reward (the opportunity) for this effort is a beautiful view that brings us joy and fulfillment for the hard-fought goal we earned. We can apply this metaphor to the challenges, threats, and opportunities for libraries in 2035.

CHALLENGES AND THREATS

The main challenge—and threat—all libraries face is becoming obsolete and irrelevant in our rapidly changing and unknown future, particularly now that print book circulation and physical visitation continue to drop. The reality is that libraries, in many cases, are being used *more*, not less, as digital access is increasing faster than print circulation is decreasing.[8] The mismatch between these realities is a real challenge and threat to libraries as decision-makers are forced to make tough budget decisions about which important community services to fund. Even if a library is well attuned and serving its community at high levels, decision-makers may deem their libraries obsolete and irrelevant and start to proactively cut budgets. One way to prevent this is to build and nurture strong relationships with decision-makers and have data and patron stories that can be shared with them continuously.

Another issue is health and wellness for all of us, especially the library frontline staff. New challenges in communication and the ways teams work together, misalignment between skills and job requirements, and new demands and services inherently cause staff anxiety and a sense of ineptitude at times. The morale of any team is essential for its success, and when one team member is struggling, it resonates throughout the team. It is imperative to ensure that staff, facilities, and the overall budget and workflow are well positioned to handle the new demands, the new ways of doing things, and the continued migration from print to digital.

OPPORTUNITIES

Our disrupted, technology-enriched society also presents libraries with tremendous opportunities. Convenience is key. If libraries can provide convenient access to resources, services, and programming that patrons want and need using technology, then digital consumption and usage should continue to grow exponentially. As broadband becomes more accessible, it is essential that all people, regardless of socioeconomic status, have access to hardware and software and develop necessary digital and information literacy and privacy skills.

> Our disrupted, technology-enriched society also presents libraries with tremendous opportunities. Convenience is key.

More libraries are offering check-out services to technologies, like cell phones, tablets, and laptops, to directly address this very real issue. Another opportunity is outreach, partnership, and collaboration with other community organizations to address literacy and to reach members of the community who do not use the library.

AN IDEAL FUTURE FOR PUBLIC, ACADEMIC, AND SCHOOL LIBRARIES

So, what do the public, academic, and school libraries of 2035 look like? For all libraries, knowing our primary users is essential so we can design resources, services, and programs for them.

For public libraries, it is paramount that their power-users (e.g., children, families, seniors, and the displaced) are well taken care of. This means engaging with children in new and novel ways, such as offering story times using virtual, mixed, and augmented reality, hybrid programming, and resources, services, and programming that are well aligned to their interests. It is also important to prepare them with the knowledge and skills their parents deem valuable (e.g., meeting authors, STEM, innovation, etc.). For seniors, providing entertainment and access to print, digital, and audio books will continue, but the specific *what* and *how* of these offerings will continue to change as technology evolves and makes many new things possible. For the displaced, effectively managing space so they can use the library while also providing high-end and modern spaces for other users will remain a priority. Furthermore, workforce development, training, and eLearning will continue to grow in libraries as AI, automation, and homeschooling increase.

For academic libraries, the primary users remain faculty and students. As print materials become less pronounced, the regained space means opportunities to reimagine spaces for reading, studying, and collaborating. AI's ability to connect faculty and students to resources they need will become more accurate, automated, and relevant. Instruction and training will also be essential for librarians and patrons as new technology, innovations, and work processes continue to evolve.

Finally, the redesign of school libraries into flexible spaces for reading, studying, collaborating, and creating/innovating will continue. Well-trained and certified librarians are key to meeting the complex demands of a K-12 school. School libraries need to ensure that budgets remain strong, decision-makers and teachers understand the role of libraries and are presented with data and stories of impact, and access to relevant books, technology, and relevant programs is made available. Top priorities include digital literacy, information literacy, and instructional technology training for teachers, students, parents, and administrators.

CONCLUSION

I like to use Global Positioning Systems (GPS) technology as a metaphor for defining, negotiating, and arriving at an ideal future. GPS systems, like the one used for navigation, use at least three different satellites, or data sources, to triangulate where any one person is at any given moment. When using GPS, a destination address is entered, and then multiple points of data are provided in real time (e.g., distance, speed, time to get there, alternative pathways). What is most valuable, however, is that it provides the user a glimpse of the future so they can make informed decisions.

The broad trends identified in this chapter are most likely to be accurate in 2035, but the specifics must be defined by user needs and preferences *and* the expertise of the LIS organizations and professionals that serve them. The bottom line for libraries: the reasons we deliver services, resources, and programming really has not changed very much. That said, how libraries can deliver and implement them and how patrons and the community want to access them has changed dramatically. GPS thinking—people, data, and goals—can help us develop the library of 2035 that our patrons need and desire. It will most definitely take a lot of work, and it will require the ability to overcome challenges, but the view from the mountaintop will be well worth it.

NOTES

1. OpenAI, "Creating Safe AGI that benefits all of humanity," accessed October 18, 2023, https://openai.com/.
2. OpenAI, "Introducing ChatGPT," accessed October 18, 2023, https://openai.com/blog/chatgpt.
3. Sabrina Ortiz, "What is ChatGPT and why does it matter? Here's what you need to know," ZDNet, April 18, 2023, https://www.zdnet.com/article/what-is-chatgpt-and-why-does-it-matter-heres-everything-you-need-to-know/.
4. Dr. Anthony Chow personal communication via ChatGPT (April 12, 2023).
5. ACRL Research Planning and Review Committee, "Top trends in academic libraries: A review of the trends and issues," *Association of College and Research Libraries* 82, no. 6 (2022), https://crln.acrl.org/index.php/crlnews/article/view/25483/33379.
6. SoftBank Robotics, "For Better Business, Just Add Pepper," accessed January 31, 2024, https://us.softbankrobotics.com/pepper.
7. Paige Tutt, "Setting Up Libraries to Be the Best Space in School." *Edutopia*, August 8, 2023, https://www.edutopia.org/article/setting-up-libraries-to-be-the-best-space-in-school/.
8. WordsRated "State of US Public Libraries—More popular and digital than ever," February 17, 2022, https://wordsrated.com/state-of-us-public-libraries/#:~:text=More%20registered%20borrowers%20than%20ever,37.39%25%20of%20all%20collection%20use.

8

The Library as Community Enthusiast, Champion, and Advocate

Patty Wong

The library of 2035 will continue to be vital to community engagement and success, but the depth of that participation will depend upon the library's ability to adapt and respond effectively.

When I was elected president of the American Library Association, I visited libraries of all types—school, public, academic, and special—across the country and the world. Each library had a common commitment to community connection and support for values of access. Those visits left a deep impression upon me. I realized—if we could overcome the fiscal challenges and turn to collaboration and partnership—we could serve more people and have a greater impact, community by community.

In the past five years, more change has impacted library services than the previous twenty-five, and we haven't always had the time, nor the practice, to prepare. Libraries will need to continually evolve in response to the human and societal needs of our immediate, statewide, and national communities. Going forward, libraries need to consider numerous societal changes, such as politically and racially motivated unrest, divides between the advantaged and the disadvantaged, incivility in our marketplaces, insecurity in our sense of personal and professional safety, and attacks on the right to read and pursue learning. More than ever, libraries must champion leadership and advocacy at all levels, and our communities must be a part of this conversation. We need to help our users make sense of the world and how to succeed through the many changes we have already experienced and those we will experience in the future.

FOUNDATIONS FOR THE LIBRARY OF THE FUTURE

Libraries in 2035 must be even more community-based and community-facing than they already are in order to maintain relevance and an elevated value in their respective environments. Libraries need to reexamine how to engage with their communities and users. This means focusing on community conversations; ensuring social justice and equity, diversity, and inclusion (EDI) in libraries; engaging in collaboration to expand access; and seeking diversified funding. It is imperative to involve staff and stakeholders deliberately in all this work.

COMMUNITY CONVERSATIONS

Taking advantage of the library's reputation as a trusted and respected entity is crucial in advancing our role as facilitators. Librarians need to go beyond the roles of data and information gatherers to become providers of authoritative analysis by helping make sense of information either on their own or by bringing together others who can. The library of 2035 will be a resource of reliable, vetted information and will continue to be a communal place of discussion to elevate understanding and give voice to those who otherwise may not have a voice.

SOCIAL JUSTICE AND EQUITY, DIVERSITY, AND INCLUSION

The library of 2035 must provide opportunities to facilitate a better world by bringing social justice and EDI into the forefront of all areas of library work, including education and information access, and exemplify this work for its partners and collaborators. This means we need to ensure that all people have free and easy access to information and technology in our libraries and that these foundations are baked into our library policies and processes. Library leaders and workers must do the hard work of reflecting on their biases and premises that determined older practices, and begin to revise, eliminate, or create new policies and processes that truly uphold the principles and practices of social justice and EDI. Services must be strategically purposeful for us to maintain and sustain relevancy and the public's support, always with an eye toward equity and free access. Mission statements, strategic plans, and goal setting should further reflect that commitment. When libraries lead this work, their commissioners, trustees, and governing boards will continue the work in their own supportive operations.

COLLABORATION AND ACCESS

Collaboration must be part of our everyday practice to support library users better and engage in better library practices. For example, users would benefit greatly from libraries that allow them to borrow materials and obtain services without formal proof of address, access library services reliably 24/7, and use shared services regardless of library jurisdictions. A universal card within each state? What about a universal card across the nation? This type of collaboration will be more of a norm in 2035—it is simply good business. We need library leaders and legislative partners to champion this work with a commitment to resources and supportive lawmaking.

The library of 2035 will provide opportunities for staff to collaborate, share ideas, and learn from other libraries in their consortium. Resource sharing will be commonplace. Libraries will be able to share an integrated library system, and possibly even staff, with a sister agency that is smaller or a joint use with another community-facing entity: police, fire, parks, recreation, schools, and more. Instead of building walls that inhibit services (e.g., requiring library membership in a consortium or local residency of patrons in order to receive library services), libraries of 2035 will share access or storage to collections and services, recognizing this benefits all.

The library of 2035 may not always be able to provide resources locally to ensure this kind of collaboration. Library consortia could and should be able to support enhanced services regionally if funding is unavailable. Resources could be directed at the state and federal levels to fill gaps. Gap analysis should be part of the state and national priorities for funding. Collaboration and partnerships could be an elevated expectation for all grant and alternative funding, including the pursuit of alternative funding for libraries through legislation that is statewide or within regional jurisdictions. Imagine if there was collaboration regionally for a library initiative involving multiple jurisdictions.

The library of 2035 will also engage in more regional collaboration and sharing. What better way to economize than to agree on resource sharing or a focused collection development plan? Imagine sharing excess shelving, furnishings, and collections within our greater library systems, cost-sharing within the state for materials and resources, and collaborative cataloging (particularly to support non-English collections) through international support. As preparation for these new ideas emerges, librarians should begin to engage in dialogue with their systems libraries today and create funding priorities for these efforts.

DIVERSIFIED FUNDING

In 2035, the community support for impactful libraries will be palpable. Advocates, library leaders, and especially government-supported institutions should work actively toward diversified funding—whether from a voter initiative, sales, parcel tax, general bond or developer impact fees, or other types of resources that add sustainable support in addition to the specified general or base funding. Grant funding and donor-funded support are always welcome. Formal, diversified, and dedicated resources are fundamental to sustainably operating in a future environment. Existing funding from a single source will be insufficient to fully support library operations. A healthy library is often one that is sustained by multiple funding sources with longer-term sunsets. Libraries of 2035 will be involved in legislation and movements toward collaborative support for longer-term funding approaches that benefit beyond immediate borders of service.

CHAMPIONING, ADVOCATING, AND IMPLEMENTING CHANGES TO ADDRESS THE COMMUNITY'S NEEDS

As library workers, we cannot and must not take for granted that our community's needs are changing—often rapidly. We must remain nimble and smart in developing sustainable and mindful services. We cannot do this alone. Community voices are incredibly valuable and essential to the continuing services libraries offer, and in many cases, libraries will be reliant on collaborations with third-party entities to provide stronger impacts and outcomes for our respective communities. Key questions include:

- Do we work effectively with our current partners?
- Whom else do we want to work with to ensure the strongest support for our community?

People work more effectively when there is an established relationship.

The library of 2035 also needs to be designed differently to better support technology and to provide an enhanced user experience for its functions and services. These actions will position libraries strongly to meet their communities' new and changing needs.

TECHNOLOGY

Technology will play a vital role in the work of the library of 2035. We will need to automate systems, broaden access, keep up with community expectations, and create environments to support training and instructions for those with limited technology experience. As an effective resource and means of delivery, technology will drive decisions from acquisition to community engagement. Communication will remain a key part of our ability to connect. Unfortunately, I do not see full equity in terms of access unless libraries and our community expect it and demand it. Librarians can and should identify ways to make this part of the public discourse.

These technology changes do not just apply to front-line service delivery, but they also apply to the ways in which libraries store materials and information; libraries will also need to continue to be mindful of equity and inclusion concerns in technology implementation. For example, libraries will:

- increase vendor access through sharing protocols,
- expand access to different formats to meet customer needs,
- support the removal of outdated subject headings and integration of inclusive language, and
- ensure the strongest broadcasting of Wi-Fi access.

All these and more will be on the minds of community-centered library leaders of 2035.

Technology plans will be focused on access, advocacy, cost containment, and collaboration. Libraries will work with their centralized information technology leaders to drive opportunities and generate projects to increase and expand access and all things related to technology. Digital equity (i.e., access, interpretation, and use of information and communication technologies) remains a critical undercurrent impacting local and national success. By 2035, I predict a national effort to create equitable access to free high-speed internet and localized means and support for implementation.

Libraries will also use technology in its broadest capacities to develop new and exciting ways to learn. Our customers will benefit from this collaborative approach. Imagine a marketplace of ideas and materials where one can instantly interface with a hologram of Mother Teresa, Frida Kahlo, or Aretha Franklin to learn about their lives and share in their experiences using AI. Imagine options for printing any article or book or a portion of a monograph on demand and having it delivered anywhere within minutes. Imagine libraries where consumers can facilitate free or reduced-cost training or learning through systems of choice vetted through their local library consortia. Entrepreneurs and startups of all kinds will come to their local library for business preparation and certification and conduct business in person or virtually with clients through the self-service shared workspaces.

USER EXPERIENCE

The library of 2035 will be intensely focused and dedicated to the user experience, including digital and physical access. Libraries should offer services where every door is the right door. User experience begins with the concept of the library as a trusted and reliable place and is then followed by the ease of transportation, parking, and access to the library. Do you work with your local public transit to make sure there are stops close to your buildings? Is the parking area comfortable, familiar, well-lit, with emergency phone access, good cell and internet access, and plenty of EV chargers? Are there various media associated with the library to encourage use? Is there good wayfinding signage in languages that share the library's commitment to the diversity of the community? Are the hours convenient? Do the staff have the tools, training, and expectations to create the best customer experience environment? Will the customer want to come again? Is there a broad range

> The library of 2035 will be intensely focused and dedicated to the user experience, including digital and physical access. Libraries should offer services where every door is the right door.

of diversity and linguistic and multicultural skills and talents amongst staff to create the strongest outreach and engagement with the community? As the economy may drive some of our local decision-making, we must make efforts to retain access and not build artificial walls with policy or process. Library use should be an opus of abundance, not limitations.

CONCLUSION

Whether it's public service hours, literacy, social services programming, or outreach, the library of 2035 must maintain a commitment to community-centered work. That commitment will almost assuredly not look as it does today. But with the evolution of our society and economy, there is an opportunity to create the substantial change that our communities have been demanding. All libraries, library leaders, and workers need to be unafraid of the new and continue to center our work around the most important person to the library: the customer, no matter their age, ethnicity, or socioeconomic status.

9

We Are Not Alone

LIBRARIES MAKING A STRONGER IMPACT IN A GLOBAL COMMUNITY

Lynn Silipigni Connaway

The library of 2035 will be dependent upon relationship building and adaptability.

One of my favorite quotes by Brian Mathews emphasizes this point, stating that "by focusing on relationship building instead of service excellence, organizations can uncover new needs and be in position to make a stronger impact."[1]

I believe that if we look at past trends, we can identify patterns and plan for the future. Therefore, when preparing to write this chapter, I decided to look back at both my submission in *Library 2020*[2] and my work at OCLC Research during the past twenty years.[3]

REFLECTING ON PAST TRENDS

Historically, the library model has considered the user to be a part of the library. Our systems, ontologies, classification schemes, descriptions, and policies were centered on the workflows and needs of the library staff. We expected users to figure out these systems or to ask us for help.

In the late 1990s through 2005, OCLC Research concentrated on the optimization and quantitative analysis of library bibliographic data, systems, and collections. Simultaneously library staff were measuring and evaluating their worth by focusing on outputs (i.e., gate counts, number of volumes and titles, and number of individuals attending library programs). The greater the number of these outputs, the better the library, its offerings, and its status.

We learned, however, that counting outputs does not necessarily bring results. If those who control the funding or are the intended users of the collections, programs, and spaces do not use or know about these offerings, these offerings probably are not what is valued, expected, or needed.

In 2005, the focus shifted to placing the *user in the life of the library* instead of the library in the life of the user.[4] Focusing on the user is not a new idea. In 1931, Ranganathan said this in the fourth law of library science: "save the time of the reader."[5] However, the user has not always been our focus.

Assessment and evaluation of collections, programming, and spaces became important to library staff for several reasons. Assessment and evaluation informed library staff about the offerings wanted, expected, and needed by both current and prospective users of the library; provided an opportunity to promote the library by seeking user input; and enabled library staff to include user needs and expectations in the library's strategic planning.

The profession began to widely promote and advocate for libraries at this time. Initiatives and professional development for library staff and leaders focused on how to articulate the value of the library to their community stakeholders. Library assessment and evaluation shifted from not only counting and reporting outputs to also measuring impact, which helped library leaders tell the library's story and focus on community engagement.

In my *Library 2020* chapter, the first sentence read: "The library in 2020 will be engagement centered."[6] While true, that engagement drastically changed with the global COVID-19 pandemic. When the physical spaces in libraries closed, some individuals in the community no longer had access to Wi-Fi, internet, computers, printers, physical materials, audio and video recordings, restrooms, or warm or cool places to relax. In response, library staff made changes to meet the needs of the community. For example, they made Wi-Fi available in their parking lots, sent materials to homes and offices, and offered outdoor material pickup.[7] This focus on engagement and meeting the community's needs exemplifies library staff's focus on relationship building.[8]

The pandemic made it clear that we are in a global society and economy. It also brought many social injustices to the forefront that previously had received less global attention. These injustices include the inequitable and exclusive practices in hiring, training, caring for, and promoting staff as well as library vocabularies, retrieval systems, and ways to access information and resources. During the pandemic, the digital divide's impact on access to spaces, resources, and information was even more damaging.

> Relationships have become more far-reaching, and our communities have expanded. Now we are part of a global society that is impacted by the constantly changing and evolving environment.

Relationships have become more far-reaching, and our communities have expanded. Now we are part of a global society that is impacted by the constantly changing and evolving environment. Currently, there are threats to democracy with materials, programs, and meeting space challenges. Some individuals do not have access to information to make decisions on voting and civic policies or on medical and legal issues. Those with access to information often do not know how to determine its credibility. In a world of data science, data analytics, and artificial intelligence (AI), privacy and ethics often are ignored or not considered.

Lepore stated, "numbers, a century ago, wielded the kind of influence that data wields today."[9] She explains how numbers had been used to identify patterns and characteristics. By the early 1930s, these facts were converted to data "to be read by machines." She attributes the beginning of the digitization of knowledge to libraries converting materials to microfiche and microfilm.[10] The discipline of AI began in the 1950s with a group of scientists, philosophers, and mathematicians, such as Alan Turing, who ideated ways to build intelligent machines based on human reasoning.[11]

NAVIGATING TODAY'S DIGITAL AND AI ENVIRONMENT THROUGH RELATIONSHIP BUILDING

So, why the history lesson, and what does this have to do with the library in 2035?

First, we have been living in a world that uses numbers and data to identify patterns for centuries. However, this world still needs people to make sense of the data—to tell the story. Second, we have been living with the concept of AI for more than seventy years. With the widespread use of AI and data for predictions and modeling (e.g., Alexa and Siri; automated chat service on websites; automated customer service for phone calls; and ChatGPT, which transfers machine learning to OpenAI's large language models [LLMs]), the importance of human interactions has become more valued in our daily lives.[12] AI makes predictions about our searches; answers our questions; proofs our work; and can write our assignments, emails, text messages, blog posts, social media posts, papers, and more. This environment calls for instruction on how to navigate these environments by evaluating the information provided and being aware of what people may be giving up in regard to their right to privacy.

Who better to provide this instruction than library staff? In this world of misinformation and disinformation, AI, and predictive modeling of our behaviors, libraries provide a neutral, welcoming place with staff who are able to help make sense of mass quantities of information and data, much of it not vetted. This is the perfect opportunity for library staff to be the "experts" in a global information society. This will require collaboration, partnerships, negotiation, and instruction.

Providing instruction or information literacy courses is not new to the library. However, the current information environment demands new ways of teaching and learning information literacy skills that depend on the relationship and trust between the instructor and learner. Mackey and Jacobson suggest that consumers of information adopt a meta-literacy approach, defined as "an overarching and self-referential framework that integrates emerging technologies and unifies multiple literacy types ... expands the scope of generally understood information competencies and places a particular emphasis on producing and sharing information in participatory digital environments."[13] Social context shapes the experience for the individuals who are key to information literacy.[14] Meta-literacy provides a participatory, interactive environment that enables learners "to continuously reflect, change, and contribute as critical thinkers."[15]

This type of participatory learning prepares individuals to use and adapt their knowledge and skills to determine the credibility of information as this landscape continues to evolve and change. It further creates the opportunity for relationship building because participatory learning requires a mutual understanding of trust between both the instructor and the learner. Relationship building has been a theme in recent focus group interviews with public library staff and leaders.[16] Creating an equitable and human-centered work environment that focuses on staff well-being demonstrates the importance of focusing on relationships with staff and the community. Library leaders also have engaged in invigorating discussions about collaborations with other libraries, agencies, and departments within their communities and the importance of developing relationships with collaborators and partners. From working with local rural fire departments to delivering hotspots and lending bicycles for transportation and recreation to providing space and staff volunteers at library branch locations for medical staff to administer COVID-19 vaccines and medical advice, library leaders and staff have been contributing to the well-being of the community while developing critical partnerships.

However, these collaborations and partnerships are not easy to initiate or cultivate. They take time, patience, and perseverance. Library staff and leaders have to first make a case for the collaboration or partnership, then explain why the collaboration is important or critical to both parties, and also identify what the library will bring to the partnership that would benefit the other party. This is where the library's outcomes become critical and are used to tell the story of the library's value to the partner or collaborator and to the community. Lankes reiterated the importance of developing relationships through storytelling when he wrote, "Knowledge is created through conversation—if you're in the knowledge business, you're in the conversation business."[17]

A leader of a large metropolitan public library in Canada stated, "The public library is a democratic institution ... not just a community hub but a civic commons."[18] This statement exemplifies the role of the library as a welcoming space that provides credible information representing different viewpoints and perspectives, instruction, technology, and programming as well as help with the discovery and access of materials and information for everyday life.

CONCLUSION

How do I envision the library in 2035? I envision great opportunities for information professionals to develop relationships in the global community and learn what changes are needed and expected by the members of this global community. By engaging with the community, library staff and leaders will be able to review and revamp metadata, ontology, collections, and staff hiring and promotion practices and policies to meet global needs. They will test, use, develop, and teach new technologies and applications.

The future is not being afraid to change and to try new ways of working, such as new ways of providing access; hiring, promoting, training, and caring for staff; developing new approaches for teaching and learning information literacy skills; providing new types of spaces; and developing and maintaining collaborations and partnerships. Library staff and leaders also will be more actively involved in sustainability and climate change initiatives at local, regional, and global levels. But none of this is relevant if it is not centered on the needs of the global community and if we fail to cultivate relationships at the broader global level.

As I said in a recent interview, "No library can do it all alone. We need to start thinking globally about our materials, policies, and practices. We need to embrace the new technologies and services that are out there and see where we fit, and where our expertise is needed. If people are going to use ChatGPT, let us teach them how. I believe we have a great future if we continue to adapt and evolve."[19] And we only can adapt and evolve if we continue to build relationships.

NOTES

1. Brian Mathews, "Think Like a Startup: A White Paper to Inspire Library Entrepreneurialism," April 4, 2012, http://chronicle.com/blognetwork/theubiquitouslibrarian/2012/04/04/think-like-a-startup-a-white-paper/.
2. Lynn Silipigni Connaway, "Meeting the Expectations of the Community: The Engagement-Centered Library," in *Library 2020: Today's Leading Visionaries Describe Tomorrow's Library*, ed. Joseph Janes (Lanham, MD: Scarecrow Press, 2013): 83–88.
3. Lynn Silipigni Connaway et al., "The Library in the Life of the Community: Twenty Years of OCLC Research," *Library Trends* (forthcoming).
4. Lynn Silipigni Connaway, ed., *The Library in the Life of the User: Engaging with People Where They Live and Learn* (Dublin, OH: OCLC Research, 2015), http://www.oclc.org/content/dam/research/publications/2015/oclcresearch-library-in-life-of-user.pdf.
5. Shiyali Ramamrita Ranganathan, *The Five Laws of Library Science* (London: Edward Goldston, Ltd., 1931).
6. Connaway, "Meeting the Expectations of the Community: The Engagement-Centered Library," 83–88.
7. Amelia Bryne and Marijke Visser, "Keeping Communities Connected: Library Broadband Services During the COVID-19 Pandemic," *ALA Policy Perspectives* 9 (March 2022), https://www.ala.org/advocacy/sites/ala.org.advocacy/files/content/telecom/

broadband/Keeping_Communities_Connected_030722.pdf; Cecelia Kang, "Parking Lots Have Become a Digital Lifeline," March 5, 2020, https://www.nytimes.com/2020/05/05/technology/parking-lots-wifi-coronavirus.html.

8. Lynn Silipigni Connaway, et al. *New Model Library: Pandemic Effects and Library Directions* (Dublin, OH: OCLC Research, 2021), https://doi.org/10.25333/2d1r-f907.

9. Jill Lepore, "The Data Delusion," *New Yorker*, April 3, 2023, https://www.newyorker.com/magazine/2023/04/03/the-data-delusion.

10. Ibid.

11. Rochwell Anyosha, "The History of Artificial Intelligence," *Science in the News* blog. Harvard University Graduate School of Arts and Sciences, August 28, 2017, https://sitn.hms.harvard.edu/flash/2017/history-artificial-intelligence/.

12. OpenAI, "Creating safe AI that benefits all of humanity," accessed October 20, 2023, https://openai.com/.

13. Thomas P. Mackey and Trudi E. Jacobson, "Reframing Information Literacy as a Metaliteracy," *College and Research Libraries* 76 (2011): 62–63.

14. Thomas P. Mackey and Trudi E. Jacobson, *Metaliteracy: Reinventing Information Literacy to Empower Learners* (Chicago, IL: ALA Neal-Schuman, 2014).

15. Trudi E. Jacobson and Thomas P. Mackey, "Proposing a Metaliteracy Model to Redefine Information Literacy," *Communications in Information Literacy*, 7, no. 2 (2013): 88. https://doi.org/10.15760/comminfolit.2013.7.2.138.

16. OCLC Research on public libraries: research in progress.

17. R. David Lankes, *The New Librarianship Field Guide* (Cambridge: MIT Press, 2016): 23.

18. Interview with public library leader (confidential), May 4, 2023.

19. Lynn Silipigni Connaway, "Not Everything Is on the Internet, and What Is on the Internet Is Not Always Credible," interview by Teresa Bau, Open University of Catalonia, May 4, 2023, https://www.uoc.edu/portal/es/news/entrevistes/2023/018-lynn-silipigni-connaway.html.

III
Equity and Inclusion

Part III: Equity and Inclusion focuses on how important it is for libraries to address diversity, equity, inclusion, belonging (DEIB), and social justice to ensure that all *people have equitable access to resources and information. The authors of chapters 10 through 14 emphasize different approaches to achieve a more sustainable and DEIB-focused future for the library of 2035, specifically noting that these libraries will:*

- uphold a diversity lens so all members of society relate, connect with, and see themselves as part of the library *(Cooke)*.
- be the trusted local space for community members to cultivate empathy about the diverse cultures of their neighbors through inclusive library experiences that ready them to fully participate in today's global culture *(Pitchford)*.
- be universal, a seamless system of libraries that positions the library profession to achieve full power and potential *(Norman)*.
- be open, inclusive, and diverse, utilizing social science and humanities methodologies, a superstructure approach, and an awareness of generational and economic influences *(Hudson-Ward)*.
- need to ensure that every student has unfettered access to the opportunities, resources, and instruction they rightfully deserve *(Valenza and Kachel)*.

In chapter 10, Cooke addresses the significant need for libraries to be equitable, accessible, and representative of the communities they serve and notes that libraries have a lot of work to do if they are to accomplish this by 2035. Librarians will need to act on behalf of others, be empathetic and understanding, and be willing to advocate for diverse programming, services, and resources that represent and meet the expectations of their community. In chapter 11, Pitchford warns about libraries creating diversity programming through their own lens, noting that this can cause more harm than good. To truly connect with and effectively serve diverse communities, she suggests that librarians co-create programming with their diverse communities in ways that foster understanding, connectivity, trust, and loyalty.

In chapter 12, Norman makes the case for allowing users to have more seamless access to libraries via a system that provides users with universal library cards. Libraries that collaborate, partner, and share resources can also utilize shared data to monitor and enable outcomes and impact at scale. Hudson-Ward, in chapter 13, discusses the importance of purposeful planning and action to build a future that is inclusive and diverse in academic libraries. Factors such as library space, generational influences, and economic instabilities can influence whether the library remains stagnant or moves closer to being an open and inclusive organization. Similarly, in chapter 14, Valenza and Kachel emphasize the struggle that school libraries have in moving beyond inequities in school systems and communities. They offer several models to help address the disparities between students who have access to library programming and those who do not, including ensuring literacy instruction is taught, programs are built through collaborations, a pipeline of trained professionals is sustained into the future, and equitable practices are incorporated throughout the district. Of most importance, they call for advocacy to sustain efforts to ensure every student can access the opportunities, resources, and instruction they rightfully deserve.

Archived webcasts of author interviews are available at: https://sites.google.com/sjsu.edu/library2035/home

10

Equity Is a Necessary Foundation

Nicole A. Cooke

The library of 2035 will uphold a diversity lens so that all members of society relate, connect with, and see themselves as part of the library.

Let us talk about equity as a primary foundational piece of our library practice and the lens through which we do our work in our library organizations. If we imagine a brick wall, with a book under one of the corners, we see how the entire wall shifts and flows. The new shape could be perceived as unexpected, or even unwelcomed, but also beautiful and unique. We can view the book as a disruptive force; we can also view it as a positive force that creates a significant difference for the whole structure. It ultimately impacts everything built upon and set on top of the wall. Similarly, equity can be seen as both a disruptive and positive force that should be a foundational brick as we imagine and predict the library profession of 2035.

When we plan for and implement equity, it benefits everyone involved. For example, when a library creates a curb cut to facilitate wheelchair use, it also facilitates caregivers using strollers as well as people with joint pain. If a library creates a "comprehensive collection of multi-format materials for children, teens, and adults featuring a wide array of characters, subjects, languages, authors, and illustrators with differing perspectives,"[1] that act can enrich the experience of everyone who uses the library, not just a specific underrepresented community group. If that same library strives to "provide technology to help bridge the digital divide,"[2] those improvements will enable better access for those inside the library and for those who rely on the library's online offerings in their homes. When library professionals endeavor to become culturally competent to better engage with a new constituent group in their community, their improved interpersonal and empathy skills will be evident in all their personal interactions.³ We should consider our professional practice as having equity, diversity, inclusion, access, sovereignty, and social justice at the core of what library and information science (LIS) professionals espouse and enact, and what our organizational lenses should be.

An equity foundation infiltrates and influences an organization's infrastructure and ensures that the environment and culture are welcoming and safe spaces for all marginalized, underrepresented, disfavored, or otherwise underserved individuals. Not having an equity foundation and lens creates a huge chasm and discrepancy between the work we do in the name of equity and the work we do to *sustain* equity. For example, suppose we do not demonstrate equity on either the inside or outside of our libraries. In that case, we will inevitably have students, patrons, and community members who do not feel welcome or see themselves in what libraries do. Similarly, this lack of equity also applies to library staff and the LIS profession's recruitment and retention issues with attracting diverse candidates.

INEQUITY IN OUR LIBRARIES

There is no shortage of inequity in our communities. This shortage manifests in our libraries and the LIS profession through the need for more culturally responsive practice and pedagogy. Libraries are microcosms of the greater society, and the issues we see in our libraries are the same as the dilemmas we see out in society at large, just on a different scale and in a different setting. So, the issues we see in our libraries take an extra toll on information professionals.

An example of how inequities trickle down and influence the library profession comes from the February 2021 cover of *School Library Journal* (SLJ).⁴ There was a great deal of controversy during Black History Month surrounding the cover, which centered on a young white girl holding up a book with a Black boy on the cover to her face. To many, the cover was reminiscent of blackface, which is historically problematic and offensive. When disdain and negative feedback built up online, the magazine editors became defensive and doubled down by saying that the cover was not about blackface—"that wasn't our intention"—and that readers had misinterpreted the illustration. However, even if the editors did not intend the cover to be offensive and did not want to *admit* it was offensive, that is how people perceived it, and harm was done. Another issue with *SLJ* is that the editors at the time were Asian American and Dominican American, and they claimed they could not be racist because they were women of color. If we examine this critically and radically,⁵ with nuance, and through a lens of cultural competence, we recognize and understand that everyone and anyone can be prejudiced, bigoted, and/or anti-Black regardless of race, ethnicity, or nationality. It does not matter if you are a person of color or not.

Critically examining the *SLJ* cover challenges LIS professionals to question their collections, services, policies, and missions. Examples of questions LIS professionals can ask to examine their practices include (and are not limited to):

- Can information consumers see themselves positively portrayed in the information we provide to them?
- Do our collections feature diverse materials representing more than just historical events? And do we offer these materials in multiple languages?
- Can Black boys and men wear hoodies in our institutions without scrutiny or fear?

Many embedded rules and policies in our organizations are implicitly and explicitly rooted in biases. If we do not critically and radically question and examine our roles and policies, the inequities are perpetuated and allowed to flourish.

Not allowing communities to see themselves represented in our institutions is terrible, and it is certainly not something that the profession should want or tolerate. At the time this chapter was written in 2023, there were evidential scenarios that demonstrated the threats to improving the equity gap in the near future. For example:

- An acute uptick in library book challenges and censorship has occurred—the likes of which has not been seen since the McCarthy era.[6]
- A dangerous rise in legislation around the United States has attempted to prohibit how information is taught to students and library patrons.
- The "Don't Say Gay Law" in Florida went into effect, which has attempted to censor teachers from talking about the LGBTQIA+ community.[7]

Our discriminatory worst-case scenarios are happening, and without staff, policies, and rules that reflect a strong sense of equity, library professionals are not able to disrupt and fight back. There is much work to do if we are to envision a library in 2035 that is equitable, accessible, and representative of the diverse needs of the community it serves. How can we accomplish this? How can we reverse the trends and build more equitable practices at all levels within the LIS field?

RADICALLY IMAGINE THE FUTURE OF LIS

As I radically imagine the future of LIS,[8] I think of the many conversations that have occurred in the profession, particularly after the murder of George Floyd in 2020. Conversations about focusing on critical self-reflection, developing critical consciousness, and engaging in action and advocacy[9] are essential, but more is needed. As the profession looks toward a more powerful and influential future, *action* in these areas is imperative. This is the only way to create and maintain an equitable professional foundation.

CRITICAL SELF-REFLECTION

Critical self-reflection (CSR) requires us to dig deep internally and assess who we are as culturally responsive human beings. It is a fluid and ongoing process that requires vulnerability. CSR challenges us to acknowledge, examine, and rectify our implicit and explicit biases, identify our knowledge gaps, pinpoint our strengths, and use this information to positively grow and change in ways that benefit those around us. As part of the CSR process, we must embrace active listening, cultural competence, and cultural humility. Through our own process of getting to know ourselves, we get closer to being able to know and subsequently care for and engage with others.

Active listening is an essential skill—one we must strengthen if we are going to participate in equity work effectively. We must listen to others; we must not just listen to respond, but we must instead listen to hear and understand. We must listen to hard things. Active listening includes listening to experiences other people have that you have never had and exhibiting empathy.

Cultural competence and cultural humility bridge that gap between critical self-reflection and critical consciousness (described below). These are ongoing and dynamic processes that we will engage in long-term. Cultural humility is having the wherewithal to know we still have things to learn, and room to grow and change. Cultural competence is much more than having cultural awareness; cultural competence is about becoming aware of people and groups who are different from us and actually celebrating those differences. Bringing everyone's rich history and culture to the table benefits everyone.

CRITICAL CONSCIOUSNESS

Similarly, we need to develop a critical consciousness (CC). CC occurs when we can acknowledge societal ills and better recognize and understand the systemic and structural barriers that sustain intergroup and intragroup inequities. We cannot address or alleviate things that we do not see or understand.

Education scholars and justice advocates bell hooks and Paulo Freire[10] have greatly informed the concept of CC. hooks wrote about teaching as a way of transgressing boundaries and transcending those differences that we might ordinarily think divide us.[11] We all have problems, points of privilege and disadvantage. However, education is one of the great equalizers and one of the ways in which we can transcend differences. Freire wrote about education as a means to liberation and to bring people together. Both Freire and hooks favored the co-construction of knowledge, which values the wisdom of teachers *and* students. Learners bring as much value and experience to the table as the teacher does, and the two groups should work together to create new knowledge and experiences. Moving past differences and focusing on similarities facilitates dialogue and the creation of things bigger and greater.

ACTION AND ADVOCACY

Once the CSR is completed and the LIS organization has developed a level of CC, the only thing left to do is act! This newfound understanding and empathy must be put into action. There are many ways to act, whether by donating to a cause, writing to elected officials, volunteering in the community, or advocating for books facing bans or challenges at your local library. Taking action could also include:

- speaking up for others in person and online,
- being an active bystander,[12]
- giving up our own power and privilege to help, and
- empowering others.

When we have a seat at the proverbial table, action and advocacy involve us making room at the table for others or perhaps even giving up our own seat. Action and advocacy, which are ongoing processes, require us to go out of our way to make things better for others, even when it is inconvenient.

CONCLUSION

Can we achieve the equitable library we envision by 2035? It is possible, but we have much work to do—work that must start now to create the desired future. We must continually act on behalf of others, and that requires advocacy, understanding, and actively acting on behalf of others—even when it is not comfortable or convenient. When we act on behalf of others, we might consider ourselves allies. However, a note of caution: we do not assume the privilege of calling ourselves allies; rather, the communities for whom we advocate must first deem us worthy of these titles. Ideally, we should strive to be accomplices. Allies may lend their voices to a cause or protest, but an accomplice will give up some of their privilege to ensure some measure of equity for others.

> An ally will mostly engage in activism by standing with an individual or group in a marginalized community. An accomplice will focus more on dismantling the structures that oppress that individual or group—and such work will be directed by the stakeholders in the marginalized group. Simply, ally work focuses on individuals, and accomplice work focuses on the structures of decision-making agency.[13]

Being an ally and an accomplice each requires effort, consistency, and action. But being an accomplice requires systemic change, not just lending support to those with less privilege.

Ultimately, as we selflessly embark on this continuous, dynamic, and sometimes isolating work, we should strive to be equity champions. Equity

> Equity champions use their voices to amplify the voices of those who do not ordinarily have the opportunity to share their perspectives. They understand that this work requires individual and collective action to be successful and sustainable.

champions use their voices to amplify the voices of those who do not ordinarily have the opportunity to share their perspectives. They understand that this work requires individual and collective action to be successful and sustainable.

When equity is at the core of professional practice, and advocating for others is a normalized and desired part of daily work, being an equity champion is inevitable. Equity champions work for everyone to be treated fairly, regardless of race, ability, sexuality, socioeconomic status, religious beliefs, cultural background, education level, etc.

Centering equity in practice strengthens the entire profession, to 2035 and beyond.

NOTES

1. South Pasadena Public Library, "Equity, Diversity, and Inclusion," City of South Pasadena, April 17, 2023, https://www.southpasadenaca.gov/government/departments/library/about-the-library/equity-diversity-and-inclusion.
2. Ibid.
3. Nicole A. Cooke (2016), *Information Services to Diverse Populations: Developing Culturally Competent Library Professionals*, Bloomsbury Publishing USA.
4. Kathy Ishizuka, "About Our February Cover I from the Editor," *Library Journal* (February 4, 2021), https://www.slj.com/story/about-our-february-cover-from-the-editor.
5. Angela Davis (2006), "Moe Lectureship in Women's Studies," Saint Peter, MN, Gustavus Adolphus College, Women's Studies Program.
6. Adriane Herrick Juarez, "103. Dealing with Book Banning with Tracie D. Hall," *Library Leadership Podcast* (April 28, 2022), https://libraryleadershippodcast.com/103-dealing-with-book-banning-with-tracie-d-hall/.
7. National Education Association (NEA), (June 2022), *What You Need to Know about Florida's "Don't Say Gay" Law*, https://www.nea.org/sites/default/files/2022-06/FL%20Dont%20Say%20Gay%20KYR%20-%20Updated2022.06.pdf.
8. Alex Khasnabish and Max Haiven (2014), *The Radical Imagination: Social Movement Research in the Age of Austerity*, London: Zed Books, excerpt, https://www.opendemocracy.net/en/transformation/why-social-movements-need-radical-imagination/.
9. Nicole A. Cooke, "Reading Is Only a Step on the Path to Anti-Racism," *Publishers Weekly* (June 19, 2020), https://www.publishersweekly.com/pw/by-topic/industry-news/libraries/article/83626-reading-is-only-a-step-on-the-path-to-anti-racism.html.
10. Paulo Freire (1970), *Pedagogy of the oppressed*, New York: Seabury Press.
11. bell hooks (2014), *Teaching to transgress*, Routledge.

12. Nicole A. Cooke (2017), "Librarians as Active Bystanders: Centering Social Justice in LIS Practice," *The Portable MLIS: Insights from the Experts, 2nd Edition.* Santa Barbara, CA: ABC-CLIO/Libraries Unlimited: 39–48.

13. Colleen Clemens, "Ally or Accomplice? The Language of Activism," *Learning for Justice* (June 5, 2017), https://www.learningforjustice.org/magazine/ally-or-accomplice-the-language-of-activism.

11

Libraries, Trust, and the Cultural Booty Call

Veronda J. Pitchford

The library of 2035 will be the trusted local space for community members to cultivate empathy about the diverse cultures of their neighbors through inclusive library experiences that ready them to fully participate in today's global culture.

A Monmouth University Poll reported that 76 percent of Americans considered racism and discrimination a "big problem," an increase of 26 percentage points from 2015.[1] The two pandemics of 2020—COVID-19 and the racial reckoning (i.e., the killing of George Floyd and other Black Americans and the 150 percent spike in hate crimes against Asian Americans and Pacific Islanders)[2]—further demonstrated the depth of division over race in the United States and the growing calls for change. Fania Davis, director of Restorative Justice for Oakland Youth, said, "We are beginning to disrupt centuries of denial of our collective biography. . . . Whenever you have such an intense crisis, it also presents an opportunity for significant or revolutionary change."[3]

Libraries have the power to be part of that change. Using heritage programming to expand understanding of communities' cultural groups directly aligns with the public library's commitment to equitable access to information and lifelong learning. However, issues such as white gaze and cultural objectification in heritage programming reflect the need for better understanding of BIPOC cultures and communities. Libraries can work in new ways to build BIPOC community trust and create partnerships with BIPOC groups for co-creation and authentic representation in library heritage programming and beyond as we look toward the library in 2035.

CULTURAL BOOTY CALL

Urban Dictionary defines the *booty call* as a disparaging title for the "lesser of two unequal partners," and a casual meeting "devoid of any meaningful social engagement."[4] Heritage Month programming is the cultural booty call of libraries because it is time-specific (occurring during assigned months), objectifies a community's sacred items and rituals, and rarely includes opportunities to cultivate trust or partnership opportunities outside of library programming throughout the year. Consequently, Heritage Month programming often unintentionally reinforces cultural stereotypes instead of serving as an opportunity to challenge them. This is not to say, however, that Heritage Month programming should disappear. In fact, with libraries having such a renowned reputation as a trusted institution, they are well positioned to rethink the future of Heritage Month programming and expand it beyond Heritage Month to cultivate empathy for communities across the country.

WHITE GAZE AND CULTURAL OBJECTIFICATION

White gaze is "the assumption that the default reader or observer is coming from a perspective of someone who identifies as white."[5] The term was coined by Toni Morrison when she began writing in the 1950s, commenting on the fact that much of African American literature and poetry were responding to the "the white gaze"—the idea of the white oppressor.[6] The impact of the white gaze can include perpetuating cultural and racial stereotypes and distorting or silencing the featured BIPOC experience—both of which are detrimental to understanding cultural experiences.

Several authors have written about white gaze and Heritage Month programming. For example, in the article "The Burden of Asian and Pacific Islander Month Under the White Gaze," Gabes Torres states:

> There was a time when I thought that API Month was meant for us to celebrate and reconnect with our wide array of identities, expressions, and histories. But over time, the month became a rigid incubator in which we are lumped into reductive categories of what it means to be Asian and Pacific Islander—as if we are the same people. Additionally, the sense of responsibility to educate others, especially White people, on racism and anti-Asian violence increasingly grew into an expectation, or even a demand, since the start of the pandemic.[7]

Authors have also written about the impact on Native American Heritage Month. In her article, "Why Native American Heritage Month can actually be a nightmare for Native people," Jana Schmieding, a Native American (Cheyenne River Lokota) writer and public educator, shared how she offered to present an alternate, non-culturally appropriative program upon hearing about a public library's annual teen dreamcatcher craft program (i.e., the dreamcatcher is a sacred Ojibwe item). Schmieding's aim was to support the Ojibwe peoples' struggle to preserve their formerly outlawed religious beliefs from appropriative practices, noting that: "Native American Heritage Month can be a yearly autumnal hellscape for Indigenous folks, one riddled with microaggressions, political incorrectness, and appropriative behavior that makes our ancestors stir in their 'haunted burial grounds.'"[8] However, while she offered to do a ninety-minute talk to the teens focusing on Indigenous history and modern Native issues as well as potentially teaching them a traditional dance, the librarian allocated only fifteen minutes for her presentation as the dreamcatcher activity would take an hour. While the librarian's intent was to offer programming and an activity for Native American Heritage Month, the lack of time devoted to Jana's talk to truly represent tribal history and culture resulted in a form of silencing—or white gazing—her.

INTENT VERSUS IMPACT

Good intentions do not always result in positive impacts. Many educators and Heritage Month program providers point to the need for examination of intent and impact when designing programming. Libraries are not to blame for the state of heritage programming.

The United States has no national model of reconciliation or racial healing. For example, there are fifty-two countries that have established Truth and Reconciliation Commissions, the "official body tasked with discovering and revealing past wrongdoing by a government (or, depending on the circumstances, non-state actors)," with the goal of resolving past conflicts.[9]

Libraries cannot, nor should they, play the role of Truth and Reconciliation Commissions. However, they can work with communities to design library programming to address the values, history, current reality, and power relationships that shape culture—and the future.[10]

THE FUTURE IS TRUST AND EMPATHY

All relationships (even booty calls) require some level of trust. Social psychologist Julian Rotter defined *trust* as "a generalized expectancy held by an individual that the word, promise, oral or written statement of another individual or group can be relied on."[11] *Harvard Business Review*'s "Begin with Trust" article lists three core drivers of trust:

- *Authenticity:* when others believe they are interacting with the real you.
- *Logic:* when others have faith in your judgment and competence.
- *Empathy:* when others feel you care about them.

When trust is lost, it can almost always be traced back to a breakdown in one of these core drivers.[12]

However, trust, like most commodities, is not evenly distributed across American society. "Race is the life experience that has the biggest impact on trust."[13] When librarians incorporate empathy and authenticity throughout the library experience, they help instill these values within the community; this can contribute to a cultural shift within that community. Empathy is valued as an individual trait—an ability to emotionally connect with another person and value their life experience in an authentic way.[14] Both trust and empathy require authenticity. The first step is practicing empathy in the library to ensure it becomes an empathetic organization.

CO-CREATING AN EMPATHETIC ORGANIZATION

So, how do libraries create empathetic organizations? One way is for libraries to learn from the outward-facing framework called trust-based philanthropy that some philanthropic organizations have adopted.[15] Started in 2014, trust-based philanthropy addresses the power structure in place between philanthropic organizations and communities and is rooted in advancing equity, shifting power, building mutually accountable relationships, and demonstrating humility and collaboration in the work. The trust-based values are: culture, structures, leadership, and practices. Though not granting agencies, libraries are departments of local government, and for some historically excluded and immigrant communities, trust in government can be dangerous. This outward-facing framework prioritizes centering relationships, working for systemic equity in the community, embracing learning about the community, redistributing power, partnering in the spirit of service, being accountable to those they seek to support, and embracing opportunities for growth.[16]

Co-creation is critical for libraries to embrace their drive to create empathetic organizations. A great example of co-creation from which libraries can learn is the Poverty Truth Network,[17] which is based in Scotland. The Poverty Truth Network leverages co-creation to develop lasting social change to address poverty through partnerships with "people who know what it means to struggle against poverty," policymakers, and nonprofit executives. They employ the following strategies to build empathy and understanding between those working professionally to address poverty and those with lived experience:

- Focus conversations on the direct experience of people who understand what it means to struggle against poverty;
- Connect and build impactful relationships between those who have experienced poverty and society's decision-makers;
- Honor the need to establish trust before difficult conversations; and,
- Seek to "humanize people and systems" to ensure everyone is treated as human beings.[18]

This powerful and effective model offers strategies that libraries can utilize with library boards and policymaking committees to demonstrate collaborative and trusting partnerships and put participatory creation in action.

CO-CREATED HERITAGE PROGRAM EXAMPLE: LIBRARY INNOVATION LAB

The California Humanities' Library Innovation Lab (LiL): Exploring New Ways of Engaging Immigrant Communities through Public Humanities Programming grant[19] is an excellent example of a co-created heritage program with the community. A cohort of programming librarians learn empathy-based design thinking strategies to deliver responsive and relevant public humanities programming for a preidentified immigrant community in their library service area. The librarians begin with interviews and conversations to understand the needs and aspirations and to gain empathy before program development begins. Program design is iterative as they work with the community to identify topics and presenters reflecting interview conversations. Community feedback throughout the process ensures programming reflects what was heard in the community conversations. These programs aim to foster creative humanities programming in and by libraries that provide welcoming experiences for immigrants, contribute to building more inclusive communities, and use collaborative learning and reflective practices.

This model and the LiL's heritage programming was so impressive that it was featured in an Infopeople webinar, "Welcoming Immigrants through Cultural Programming: Lessons from the Field."[20] After engaging with community members, a LiL librarian identified that local parents, whose primary language was Arabic, were eager for their children to hear Arabic spoken outside the home. The resulting programs included a bilingual Arabic/English story time and an intergenerational game night for teens and parents featuring games from their home countries and the United States. The programming met the interviewed parents' stated needs and also served as a fun and culturally enriching program for everyone in the community.

CONCLUSION

There is a chasm filled with misinformation, misunderstanding, and misperceptions dividing communities. Remaining naive against these issues puts libraries at risk in remaining relevant and resilient to the diverse needs—and unique cultural opportunities—of the communities they serve. As we envision the library of 2035,

> Hosting Heritage Month events, activities, or story times is not enough. Cultivating empathy in library communities, and co-creating library experiences with members of that community, is necessary to create understanding and connectivity.

we must avoid cultural objectification and cultural booty calls and instead keep the community's core cultural heritage in mind when developing programs throughout the year. Hosting Heritage Month events, activities, or story times is not enough. Cultivating empathy in library communities, and co-creating library experiences with members of that community, is necessary to create understanding and connectivity. So, as we look to the future, how can we build a more empathetic library by 2035?

The answer lies within Octavia Butler's quote in *Parable of the Sower*: "The only lasting truth is change."[21] As trusted community partners, libraries have successfully supported community needs as they have evolved and changed throughout history. Given this, I am confident that libraries are more than up to the challenge.

NOTES

1. Monmouth University, "Protestors' Anger Justified Even If Actions May Not Be," (June 2, 2020), https://www.monmouth.edu/polling-institute/reports/monmouthpoll_us_060220/.
2. As reported by the Center for the Study of Hate and Extremism at California State University at California State University, San Bernardino.
3. Sarah Souli, "Does America Need a Truth and Reconciliation Commission?" *Politico*, August 16, 2020, https://www.politico.com/news/magazine/2020/08/16/does-america-need-a-truth-and-reconciliation-commission-395332.
4. *Urban Dictionary*, "Booty Call," accessed October 2, 2023, https://www.urbandictionary.com/define.php?term=booty%20call.
5. Wikipedia, "White Gaze," accessed October 2, 2023, https://en.wikipedia.org/wiki/White_gaze.
6. Ibid.
7. Gabes Torres, "The Burden of Asian and Pacific Islander Month Under the White Gaze," *Yes!*, (May 25, 2022), https://www.yesmagazine.org/opinion/2022/05/26/asian-pacific-islander-month-white-gaze.
8. Jana Schmieding, "Why Native American Heritage Month can actually be a nightmare for Native people," *Hello Giggles*, November 22, 2018, https://hellogiggles.com/native-american-heritage-month-nightmare-for-native-people/.
9. Wikipedia, "Truth Commission," accessed October 18, 2023, https://en.wikipedia.org/wiki/Truth_commission.
10. Deborah J. Menkart, "Deepening the Meaning of Heritage Months," *ascd* April 1, 1999, https://www.ascd.org/el/articles/deepening-the-meaning-of-heritage-months
11. J. B. Rotter, "Interpersonal trust, trustworthiness and gullibility," *American Psychologist*, 26 (1980): 1–7.
12. Frances X. Frei and Anne Morriss, "Begin with Trust," *Harvard Business Review* May–June 2020A), https://hbr.org/2020/05/begin-with-trust#:~:text=In%20our%20.
13. E. M. Uslaner, *The Moral Foundations of Trust* (Cambridge University Press: Cambridge, UK, 2022).
14. The Empathetic Museum, "Maturity Model," accessed October 2, 2023, http://empatheticmuseum.weebly.com/maturity-model.html.

15. Trust-based philanthropy project, "A Trust-Based Approach," accessed October 18, 2023, https://www.trustbasedphilanthropy.org/overview.
16. Ibid.
17. Poverty Truth Network, "nothing about us, without us, is for us," accessed October 18, 2023, https://povertytruthnetwork.org/.
18. Poverty Truth Network, "The distinctives of our work," accessed October 2, 2023, https://povertytruthnetwork.org/the-network/the-distinctives-of-our-work/.
19. California Humanities, "Library Innovation Lab: Exploring New Ways of Engaging California's Immigrant Communities," last accessed June 22, 2023, https://calhum.org/programs-initiatives/programs/library-innovation-lab/.
20. Veronda Pitchford, Felicia Kelley, Bobbi Luster, Curita Tinker, and Denise Lopez, "Welcoming Immigrants through Cultural Programming: Lessons from the Field," *Infopeople* (February 24, 2022), https://infopeople.org/content/welcoming-immigrants-through-cultural-programming-lessons-field.
21. Octavia Butler, *Parable of the Sower* (Warner Books, 1993).

12

The Library in 2035 Will Be Universal

Annie Norman

The library of 2035 will be universal, a seamless system of libraries that positions the library profession to achieve full power and potential.

Since its inception, the library profession has survived fairly well by navigating technology whitewater, pivoting during the COVID-19 pandemic, and adapting to numerous other evolutions. Time and again, librarians go with the flow. But could librarians be more proactive in getting out in front of future disruptions? The library profession is small and must leverage its energies collectively and strategically in order to elevate from surviving to thriving. Librarians are typically middle managers, providing library services within a government hierarchy or other governance, and they are perpetually dependent upon the goodwill of leaders in other professions for support. However, as Michael Moore discovered, librarians have power potential: "[Librarians] are subversive. You think they're just sitting there at the desk, all quiet and everything. They're like plotting the revolution, man. I wouldn't mess with them."[1] Librarians are excellent at the servant part of servant leadership, but they need to prioritize their own strategic needs as well as the needs of others. How might librarians build their own empire, so to speak, and become societal leaders at the highest level?

THE LIBRARY IN 2035 WILL BE A UNIVERSAL, SEAMLESS, AND NATIONAL SYSTEM OF LIBRARIES

While the nation works to repair outdated infrastructures, the library profession has an opportunity to revisit and update its infrastructure as well. In an ideal universal library system, libraries are members of a single consortium, are seamlessly connected with shared technologies, and share common policies, consistent services, and live data to monitor and enable outcomes and impact at scale. The public now expects library infrastructure to be strong and technologies to be seamless, with no excuses about barriers due to governance or funding source.

In response to the prompt, "What are the benefits of library consortia over a single library?" ChatGPT summarized:

> Overall, library consortia offer many benefits to member libraries and their patrons, including increased purchasing power, expanded collections, improved efficiency, enhanced services, and increased collaboration. By working together, libraries in a consortium can achieve greater impact and provide more comprehensive and effective services to their communities.[2]

Small, stand-alone libraries cannot match the capacity of a library system to provide the variety of content and services needed by the public. Libraries have always obtained their strength from sharing; therefore, when libraries are seamlessly connected, libraries and the public have access to even more. A universal library system with a universal library card established and funded at the highest, broadest level ensures equity of access and capacity, provides a leadership platform for the library profession, and supports the best local and national outcomes.

> A universal library system with a universal library card established and funded at the highest, broadest level ensures equity of access and capacity, provides a leadership platform for the library profession, and supports the best local and national outcomes.

Delaware Libraries has adopted this strategy and migrated into a single library catalog and consortium, a universal seamless system of multitype libraries across the state. All public libraries, several academic and special libraries, and a few school libraries are participating so far. The Delaware Library Consortium[3] was first modeled after other state consortia (Georgia Library Association[4] and Wyoming State Library[5]), and it has learned a lot from its own implementation. Specifically, it found that the more tools that are connected, and the deeper the integration, the more powerful, effective, and better funded the Delaware Library Consortium has become. For instance, the state of Delaware now fully funds and supports the library technology infrastructure, and it funds up to 50 percent of the library building's infrastructure with a shared goal of one square-foot per capita, to address population capacity and ensure equitable, quality services statewide.

Delaware Libraries embarked on creating a statewide library infrastructure, in part, to have shared live data. Now when public officials and journalists ask questions about public library use, Delaware Libraries have answers! Nationally, having live universal big data for libraries should be a given. Trend and current data are essential to track progress, make improvements, and demonstrate impact. Public officials want evidence that libraries are part of community solutions, and funding is a result of delivering and measuring at scale that value to the community.

THE LIBRARY IN 2035 WILL BE UNIVERSAL ACROSS THE LIFESPAN

For many years, literacy rates have been declining nationwide. While one of the fundamental and historic roles that libraries provide is to help ensure a literate society, it has become even more of a challenge to address literacy needs. When the Delaware Library Consortium was first formed, about one-third of Delawareans had a library card; the number of library card holders then increased to about half of Delawareans. But now the number of library card holders in Delaware is starting to decline. Delaware school libraries have been in crisis for decades, contributing to generations of Delawareans who have not been raised to be library users or fully literate. School librarians are on the front lines, but they do not have the authority or leverage within education to solve their issues. Likely as a result of the poor condition of the school library collections, inconsistent alternatives cropped up in schools and among literacy partners, such as classroom libraries, book giveaways, and education software tools with excerpts from books and articles. For libraries' traditional role of literacy support, Delaware public and school libraries have been overlooked and excluded, and a new approach is needed to resolve the literacy challenge and elevate respect for the library profession.

New funding from the state supports integrating all school libraries in the Delaware Library Consortium. By adding school libraries, Delaware now can complete the system of libraries and can achieve the last mile in ensuring equity of access to books for students who lack access to public libraries. Delaware school librarians have been isolated from their librarian colleagues in schools and other sectors, and now will benefit from being seamlessly connected with colleagues and resources in the Delaware Library Consortium.

Additionally, Delaware Libraries established the Delaware Literacy Alliance, a Communities of Excellence[6] initiative, to connect and align services of the literacy partners. Although libraries support all aspects of literacy, libraries' greatest advantage over any other partner is the magnitude of the quantity and quality of physical and electronic books available to spark individual serendipity and equity of choice, at no cost to the patron. Additional funding for shared collections in the Delaware Library Consortium with a focus on reviving the school libraries has been requested and is under consideration. Literacy emerges and is sustained in part through developing the habit and joy of reading and library use, ideally beginning at a young age and across the lifespan. Universal public access across all libraries can quietly circumvent local book banning and address societal polarization in support of cultural inclusion. All libraries must rise together, apply the latest in literacy research, and ensure the library profession is effective, earning and receiving the respect it deserves.

THE LIBRARY IN 2035 WILL BE THE RECOGNIZED LEADER IN SOCIAL INFRASTRUCTURE

Libraries offer a lengthy laundry list of services, often without sufficient framing to connect them to community impacts. The library profession developed classification systems (e.g., OCLC's Dewey Decimal Classification System) that support collection organization and management. Libraries can expand on the collection organizer to develop a more robust universal framework for libraries to unify their work and collaborate at a more mature level, while continuously improving the framework to keep pace with societal changes. Using this universal framework, all libraries contribute to the whole and enable shared live data for decision-making and collective impact to benefit their communities.

In Delaware, the framework that has been developed consists of updated and modified versions of Dewey, representing the world's knowledge, connected with Maslow's hierarchy of needs (i.e., Find, Connect, Learn, Inspire, and Transform), signifying libraries' role to help individuals and communities achieve their full potential. The Dewey/Maslow framework aligns data by subject across all library services, collections, programs, reference services, and so on, including partner services (i.e., registration for social services, literacy tutoring). The Dewey/Maslow framework organizes the services and the data practically, conceptually, and strategically.

As Delaware Libraries deepen their learning across the state, patterns have emerged, particularly at the lower level of the framework, informing next steps regarding literacy and other basic social service needs. For example, Delaware Libraries have learned there is an ideal sequence for social services support. People in crisis may not be able to focus or think clearly. Self-service referrals and workshop series do not solve the critical need. Instead, considerable library staff and partner time is invested to provide hand holding and just-in-time assistance to help individuals find and take their next step for housing, health care, child care, job applications, digital literacy, and more. Open labs for walk-ins effectively manage all the immediate social services demands with individualized attention from partners, AmeriCorps volunteers, and interns. Changes in state and national programs are monitored to connect patrons to services that are needed. Libraries have also supported internet access, digital literacy, and equity since the 1990s. This focus on access is "in vogue" again, as federal funding for broadband and digital literacy has become available.

Delaware public officials have invested in Delaware Libraries' universal technology and facilities infrastructure, and they are just beginning to appreciate the power of this infrastructure to effectively deliver the variety of services needed by Delawareans to improve their lives. The partnerships, learning, and visibility of the Delaware Libraries' system to date ensure that libraries are well positioned to be leaders in social infrastructure by 2035.

CONCLUSION

The next evolution is for library consortia to scale up and integrate, perhaps via blockchain, into a nationwide, and then worldwide, universal library system. Leading at a higher level requires working together seamlessly at a macro scale across the profession, serving the majority of the population, and addressing the long view across time.

Libraries today are universally loved, and they will be universally powerful by 2035. The universal library system enables integration, learning, impact, and leadership—all at scale. The network of libraries, further strengthened by a network of partners, will enhance the social infrastructure of public life.

Librarians share freely, such as the ideas shared here. But sharing takes time, and not everyone is reading this book. A universal library system will enable librarians to fully live up to their slogans. Beyond providing the universal "Smartest Card" for library patrons, librarians can become the universally "Smartest Profession."

How likely will libraries achieve a universal library system within a decade? It took Delaware Libraries a quarter of a century to evolve to this point. The technology exists; what is needed now is a universal, or critical mass, consensus among library professionals. Library consortia of all types, in addition to the Delaware Library Consortium, should be studied, quickly. There are more possibilities and much more to learn between now and 2035.

Spread the word and begin today! Librarians can start now to plot the revolution, build the universal library empire, and truly scale to be the universally smartest, most effective profession.

NOTES

1. Buzzflash, "A Buzzflash Interview with Michael Moore, Filmmaker, TV Host, and Author of 'Stupid White Men,'" March 13, 2002, https://buzzflash.com/flashback/moore-2002.
2. ChatGPT, "What are the benefits of library consortia over a single library," 13 Feb version: 11 (March 2023), chat.openai.com/chat.
3. Delaware Libraries, "About DLC," accessed October 20, 2024, https://lib.de.us/about-us/about-dlc.
4. Georgia Library Association, "About," accessed October 20, 2023, https://gla.georgialibraries.org/about/.
5. Wyoming State Library, "WYLD Network," accessed October 20, 2023, https://library.wyo.gov/services/wyld-network/.
6. Communities of Excellence 2026, accessed April 9, 2023, https://communitiesofexcellence2026.org/.

13

Open, Inclusive, and Diverse

THE ACADEMIC LIBRARY OF 2035

Alexia Hudson-Ward

The library of 2035 will be open, inclusive, and diverse, utilizing social science and humanities methodologies, a superstructure approach, and an awareness of generational and economic influences.

A more open, inclusive, and diverse future for academic libraries is on the horizon within the next decade. A series of circumstances have and will continue to converge, setting this new version for the library of 2035 into motion. These circumstances include demographic changes internationally,[1] heightened and scalable sustainability efforts, lessons learned from the 2020 COVID-19 pandemic crisis,[2] the promise of various forms of artificial intelligence (AI) and new types of machine learning, current open scholarship investments, and the rise of Generation Z,[3] who, by data-centered accounts, are deeply committed to equity and social justice.

This chapter outlines open, inclusive, and diverse as three distinct yet intersecting phenomena that will positionally and directionally guide the future of academic libraries in 2035. The assertions made in this chapter are based on trends data and are intentionally aspirational. The concepts presented aim to spark new dialogue, innovative workflow development, and research on the forces impacting the library of 2035. While written primarily for those employed (or who desire to be employed) in academic libraries, readers from other libraries, research centers, labs, archives, and independently managed special collections will find the insights highlighted in this chapter valuable.

OPEN INITIATIVES: GUIDED BY SOCIAL SCIENCES AND HUMANITIES METHODOLOGIES

The library of 2035 will benefit from decades of capacity building in support of open infrastructure. Gone will be lingering concerns about intellectual property and research confidentiality agreements as open scholarship will be socialized as a standard practice both within the field and globally. Academic libraries will lead in supporting, developing, and communicating more synergistic research outputs that align open scholarship, public scholarship, and institutionally led justice efforts due to political criticism and general critique about the value of higher education.

The advancement of open scholarship will continue to be primarily led by STEMM (science, technology, engineering, mathematics, and medicine) faculty and researchers to teach, fortify, and protect the world's citizens from the inevitable global pandemic in the next decade. Yet another circumstance within the research ecosystem will elevate the importance of social sciences and the humanities. Research methodologies long championed by social sciences and humanities faculty and researchers, such as ethnography, text and content analysis, the history-of-ideas, connoisseurship, phenomenology, and action research, will come to the fore more as building-block principles for open humanistic scholarship.[4]

THE DEMOCRATIZING VALUE OF AI FOR RESEARCH, DATA MANAGEMENT, AND HUMAN CAPITAL

Generative and traditional AI will further democratize resource access and creation. Similar to the advent of the internet and the internet age, academic libraries will lead in developing evolving educational guidelines for ethical AI usage, including clarifying current blurry lines about plagiarism. By 2035, international case law will provide more context, structure, and boundaries concerning how AI-generated assets can be legally incorporated into cross-disciplinary coursework.

Recognizing academic libraries' reputational girth, focus on strategic data management, resources quality control, consortia relationships, campus political acumen and skill with grants stewardship, partnerships with offices of vice presidents and vice provosts of research (VPRs), and academic libraries will be strengthened and expanded. These partnership expansions between academic libraries and universities' center research units will include AI-focused positions shared between the two entities.

These new roles will encompass duties in data science, research data management, human-computer interaction, large language models, and machine learning across all major libraries' functions. While some of the new shared positions between university research units and academic libraries will include aspects of collections, reference, instruction, and access services, library administrators' roles will be re-envisioned to development and advance organizational strategy through DEI, ongoing organizational design, and IT technology positions charged with culturally inclusive discovery. Furthermore, these collaborations between VPRs and academic libraries will spur more temporary and permanent joint research centers that will function in a consortia-like fashion by publicly sharing insights-to-action research that will have a trans-sector impact.

These changes will result in critical shifts in the work of academic library staff members within the next ten to twelve years. As the world and higher education move toward a more automated AI-enabled future, essential questions arise about how much human labor may be devalued and replaced by machines. Work that can be automated within academic libraries will likely occur in the next decade. Yet, this change will translate into more job redesign with higher degrees of frequency versus massive job elimination.

By 2035, more academic library staff will have transitioned into data quality management and research data management roles supporting their institution's research enterprises.[5] Less emphasis will be placed on physical book acquisition and current catalog management methodologies, with more emphasis on supporting faculty and students to create and sustain their digital assets used in the classroom and for research. In addition, more academic libraries' staff duties will change to help students determine quality data and how to manage data across various cloud-based management systems. These staff members will also assist faculty in sustaining assets derived from and used in support of their research.

PRESERVING AMERICA'S, CANADA'S, AND THE GLOBAL SOUTH'S CULTURAL HERITAGE

Climate changes, sociopolitical disruptions, economic fractures, and wars will continue to threaten and destroy critical cultural heritage assets in the next decade.[6] Drawing from more than thirty years of knowledge on how to manage environmental and war-derived threats to cultural heritage assets, academic libraries will enter into a new UNESCO agreement to preserve Indigenous, African, African American, Latino/x, Asian, and rural populations' oral and material culture, including language, dance, physical artifacts (such as quilts), and foodways. The future UNESCO agreement will be further strengthened by representation and alignment from various countries' national archives.

Academic libraries in the Global South will assert their preservation efforts as a vital pillar of open scholarship internationally. More academic library staff in this region will engage in sustainability, preservation, and objects-based pedagogical research by creating one or more multimedia open-access journals to document real-time efforts to digitize large corpuses of cultural heritage elements, especially in conflict-ravished locations. Global South academic libraries will also develop technologically enabled solutions that ensure ancestral, ancient language is reproducible to create a series of multidisciplinary digital learning objects.

The Global South's academic libraries will form alliances by 2035 to further assert the significance of non-Western-centered knowledge creation and preservation. This effort will position these libraries as international leaders on innovative approaches to solve wide-scale community challenges beyond cultural heritage asset management. For example, cultural heritage asset management practices of Global South academic libraries (most specifically, development of new metadata versions) will be replicated in support of other regional challenges, such as agricultural data management and health-care data collection.

INCLUSIVITY AND DIVERSITY ENTAIL A "SUPERSTRUCTURE" APPROACH

In many ways, academic libraries currently function as an intricate service system tasked primarily to deliver resources to end users. Within an academic library service system are micro-systems and micro-cultures that, at times, struggle to fully align to advance a unified service delivery model. The academic library literature points to several decades of internal organizational conflicts regarding which division leads which portion of intersecting workflows and who is the authority voice in service delivery decision-making. These conflicts compromise inclusive workplace efforts, including increasing and retaining a compositionally diverse staff, by thwarting creativity and innovative concepts. The thwarting of creative and innovative approaches to solving academic libraries' long-standing DEI-related issues has reached a breaking point. The library profession is aging quicker than it is replenishing its ranks with a workforce representing diverse communities within the United States.

The library of 2035 will address operationalizing inclusivity and diversity by adopting a superstructure model that draws on quality design from science, management, and engineering principles.[7] These building construction and space design concepts will be applied by future academic libraries' leadership to clarify and disentangle the DEI problem space with strategies intended to harmonize roles and functions that are critical to the success of inclusive workplace practices.

By adopting a "superstructure" model that explicitly outlines foundational, first-, second-, and third-level strategy bearers, decision-makers, and executional processes leads, leaders within the library of 2035 will turn their continuous attention on related dependencies to the success of DEI efforts. Planning for a future in which all parts of the symbolic academic library building structure must be coordinated and synchronized so that the "building" is sturdy and functional will ensure that DEI is centered as standard operating procedure rather than marginalized into meaningless checklists of non-transformational activities.

GENERATIONAL INFLUENCES AND ECONOMIC INSTABILITY

Generation Z will continue to place their generational imprint on the sociopolitical landscape in 2035. This generation began articulating their desire for a more values-aligned existence—first as students, and later as workplace professionals and parents. Their expectations include how academic libraries will serve as campus-wide examples for what belonging and mattering in the workplace means.

Many Gen-Zers are the children of Gen X, a small yet quietly influential generation that navigated new technologies and a complicated post-9/11 world. By 2035, the majority of Gen X will have entered into their early to mid-sixties. This generation, in combination with the Boomer generation, will equate to one in every four Americans being aged sixty-five and older.

An interesting circumstance is currently unfolding that will further guide the library of 2035. Points of strategic unification and points of divide between the so-called creative, political, entrepreneurial, and traditional worker classes[8] based on global economic inequality will continue to become more pronounced. These four classes agree on the importance of unfettered information access within libraries, yet they remain divided on "ownership" and "authorship" of freedom of expression, the role of collective bargaining, how institutions enable income instability and gentrification in surrounding communities,[9] and the value of DEI initiatives on campuses.[10] Consequently, academic libraries will lead the way in how to successfully work within and convene educational experiences to bridge-build between these four distinct classes.

CONCLUSION

The objective of this chapter balances my optimistic vision of the library of 2035 with a clarion call for today's academic libraries to scale *now* to address the complex challenges facing us globally. The current academic library landscape (compounded by climate change, massive retirements, emerging technologies like generative and traditional AI, increasing emphasis on DEI, and complex global challenges that threaten the future of cultural heritage assets) was predicted at the end of the twentieth century. Yet many academic libraries appear to be currently "scrambling" to create and implement short- and long-range strategic plans in support of the impending library of 2035.

> Stubbornly holding on to comfortable legacy practices for the sake of "this is the way we've always done it" disables expansive thinking and preparedness to be better global partners.

What's missing at this critical juncture is introspection and assessment on how academic libraries must best prepare for new learning and operational modalities in a rapidly paced, changing environment. Stubbornly holding on to comfortable legacy practices for the sake of "this is the way we've always done it" disables expansive thinking and preparedness to be better global partners. A more open, inclusive, and diverse future for academic libraries will not come from wishful thinking, bogged down by iteration. Purposeful planning and action to support wide-ranging change is the key to an impactful future that is open, inclusive and diverse.

NOTES

1. United Nations, "Shifting demographics," n.d., https://www.un.org/en/un75/shifting-demographics#:~:text=WE%20ARE%20GETTING%20OLDER,(ages%2015%20to%2024).
2. Murtaza Ashiq, Farhat Jabeen, and Khalid Mahmood, "Transformation of libraries during Covid-19 pandemic: A systematic review," *Journal of Academic Librarianship* 48, no. 4 (2022): 1-10, https://doi.org/10.1016/j.acalib.2022.102534.
3. Shilpa Gaidhani, Lokesh Arora, and Bhuvanesh Kumar Sharma, "Understanding the attitude of generation Z towards workplace," *International Journal of Management, Technology and Engineering* 9, no. 1 (2019): 2804-12.
4. Paul Longley Arthur and Lydia Hearn, "Toward open research: A narrative review of the challenges and opportunities for open humanities," *Journal of Communication* 71, no. 5 (2021): 827-53.
5. Andrew M. Cox, Stephen Pinfield, and Sophie Rutter, "The intelligent library: Thought leaders' views on the likely impact of artificial intelligence on academic libraries," *Library Hi Tech* 37, no. 3 (2019): 418-35.
6. Kate Crowley, Rowan Jackson, Siona O'Connell, Dulma Karunarthna, Esti Anantasari, Arry Retnowati, and Dominique Niemand, "Cultural heritage and risk assessments: Gaps, challenges, and future research directions for the inclusion of heritage within climate change adaptation and disaster management," *Climate Resilience and Sustainability* 1, no. 3 (2022): 1-12.
7. Zdenek Dytrt, "Leadership—Management Superstructure," *Economics World* 5, no. 4 (2017): 354-61.
8. Amanda Coles, "Creative class politics: Unions and the creative economy," *International Journal of Cultural Policy* 22, no. 3 (2016): 456-72.
9. Davarian L. Baldwin, *In the shadow of the ivory tower: How universities are plundering our cities* (Bold Type Books, 2021).
10. Chelsea Guillermo-Wann and Marc P. Johnston-Guerrero, "Contextualizing multiraciality in campus climate: Key considerations for transformative diversity, equity, and inclusion," in *Multiracial Experiences in Higher Education* (Routledge, 2021): 141-60.

14

The Future of School Libraries

IT'S ABOUT EQUITY

Joyce Kasman Valenza and Debra Kachel

The library of 2035 will need to ensure that every student has unfettered access to the opportunities, resources, and instruction they rightfully deserve.

Science-fiction writer William Gibson famously predicted, "The future is already here—it's just not very evenly distributed."[1] As we forecast a future for school libraries, we also see an uneven future. For a profession foundationally based on the conviction that *all* learners deserve robust school library programs led by skilled school librarians, this recognition is a call to action. Whether and how well we address inequities could shape the preparedness of current and future generations for active citizenship and societal participation.

THE RESEARCH: IT'S ABOUT EQUITY

Decades of school library research correlate the impact of effective school library programs with improvements in reading, writing, and graduation rates.[2] In addition, a study of New Jersey college students discovered that first-year students who experienced strong high school library programs transferred critical information and media and digital literacy skills into their academic experiences.[3] Sobering data revealed that over the 2021-2022 academic year, 35 percent of all school districts in the United States had no school librarians—affecting 7.1 million students.[4] Another 35 percent of school districts reported having less than one full-time equivalent of a school librarian, impacting another 5.5 million students.[5] An examination of federal data from over thirteen thousand public school districts reveals that these inequities of access are clearly associated with race and ethnicity and were even more pronounced among students residing in extreme poverty, in isolated areas, or within smaller districts. The prevailing condition of unequal access should also serve as a pressing call to arms for policymakers and library professionals.

The access gap is just a single indicator of information poverty. Robust library programs yield advantages for students throughout their academic and personal journeys, equipping them with skills to thoughtfully navigate vast streams of media and information and use them to ethically create information products. Students who benefit from experiences with qualified K-12 school librarians gain access to a diverse array of literature, engage with inquiry and research tools regularly, explore emerging information technologies, and become acquainted with academic reading and writing frameworks. Others do not. Access to an effective school library program is a manifestation of *information privilege*.

CHALLENGES HEIGHTENING INEQUITIES

Looking forward to 2035, it is likely that the gap between students who benefit from school library programs and those who do not will widen if key challenges continue unabated.

WIDESPREAD CENSORSHIP CAMPAIGNS

In 2022, the American Library Association (ALA) documented an alarming surge in book bans, marking the highest level in the past two decades.[6] Driven by politically motivated attempts, this upsurge also threatened librarians' jobs and reputations. Some states proposed fines or imprisonment for librarians based on the contents of their collections. Despite courageous examples of librarians and library organizations mobilizing communities and advocating for students' freedom to read, as well as innovative legislative measures like those in Illinois designed to curtail book banning,[7] well-coordinated censorship campaigns have resulted in compromised collections and early retirements.

THE NECESSITY FOR CONTINUAL TECHNOLOGY LEARNING, ASSESSMENT, AND INTEGRATION

Students face an increasingly complex information landscape. Heuristics learned years ago in pre-service programs may have limited value and relevance. Generative artificial intelligence applications now impact the ways we search, write, and create media. School librarians must lead their colleagues in discovering and vetting promising information and communication technologies for integration in learning and establishing norms for thoughtful, ethical, and creative use. Especially for large numbers of veteran library professionals, continued, high-quality professional learning is essential and a personal responsibility.

THE PIPELINE

Data from the National Center for Education Statistics confirms an almost 20 percent loss of school librarians between 2009-2010 and 2018-2019; in addition, fewer states now offer school library certification programs.[8] An examination of 2020-2021 data also shows that districts with majority non-white districts and majority Hispanic districts with fewer than one thousand students, and those located in more rural areas, are the districts most likely not to have any school librarians.[9] Districts with lower enrollments and those located in rural areas may find it more difficult to recruit and hire capable school librarians. In addition, school librarian credentialing programs in universities have been closing due to limited enrollment. According to SLIDE research completed in January 2021, thirty of the fifty states, in addition to the District of Columbia, had two or fewer higher education institutions that prepared school librarians.[10] Five states no longer have any such university programs, and some have seen programs eliminated. Over the course of ten years, Pennsylvania closed three of its five university school librarianship programs.[11] While online programs somewhat mitigate the issue, complex and state-specific certification requirements continue to present barriers. School librarian candidates quite reasonably wonder about their investment in acquiring a K-12 credential at a time when many schools are not hiring/replacing school librarians.

ADMINISTRATOR PRIORITIES AND TURNOVER

School leaders who control budgets directly determine the effectiveness of school library programs. Not every leader has had opportunities to work with exemplary school librarians or witness an effective school library program. Many lack instructional leadership experience as well as any experience supporting school libraries to lead student learning. High turnover rates of both superintendents and principals threaten even exemplary school programs and librarian positions when priorities change.[12]

MODELS OF CHANGE

Existing models for ensuring learner equity demonstrate that when strategic activism and coalition building are commonplace, trends are reversible, suggesting a bright(er) future.

MODEL #1: ENSURING INFORMATION LITERACY INSTRUCTION IS REQUIRED AND TAUGHT

While some states recognize the need for a planned K-12 program of information, media, and digital literacy instruction, many do not. The curricular knowledge school librarians offer is as valuable as math, science, and other disciplines. According to Media Literacy Now,[13] eighteen states have enacted legislation promoting or requiring media or information literacy in schools. For example, the New Jersey Student Learning Standards in Information Literacy[14] is the result of a five-year collaboration led by the New Jersey Library Association[15] and the New Jersey Association of School Librarians,[16] which engaged the teachers union, principal and administrator associations, the state school boards association, and other education coalitions. This broad base of support led to the success of state legislation requiring K-12 information literacy instruction and school librarian leadership in developing the state standard and its implementation.[17]

While not legislatively mandated, other states also support comprehensive K-12 frameworks. In New York, the Empire State Information Fluency Continuum[18] continues to be broadly shared and has evolved to include digital fluency alignments in its rich collection of lessons, scaffolds, assessments, and culminating projects.

MODEL #2: SUSTAINING PROGRAMS AND FUNDING BY BUILDING COALITIONS

A sustained and institutionalized role for school libraries will depend on whether influential stakeholders (e.g., administrators, teachers, parents, nonprofits, and librarians outside our schools) work together to advocate for and defend school libraries and librarians as essential for all students—rather than competitors for funding. Librarians cannot sustain a quality library program on book fair money. Likewise, school librarians and their associations need to become true education partners, reaching beyond their silos and working with their partners. Two examples that demonstrate the success of strong partnerships and shared goals include the coalition that sought to address equity in the District of Columbia[19] and the partnerships developed in Nashville's public/school Limitless Libraries program.[20]

MODEL #3: ENSURING A PIPELINE OF TRAINED AND AVAILABLE SCHOOL LIBRARIANS

To ensure the future of our profession, we need to address barriers that discourage promising professionals from preparing for this career. Recruitment measures may include financial incentives and the intentional recruitment of professionals who look like the students they will serve. Not only do today's school librarians need to come armed with strong advocacy skills and strategies for ensuring students' intellectual freedom rights, they also need continual professional development to lead schools in the thoughtful integration of emerging technologies.

In New York City, a coalition of partners, including two universities, the city's Department of Education, and an education foundation, formed the Teacher-2-Librarian Scholarship Program. The program seeks candidates from a diverse population of existing New York City teachers. To date, it has reopened eighty-six campuses with vital school library programs directly and effectively addressing the pipeline.[21]

MODEL #4: ENSURING EQUITY WITHIN SCHOOL DISTRICTS

In districts adhering to site-based management (SBM), principals determine the allocation of their building budgets. This budgetary strategy offers school leaders autonomy to invest funds to meet individual school needs. Because libraries are a costly, long-term investment, SBM often leads to considerable inequities in library services across districts. Recognizing that these inequities often impact schools in the poorest communities with the neediest students, some districts have returned to centralized budgeting and decision-making.

Boston Public Schools is implementing an initiative that promises every public school will have an effective school library program by 2026. In 2022, only 25 of Boston's 125 campuses had a full-time licensed school librarian with schools in less-privileged communities without librarians.[22] A supportive superintendent, along with school and community stakeholder groups, produced a Library Services Strategic Plan[23] that includes funding for school librarians, opening day collections, improvements to existing spaces, and funding to support and sustain growth.

CONCLUSION

While there has never been a more exciting time to lead in new information and communication landscapes and explore an increasingly diverse bounty of literature, forecasting the future of school librarianship in 2035 imposes today's librarians with an urgent call to action. The current state of school library programs reflects deep-seated and persisting educational inequities. To ensure a future where every student experiences a rich, school-based reading culture as well as instruction in information, media, and digital literacy nurtured by school librarians, we must transcend hyper-local advocacy and promote systemic change.

> To ensure a future where every student experiences a rich, school-based reading culture as well as instruction in information, media, and digital literacy nurtured by school librarians, we must transcend hyper-local advocacy and promote systemic change.

The future of school librarians hinges on others recognizing their role as an indispensable component of education, just as valued as our science, math, and English programs. Such a shift requires organized, large-scale approaches that reach beyond the confines of our profession. The preservation of school library programs lies in aligning with influential allies who possess the power to effect change. Without these connections, our programs, however excellent, risk being eliminated by a tide of indifference.

Local advocacy is critical, but it alone is insufficient. Disparities will continue unless we dare to think bigger. The success stories we share underscore the transformative potential of alliances between librarians, teachers, administrators, unions, politicians, parents, and other stakeholders who value the educational impact of school library programs. Despite obstacles, these examples demonstrate that our commitments and collaborations can generate innovative solutions. Looking toward the future in 2035, we will move closer to the reality where every student gains unfettered access to the opportunities, resources, and instruction they rightfully deserve.

NOTES

1. National Public Radio (1999), NPR: Talk of the Nation, "The Science in Science Fiction," Interview with William Gibson [Quotation is spoken around 11:50], https://www.npr.org/2018/10/22/1067220/the-science-in-science-fiction.
2. Keith Curry Lance and Debra E. Kachel, "Why School Librarians Matter: What Years of Research Tell Us," *Phi Delta Kappan* 99, no. 7 (2018): 15–20, https://doi.org/10.1177/0031721718767854.
3. Joyce Kasman Valenza et al. (2022), "First Years' Information Literacy Backpacks: What's Already Packed or Not Packed?" *Journal of Academic Librarianship* 48, no. 4: 102566, https://doi.org/10.1016/j.acalib.2022.102566.
4. M. K. Biagini, and D. E. Kachel (2023, May 9), "School libraries link students to literacies: What we know now," [PowerPoint slides], Indiana Libraries and Literacies Symposium.
5. K. Lance, Personal communication, August 6, 2023.
6. American Library Association, "2022 Book Ban Data," March 20, 2023, http://www.ala.org/advocacy/bbooks/book-ban-data.
7. Alexi Giannoulias (2023, May 3), "First-in-the-Nation Legislation to Prevent Book Bans Approved by General Assembly: House Bill 2789 passes Senate today," https://www.ilsos.gov/news/2023/may/230503d1.pdf.
8. Debra E. Kachel and Keith Curry Lance. "Contexts of School Librarian Employment." *SLIDE: The School Librarian Investigation—Decline or Evolution?* (January 26, 2021): 9. https://libslide.org/pubs/contexts.pdf.
9. Keith Curry Lance, Debra E. Kachel, and Caitlin Gerrity, "The School Librarian Equity Gap: Inequities Associated with Race and Ethnicity Compounded by Poverty, Locale, and Enrollment," *Peabody Journal of Education* 98, no. 1 (2023): 85–99, https://doi.org/10.1080/0161956X.2023.2160112.
10. Debra E. Kachel and Keith Curry Lance. "Contexts of School Librarian Employment." *SLIDE: The School Librarian Investigation—Decline or Evolution?* (January 26, 2021): 9. https://libslide.org/pubs/contexts.pdf.
11. Ibid.
12. Rachel S. White (2023), "Ceilings Made of Glass and Leaving En Masse? Examining Superintendent Gender Gaps and Turnover over Time across the United States," *Educational Researcher*, https://journals.sagepub.com/doi/10.3102/0013189X231163139; Melissa Kay Diliberti and Heather L. Schwartz, "Educator Turnover Has Markedly Increased, but Districts Have Taken Actions to Boost Teacher Ranks: Selected Findings

from the Sixth American School District Panel Survey" (Santa Monica, CA: RAND Corporation, 2023), https://www.rand.org/pubs/research_reports/RRA956-14.html.
13. Media Literacy Now, "Putting Media Literacy on the Public Policy Agenda," accessed October 20, 2023, https://medialiteracynow.org/impact/current-policy/.
14. State of New Jersey Governor Phil Murphy, "Governor Murphy Signs Bipartisan Legislation Establishing First in the Nation K-12 Information Literacy Education," January 4, 2023, https://www.nj.gov/governor/news/news/562022/20230104b.shtml.
15. New Jersey Library Association, "Home," accessed October 20, 2023, https://www.njla.org/.
16. New Jersey Association of School Libraries, "Home," accessed October 20, 2023, https://www.njasl.org/.
17. LegiScan, "New Jersey S588. Regular Session," January 4, 2023, https://legiscan.com/NJ/text/S588/2022.
18. New York City School Library System: Connect, Create, Lead, "NYC School Librarian Guidebook," accessed October 20, 2023, https://nycdoe.libguides.com/librarianguidebook/esifc.
19. Colleen Grabnick (September 28, 2021), "A School Librarian Is a 'Jack of All Trades.' Now Every DCPS Student Has Access to One," NPR/WAMU 88.5.
20. Metro Nashville Public Schools, "Limitless Libraries," accessed May 21, 2023, https://www.mnps.org/learn/academics/library-services/limitless_libraries.
21. New Visions for Public Schools, "Teacher 2 Librarian Second Certificate Initiative," April 25, 2023, https://advance.newvisions.org/teacher-2-librarian/.
22. Andrew Bauld (December 20, 2022), "Boston's Revolutionary Pledge: A School Library for Every Student by 2026," *School Library Journal*, https://www.slj.com/story/bostons-evolutionary-pledge-a-school-library-for-every-student-by-2026.
23. Boston Public Schools, "Library Services," accessed October 20, 2023, https://www.bostonpublicschools.org/libraryservices.

IV
Organizations

Part IV: Organizations focuses on the challenges and opportunities that are, and will be, present for various types of libraries: public, academic, community college, and school libraries. Key themes throughout this section include the importance of collaboration and partnerships, advocacy, innovation and change, as well as the library's role in literacy instruction and resource sharing and access. The authors of chapters 15 through 18 share their vision for how the library of 2035 will respond and adapt to changes in their organizational environments, specifically noting that these libraries will:

- reinvent their role as society's great equalizers (Watson).
- offer more efficient resource-sharing abilities empowered by enhanced digitization, increased interoperability, and improved open access policies (Pun and Anantachai).
- continually adapt, innovate, and collaborate with other campus services expanding the library's relevance and value to the institution (Hepburn).
- collaborate with community leaders and policymakers to provide diverse collections of resources and safe spaces while also advocating for acceptance and tolerance (Dziedzic-Elliott).

Part 4 opens with Watson, in chapter 15, who highlights the importance of advocating and promoting the library brand—something that touches upon every aspect of the library as an organization: its space, partnerships, workforce, and services. He advocates for "awe-inspiring" spaces that welcome and connect with people from all walks of life and support opportunities for connection, exploration, and learning. To accomplish this, he emphasizes how libraries will need to build effective partnerships throughout the community and continuously innovate programming that is built upon nontraditional ideas, a theme that the other authors of Part 4 echo.

In chapter 16, Pun and Anantachai highlight developments they expect to see within research and academic libraries. They note some of the key challenges are incorporating and managing multiple types of collections, ensuring interoperability across systems of shared collections, and doing so with constrained budgets. Resource sharing systems will be necessary to expand the library's collections, and this means that effective partnerships will need to be established. The authors advocate for effective policies that can address these challenges and suggest that their work in scholarly communications and open access will grow in importance.

In chapter 17, Hepburn highlights the effect of declining enrollments of community colleges and the pressures it places on budgeting as well as advocating for the library's value. The challenge, he notes, is that college leaders and policymakers tend to focus on what they see: fewer visits, quieter spaces, fewer books on shelves, etc. An opportunity to address this challenge is offered through accreditation standards, which identify the library as a necessary entity for the college; this gives libraries a chance to continue reinventing their services and relevancy to the college. Hepburn also emphasizes the uncertainty of the future and how building effective partnerships and collaborations could be what helps the community college library thrive in the future—not merely survive.

In chapter 18, Dziedzic-Elliott uses the New Jersey school libraries to exemplify the important role of school librarians in becoming leaders who have a seat at the table when school education is being discussed. New Jersey school librarians successfully advocated for legislation of a new statewide standard focused on information literacy in schools. Their success came down to the partnerships they built with multiple organizations and key stakeholders. The chapter provides important learnings that could be used to help other libraries advocate for more resources and support for their users and staff.

Archived webcasts of author interviews are available at: https://sites.google.com/sjsu.edu/library2035/home

15

The Future of Libraries

ADAPTING OUR MISSION AND OUR BUILDINGS TO DEMOGRAPHIC GROWTH AND CHANGE

Kelvin Watson

The library of 2035 will reinvent its role as society's great equalizer.

America is changing. We have always been a melting pot of nationalities, religions, ethnicities, and gender identities, but historically, many of these segments have been blocked from realizing their full potential. Part of the change we have witnessed of late is that of diverse voices, raised to assert their rightful share of the American dream.

The 2020 Census has brought into sharp relief the demographic shifts behind these voices. An in-depth report by the *New York Times* found that while the total population is growing at a slower pace, the share of people who identify as white has decreased over the past ten years for the first time.[1] The population growth that did take place, some twenty-three million people, was comprised of those who identify as Hispanic, Asian, Black, or more than one race. Nearly one in four U.S. residents identifies as Hispanic or Asian; and Black residents increased by 6 percent.

Contributing to slower growth is a lower birth rate in the United States, which demonstrates the economic pressure on young families, from the lack of living-wage jobs and the need for technical training and quality child care, to high student loan debt, an unstable housing market, and the ongoing uncertainty brought on by the pandemic. By 2030, one in every five Americans will be sixty-five or older, as the outsized Baby Boom generation continues to influence the country's demographics. The U.S. Census Bureau predicts that because such a large percentage of the population will be aging, immigration will become the primary source of growth and will expand the number of non-English-speaking residents. Racial and ethnic diversity will also increase, with the total population expected to cross the four hundred million mark by 2060—an additional seventy-six million people.[2]

PROMOTING THE LIBRARY BRAND

This is the future reality in 2035 that libraries must plan for, but I see only endless opportunities to create new relevance in American society. By 2035, the majority of the population will either have never entered a library (even as children) or have an outdated view of what libraries are. Establishing and promoting a dynamic and positive perception of the "Library Brand" is critical as digital information options compete for our customers. However, we cannot do it alone. It will take commitment and investment on multiple levels:

- Elected officials, philanthropists, and educators must partner with library systems to invest public and private dollars in designing new building models and retrofitting existing structures to adapt as technology continues to evolve. These infrastructure investments will become catalysts for urban revitalization, creating civic pride in these new community centers. Consequently, these new community centers will uplift lives by providing free educational support and access to free services such as job training, after-school nutrition, legal advice, and public displays of art, music, dance, and theater performances.
- By creating the library workforce of the future, we must broaden our library and information science degrees to include more courses in business, technology, social work, and public policy. This expanded coursework will broaden the knowledge base we have and create advocates from a variety of perspectives. We also need more scholarships aimed at recruitment and training a more diverse workforce in the field. This pivot toward diversity, equity, inclusion, and accessibility (DEIA) among librarians is critical in making our spaces more welcoming for future customers who will be more ethnically, racially, and gender-diverse than ever before. In order to build trust and engagement, our diverse audiences need to see themselves reflected in our library staff members.
- The importance of expanding and exploring new partnerships cannot be overstated. Beyond the traditional community groups, we must think outside the norms to deliver our services in new ways while developing advocates who know our value firsthand. Meeting people where they are introduces and enlightens new audiences on the revolution taking place for our libraries. I have personally seen the positive results of providing library access in parks, prisons, hospitals, airports, seaports, and most importantly, within school districts. As the population grows and diversifies, our educational systems will be stretched beyond the breaking point. Making the library experience a fundamental part of a child's education beginning

in pre-K will help to ease this burden. Libraries can help by providing free homework help, tactile STEAM (science, technology, engineering, arts, and mathematics) learning, and access to computers and broadband access. Libraries in low-income and rural areas can also work to extend their broadband access reach into the neighborhoods that they serve.

- We must continually search for nontraditional ideas and unique programming that will reach those who feel disenfranchised in our communities and libraries. We must "invite the uninvited," which is how I refer to those who do not frequent libraries. They perceive themselves as outsiders and view our buildings as being for "other people" who look different from them, are educated, or enjoy a higher standard of living. They are intimidated by libraries due to the barriers of access, and so they exclude themselves. We could be describing veterans, unguided children and teens, the previously incarcerated, those with low incomes or education levels, people experiencing homelessness, and people with disabilities. These people might be foreign-born, BIPOC, LGBTQIA+, and others who are perhaps unsure of how they will be received when they walk through our doors. As we design, build, and program our future buildings, we must study the surrounding neighborhoods and incorporate the cultural vibe and sense of place.

These are not lofty goals for a remote future. They are critical steps that must begin today in planning for the need that is already here, which will surely impact the future by 2035.

LIBRARY BUILDINGS AND COLLECTIONS

As we look toward the future of our buildings and our collections, we can borrow inspiration from the visionaries who helped to create our grand American library system. While there have been many contributors to this legacy, certainly Andrew Carnegie was the principal architect, both literally and figuratively. As a boy, he arrived penniless from Scotland, but he worked in a Pennsylvania factory and dreamed of a better life. He fought for and won free access to the local public library, and ever after, it was open to the working people of the city. He became one of the wealthiest men in the United States, but he never forgot how the library contributed to his education. His vision was to provide this same access to all U.S. residents, and in the early 1900s, he donated sixty million dollars of his fortune to build 1,689 libraries across the nation.[3] Many of those buildings are

> We must continue to design awe-inspiring spaces in this model, which honor and welcome people from all walks of life and make room for activities, conversation, discovery, makerspaces, and hands-on learning for all ages.

still the most admired and patronized in their communities. For example, the Carnegie Library in Washington, D.C., is a beautiful Beaux Arts building, which cost $300,000 and opened in 1903 to women, children, and people of all races.[4] In fact, Black residents still remember that it was the only public restroom available to them downtown.

Carnegie made libraries community anchors for all Americans, rather than luxuries for the wealthy. Another of his buildings became a home for me in St. Louis, Missouri. Aside from my church, as a young boy, the Central Library was the grandest, most sacred space I had ever seen. I felt like a king every time walking those hallowed halls. Nearly all of Andrew Carnegie's libraries were built using the "Carnegie formula," which continues to be a model of public/private partnerships. We must continue to design awe-inspiring spaces in this model, which honor and welcome people from all walks of life and make room for activities, conversation, discovery, makerspaces, and hands-on learning for all ages.

DIVERSITY, EQUITY, INCLUSION, AND ACCESSIBILITY

I am also inspired by Augusta Braxton Baker,[5] a remarkable woman who began her career in 1937 at what is now known as the New York Public Library's (NYPL) Countee Cullen Branch in Harlem. She led the way in DEIA even then, creating one of the first collections that ignored the racist stereotypes of the time and portrayed the real-life experiences of Black children. Her collection demonstrated to publishers the need to expand their titles for children of color. Ms. Baker was also an author, a consultant on the TV show *Sesame Street*, and the first Black woman to serve as NYPL's coordinator of children's services. Her advocacy that children need to see positive representations of themselves in literature and culture helped to jump-start this movement, which is more important than ever for children of all racial, ethnic, and gender identities.

As Ms. Baker knew well, inclusion and diversity are concepts that must be paired with education. Even in the twenty-first century, not everyone has embraced an enlightened way of thinking, and sadly, we are witnessing a surge of intolerance and racism that for a long time was latent. To counter this negativity, our role is to be educators. We are guided by public policies that underscore our values of DEIA, and we must seek out programming for our library spaces that create enlightenment and empathy.

RETHINKING HOW THE LIBRARY'S PHYSICAL SPACES ARE USED

We must also rethink the physical spaces within our buildings, with an eye toward developing skills for twenty-first-century jobs. In our schools today, it is rare to nonexistent to find 3D printers, podcasting, music and sound production studios, video production and green screen editing, robotics, virtual reality goggles, and other cutting-edge technology. These are the hands-on experiences that students must experience to prepare for the next wave of digital and artificial intelligence (AI) careers. As the Las Vegas–Clark County Library District plans new library buildings to serve our growing, underserved neighborhoods, we are called upon to create libraries of the future and imagine what will be required of us in ten, twenty, or more years.

I believe that the library's mission is the same since the time of Alexandria, specifically to retain and transfer knowledge across generations. We are so fortunate that the digital revolution enables us to maintain fewer books on our shelves while still providing a robust collection of online titles—books, movies, and music to stream or download. Library systems today are working to serve needs and preferences beyond books, including seed packets, tools, cookware, toys, board and video games, fishing poles, blood pressure monitors, and so much more.

The reduction of bookshelves also frees librarians to imagine our buildings as learning, celebrating, and gathering spaces. As libraries update their existing infrastructure and plan for new structures, they will create hubs of activity around courtyards, common areas, art galleries, and event and performance centers to enrich and encourage community connections—which, if libraries do not step up, we are in grave danger of losing as a society in 2035. Libraries will also still offer quiet rooms where our customers can study or just escape the demands of the day by reading, rejuvenating, or creating. I believe that this is how you get a building to build a community.

CONCLUSION

I believe that as librarians, we are key community influencers. To create the library of 2035 we desire, we must create the conversations we want to have today, not only with our local and state leaders, but also with grassroots groups that are affecting change. These discussions are what make our libraries true community forums and civic centers. As a library director, I am in our community libraries as a presence and a participant. I do not just monitor community developments; I create what I want to see and initiate the discussions that I want to hear. Since I represent my institution, I want the public to know who I am, and what my vision is for the future of our library district, and in return, I want to listen to their hopes and dreams so my staff and I can provide pathways for their goals.

I applaud this collection of essays from such a diverse group of leaders in the library industry. The timing to have these conversations could not be better. The 2020 Census projects a demographic sea change in the United States, so as our democracy becomes more diverse, our buildings are ideally poised to become community-service delivery centers. And once again, we will be called upon to reinvent our role as society's great equalizers.

NOTES

1. Sabrina Tavernise and Robert Gebeloff, "Census Shows Sharply Growing Numbers of Hispanics, Asians, and Multiracial Americans," *New York Times*, August 21, 2021, https://www.nytimes.com/2021/08/12/us/us-census-population-growth-diversity.html.
2. Jonathan Vespa, Lauren Medina, and David M. Armstrong, "Demographic Turning Points for the United States: Population Projections for 2020 to 2060," Census.gov (February 2020), https://www.census.gov/content/dam/Census/library/publications/2020/demo/p25-1144.pdf.
3. Susan Stamberg, "How Andrew Carnegie Turned His Fortune into a Library Legacy," NPR, August 1, 2023, https://www.npr.org/2013/08/01/207272849/how-andrew-carnegie-turned-his-fortune-into-a-library-legacy.
4. DC History Center, "About the Carnegie Library," accessed October 20, 2023, https://dchistory.org/about/carnegielibrary/.
5. Wikipedia, "Augusta Braxton Baker," accessed October 20, 2023, https://en.wikipedia.org/wiki/Augusta_Braxton_Baker.

16

Collaborative Collections and Content Considerations in Research and Academic Libraries

POSSIBLE PATHWAYS BY 2035

Raymond Pun and Tarida Anantachai

The library of 2035 will offer more efficient resource-sharing abilities empowered by enhanced digitization, increased interoperability, and improved open access policies.

During the 2020s, research and academic libraries (RALs) saw many austerity measures and financial shocks that challenged their institutions' budgets and priorities. The enrollment declines in higher education—already taking shape before the global pandemic, but further exacerbated since then—have only added to RALs' financial concerns as they grapple with flattening (and even decreasing) budgets, alongside the ballooning prices of collection subscriptions.[1] A system of inequitable access now exists; some institutions have inherently robust budgets, and others have smaller budgets that require strategically prioritized spending. By 2035, in order to thrive, RALs will need to embrace other sustainable budgetary models, including collaborative collection building and resource sharing, loanable content, scholarly communications and open access, and interoperability within these workflows.

COLLECTION BUILDING AND RESOURCE SHARING

RALs will need to think creatively about ways to build collections and share resources in order to provide access to content in increasingly financially constrained environments. One approach is to renew attention to building collections through expanded partnerships and other resource-sharing opportunities.

Resource sharing will need to scale up drastically to account for collections gaps. Partnerships will further expand the scope of RALs' support for faculty's research and teaching needs.

Consortiums and library associations will also devise more collaborative frameworks, and due to increasing costs of collections subscriptions and shrinking collections budgets, they will work together more collectively to negotiate with vendors in order to enable multi-institutional access. As a result, vendors not agreeing to the negotiation terms may be omitted completely from consortium subscription deals. Unfortunately, this may also impact vendors with smaller budgets and presence. A consortial, or other similar partnership, could potentially provide support to these smaller vendors in order to allow for more equitable access to their materials between their institutions. Consolidations and mergers between these vendors could increase and result in expanded opportunities, but they may also invite scrutiny with questions around competitor dominance.[2]

We are already seeing some encouraging efforts to support collective collection development models. For example, one of the aims of the Collaborative Collections Lifecycle Project (CCLP) launched in 2022 is to enhance sharing opportunities between RALs and institutions serving historically marginalized communities or those that have limited resources.[3] Other collective-collection development models include partnering with collaboratives, such as tribal land-grant colleges and the Historically Black Colleges and Universities (HBCU) Library Alliance.[4] The latter is already actively exploring several partnership projects, including collections and digitization initiatives aiming to create a framework around collaborative HBCU collection access.[5]

LOANABLE CONTENT FORMAT, TECHNOLOGIES, AND POLICIES

In 2035, collections assessment and analysis librarians, or similar roles, may collaborate even more intentionally with interlibrary loan librarians and their teams to assess needs and requests from users and researchers. They will also identify and work with vendors to align such content for specific usages, ensuring that licensed content will be loanable without penalty or policy violations. In the future, internal partnerships will further help libraries demonstrate their academic impact or return on investment (ROI) on their universities' budgets, emphasizing their alignment with their universities' missions, curricula, and research interests.

RALs will be able to loan e-books and multimedia/streaming content between institutions more seamlessly, in addition to the content they have traditionally offered (e.g., physical books and journals).[6] Digital loaning could be simplified due to revised and more flexible multi-institutional licensing agreements provided by vendors and distributors. Furthermore, as a result of the library community's advocacy for increased accessibility over the past few decades, vendors will be increasingly expected to provide accessible loanable content at the outset,[7] rather than relying on the loaning institutions to either remediate this content or make additional vendor requests to do so after the fact. Other efforts include the recent establishment of groups such as the Library Accessibility Alliance,[8] which will continue to build upon a number of valuable resources and toolkits for libraries to advocate for this accessible content.

During the 2020s, some materials such as e-books were loaned out from select institutions, but streaming content had not yet been made available due to vendor policies and copyright laws.[9] However, by 2035, more efforts will be made to ensure that this licensed content can be loanable and accessible to faculty and students for teaching and learning purposes under Fair Use. Given these potentially shifting lending models, RALs will have a vested interest in providing funding and resources to support such cross-institutional partnerships. They could also, perhaps, expand interlibrary loan and collections analysis roles across the field, particularly for institutions that can afford them.

In addition to e-books and streaming content, special collections will also be more loanable through enhanced digitization efforts by 2035. For example, requests from faculty at one institution to another may expedite the process of digitizing content and making their content viewable remotely as well as at a higher resolution. Institutions performed similar work during the COVID-19 pandemic shutdown through virtual reading rooms, where users could temporarily access digitized items.[10] By increasing support for these activities, scholars may be able to access additional special collections materials without having to travel to see them. Of course, seeing the object in its physical manifestation is a very different experience than interacting with its digital version. However, newer technologies could allow institutions to print the scans into a 3D facsimile and/or create 3D imaging that could be viewed and interacted with in different and multidimensional ways. These technologies were experimental and costly in the 2020s, but by 2035, they will become more normalized and available ubiquitously, including through smartphones and tablets. Still, some physical materials and objects in special collections will continue to be restricted to on-site visits due to their fragility, rarity, or other permissions considerations. With new technologies, the access and discovery of materials has already become more user-friendly and adaptive, and as additional opportunities (e.g., Internet of Things) become more embedded in everyday life, materials will become even more accessible to a wider audience.

SCHOLARLY COMMUNICATIONS AND OPEN ACCESS

Scholarly communications will also become a more standard function in RALs by 2035. Building off the impact of groups such as Coalition for Diversity and Inclusion in Scholarly Communications,[11] copyright and open access support will be extended to all academic departments, curriculum planning will be better supported, and equity and inclusion in publishing will be better realized.

Like research services and library instruction, scholarly communications work will be even more embedded within subject liaison librarians' daily duties and expectations. Up through the 2020s, scholarly communications have often been the responsibility of one individual, such as a scholarly communications or open education librarian. By 2035, elements of this critical work will be more team coordinated, distributed, and expected of additional public services librarians engaged in faculty support and academic programs. Subject liaison librarians will partner with faculty in developing open access and course content through their institutions' or disciplines' repositories (e.g., Earth and Space Science Open Archives,[12] arXiv,[13] and PubMed Central[14]). This content will continue to support students' learning and help alleviate the financial burdens of rising textbook and tuition costs.

Furthermore, open access initiatives and the work of open educational resources library workers will also become more standardized. With the advent of the 2022 White House Office of Science and Technology Policy (OSTP) under the Biden administration, federally funded research will be made widely available in 2025, and this trend will continue into the 2030s.[15] Subject liaison librarians will continue to serve as key collaborators with faculty on federally funded research and to support efforts to preserve and disseminate their data and output into open repositories. These librarians will also more intensely monitor federal and state policies and how these policies may impact their work.

When COVID-19 surged in 2020, copyright law and fair use was leveraged to provide digital access to content for teaching purposes.[16] Libraries were able to digitize physical content to ensure faculty and students had access to their course materials in a timely manner. With a major shift toward digital content licensing, physical general collections also have been shrinking or weeded out to create space for teaching and learning activities. In libraries, spaces for compact shelving will be replaced with collaborative and technology-rich learning spaces that actively engage faculty and students in interactively exploring their libraries' digital content, emerging technologies, and special collections. In order to facilitate these different areas, more communication and prioritization on teaching and learning will be needed to help promote the library's impact and ROI on campus.

INCREASED INTEROPERABILITY

Interoperability among systems of shared collections will also be increasingly crucial, particularly in better ensuring the seamless and accessible discovery of content across institutions, using both in-house and/or vendor-designed systems. Digital access to content expanded in the 2020s due to COVID-19, and again, through strategic decisions around this made through consortiums.[17] These developments have enabled access to content that was largely neglected—particularly content from historically minoritized voices and experiences. However, bias within these systems will still exist, and the role of artificial intelligence (AI) will heighten and further enable such biases if not critically acknowledged and addressed.[18] With libraries starting to employ machine learning programs to analyze collections as data, library policies will need to adopt and prioritize ethics in AI.[19]

Similarly, both special and general collections will be more easily searchable within a library's search system. Historically, integrating library and archival materials into a central platform for research and discovery purposes has been challenging.[20] This ongoing struggle to fuse multiple collections with different standardizations from the front and back end will be addressed through integrated library systems harnessing AI. Such systems will gather, ingest, and analyze metadata from these sets of collections and then repopulate the information in a discovery tool. Of course, the issues of accuracy, precision, and biases will also come to light here—that is, no system designed by humans will provide completely unbiased, inclusive, and equitable results. However, the possibilities of these tools will allow researchers to dive into various content without being redirected to numerous other platforms. This will inevitably change the roles of metadata librarians and catalogers, in which their roles will require content knowledge on AI and AI ethics, as well as an ongoing commitment to reparative description.

CONCLUSION

By 2035, major changes in RALs may also come from other external forces—including the ever-present pulls of capitalist and geopolitical systems—which will similarly influence and increase pressure for internal reorganization and reassessment. Leveraging libraries' current expertise and strengths, and focusing on expanded collaborations and partnerships, will have the potential to result in significant changes across RALs. In the end, the more things change, the more they stay the same.

> Leveraging libraries' current expertise and strengths, and focusing on expanded collaborations and partnerships, will have the potential to result in significant changes across RALs.

NOTES

1. Stephen Bosch, Barbara Albee, and Sion Romaine, "Are We There Yet? | Periodicals Price Survey 2022," April 14, 2022, https://www.libraryjournal.com/story/Are-We-There-Yet-Periodicals-Price-Survey-2022.
2. Marshall Breeding, "2022 Library Systems Report," *American Libraries*, May 2, 2022, https://americanlibrariesmagazine.org/2022/05/02/2022-library-systems-report.
3. Oya Y. Rieger, "Collaborative Collections Development: A New IMLS-Funded Partnership," last modified December 19, 2022, https://sr.ithaka.org/blog/collaborative-collection-development.

4. "HBCU Library Alliance," last accessed May 28, 2023, https://hbculibraries.org.
5. HBCU Library Alliance, "A Call for Cooperation among HBCU Libraries," last accessed May 28, 2023, https://www.hbculibraries.org/cooperation.html.
6. Library Copyright Alliance (LCA) will play a major role in bridging these efforts for educational uses. Danielle Miriam Cooper and Katherine Klosek, "Copyright and Streaming: Audiovisual Content in the US Context," Ithaka S+R, January 5, 2023, https://sr.ithaka.org/publications/copyright-and-streaming-audiovisual-content-in-the-us-context.
7. Beth Ashmore et al., "TRLN Guide to Negotiating Accessibility in E-Resource Licenses," December 14, 2022, http://bit.ly/trln-a11y-eresource-license.
8. "Library Accessibility Alliance," last accessed May 28, 2023, https://www.libraryaccessibility.org.
9. SUNY Library Services, "EBC eBook Lending Project," last modified May 18, 2023, https://slcny.libguides.com/sls/ebc_lending.
10. University of Sydney, "University of Sydney and University of Melbourne Launch Virtual Reading Room," December 14, 2022, https://www.sydney.edu.au/news-opinion/news/2022/12/14/university-of-sydney-fisher-library-launch-virtual-reading-room.html.
11. "Coalition for Diversity and Inclusion in Scholarly Communications," Latest News: Upcoming Events, last accessed May 28, 2023, https://c4disc.org.
12. ESS Open Archive, "Home," accessed October 20, 2023, https://essopenarchive.org/.
13. Cornell University, "arrxiv," accessed October 20, 2023, https://arxiv.org/.
14. National Library of Medicine, "PubMed Central," accessed October 20, 2023, https://www.ncbi.nlm.nih.gov/pmc/.
15. The White House, "OSTP Issues Guidance to Make Federally Funded Research Freely Available Without Delay," August 25, 2022, https://www.whitehouse.gov/ostp/news-updates/2022/08/25/ostp-issues-guidance-to-make-federally-funded-research-freely-available-without-delay.
16. "Public Statement of Library Copyright Specialists: Fair Use and Emergency Remote Teaching and Research," March 13, 2020, https://tinyurl.com/tvnty3a.
17. Lenka Pokorná et al., "Silver Lining of the COVID-19 crisis for Digital Libraries in terms of Remote Access," *Digital Library Perspective* 36, no. 4 (2020): 389–401, https://doi.org/10.1108/DLP-05-2020-0026.
18. Safiya Umoja Noble, "Algorithms of Oppression," in *Algorithms of Oppression* (New York University Press, 2018).
19. Thomas Padilla, "Collections as data: Implications for enclosure," *College & Research Libraries News* [Online] 79, no. 6 (5 June 2018).
20. Tessa Brawley-Barker, "Integrating library, archives, and museum collections in an open source information management system: A Case Study at Glenstone," *Art Documentation: Journal of the Art Libraries Society of North America* 35, no. 1 (2016): 86–113.

17

Survive or Thrive

CAN COMMUNITY COLLEGE LIBRARIES SURMOUNT THE CHALLENGES THEY FACE?

Peter Hepburn

The library of 2035 will continually adapt, innovate, and collaborate with other campus services, expanding the library's relevance and value to the institution.

In late January 2023, I shared a proposal to build special and digital collections at the College of the Canyons library with my dean. The proposal addressed two of several possibilities from a list given to us by the upper administration. Both possibilities seemed feasible, though they would require an investment of space, equipment, additional supplies, and staffing. In short, we would need money to make either of the possibilities a reality. Still, they fit well with what the library could and should offer to our students and the community where the college resides.

What spurred the proposal was a *Chronicle of Higher Education* report on the transformation of academic libraries.[1] It led me to think about how my college library could include other things: makerspaces, galleries, media rooms, tutoring centers, and more. While some of these ideas are pretty cool, they already have perfectly fine homes elsewhere on my campus (e.g., STEM labs, art galleries, and studios). As a result, there is less impetus for my library to embrace them and not just keep doing what we are currently doing (e.g., reference services, resource sharing, research, and access to physical and digital collections).

And that, I fear, is how community college libraries like mine continue to merely survive, rather than thrive, as we consider what the community college landscape will be in 2035.

THE CHALLENGES

I come from a distinctly California perspective. The California community colleges comprise the country's largest public higher education system, with almost two million students at 116 colleges across the state. While interesting and innovative work occurs in all library communities, far too many libraries are just surviving, especially as their colleges emerge into a post-pandemic landscape. The challenges for community colleges and their libraries, at least in California, started before the pandemic.

Consider community college enrollment data from California (see Table 17.1). Even in the decade prior to the pandemic, numbers had been declining. However, when COVID-19 hit, community colleges experienced a *dramatic* decrease in enrollment. It is too soon to tell whether and to what extent enrollment may recover. The first full year of the pandemic saw enrollment at 26.9 percent below the 2009–2010 FTES (full-time equivalent students) and 31.7 percent below that year's headcount, a thirty-year low[2] and an extraordinary deficit to make up.

Community college libraries' current and future vulnerability to enrollment trends concerns me. Funding for colleges varies from state to state, but where funding is tied to apportionment, declining enrollments mean declining

Table 17.1 Aggregate enrollment, California community colleges, 2010–2022

Year	Credit FTES	Non-Credit FTES	Total FTES	Head Count
2009–2010	1,232,088	83,242	1,315,330	2,689,644
2010–2011	1,201,081	78,552	1,279,633	2,483,787
2011–2012	1,113,325	70,714	1,184,038	2,316,400
2012–2013	1,063,468	64,741	1,128,209	2,189,503
2013–2014	1,097,233	68,825	1,166,058	2,202,198
2014–2015	1,107,301	67,856	1,175,157	2,209,445
2015–2016	1,119,091	67,890	1,186,981	2,235,443
2016–2017	1,116,146	67,145	1,183,291	2,259,676
2017–2018	1,118,242	70,711	1,188,953	2,267,095
2018–2019	1,108,682	68,702	1,177,384	2,257,685
2019–2020	1,092,226	57,438	1,149,664	2,206,441
2020–2021	1,012,643	53,188	1,065,831	1,915,046
2021–2022	913,476	61,273	974,749	1,837,331

Data derived from the California Community Colleges Chancellor's Office Data Mart (n.d.)

Table 17.2 Aggregate door count, circulation, and reference transactions, California community college libraries, 2010-2019

Year	Door Count	Circulation of Physical Materials	Reference Transactions
2009-2010	20,378,974	4,276,400	704,202
2010-2011	20,344,505	4,254,881	715,503
2011-2012	19,809,163	3,973,662	721,384
2012-2013	19,548,961	3,432,500	669,977
2013-2014	17,425,041	3,093,261	564,472
2014-2015	16,903,715	3,076,281	561,398
2015-2016	16,560,909	2,171,028	489,033
2016-2017	16,164,436	2,064,869	434,454
2017-2018	13,977,318	2,077,614	371,622
2018-2019	11,533,330	1,878,972	342,717

Data derived from Council of California Community Colleges Chief Librarians (2022). For each category, only data from institutions for which all ten years were available were included.

monies, which means making decisions to save money.[3] So, how do colleges save money? Institutional leaders might ask, do we need a building dedicated solely to a non-revenue-producing unit like a library? Do we need books in that building? Do we require specialized, degreed staffing?

We can be optimistic. We can hope and plan for waves of students returning to community colleges. However, we probably should stop to recognize a phenomenon that will exacerbate the enrollment problem: we are fast approaching a precipice, a demographic cliff that spells challenges for enrollment and, consequently, funding. In short, there are fewer students of traditional age in graduating cohorts in upcoming years.[4] The population of eighteen-year-olds will shrink, and colleges of all types will compete for them all the more. Community colleges attract many students who are later in life, beginning or returning to school sometime after graduating from high school. However, there is nothing to suggest that community colleges will fare better than other institutions of higher education in avoiding the impact of the demographic cliff (the drop in the college-aged population)[5] and its negative implications for funding.

Nevertheless, let us focus on the students we do have and how they use libraries (see Table 17.2). For one thing, students are not physically coming into the community college library as they used to. Even though today's libraries are more than just buildings or collections of books, college administrators continue to assess the library's value based on how busy the library is (i.e., how many people are accessing the physical library building). In addition, data collected through the annual chancellor's office survey is not reassuring.[6] Even before the pandemic, the number of visitors to community college libraries was dropping annually, going from 20,378,974 in 2009-2010 to 11,533,330 ten years later, a decline of 43.4 percent. That is noticeable, and it is difficult to sugarcoat the decline by claiming that online usage of libraries makes up for it (I do not believe it does).

Just as students are not entering our building as much, their use of physical collections is also dwindling. The aggregate circulation of physical materials housed within the California community college libraries in 2018-2019 represents a decline of 56.1 percent in a ten-year period (Table 17.2), and the pandemic years (2020-2022) will likely show an utter collapse, from which recovery will be slow. At my library alone, circulation was 44,399 in 2009-2010, 24,705 ten years later, and 2,109 in 2021-2022. There is some balance to be found here in the usage of electronic resources, of course, but those numbers are wrenching.

There are other factors to consider when measuring the library's value. For example, reference support has long been core to our work in community college libraries. How are the numbers there? The data show that reference support is trending unhealthily downward over time. As is evident in Table 17.2, 2011-2012 was the peak year for reference support. However, by the end of the decade, library users were requesting reference assistance far less often, a 52.5 percent decrease from the greatest annual total.

The data reflect the long-standing, conventional roles that community college libraries perform. That said, community college libraries have also made great strides to accommodate online modalities of instruction and to work with students beyond the library's physical space. Faculty, administrators, and even students are aware of some of these efforts. Nevertheless, people tend to believe what they see; quieter buildings, books sitting on shelves, and a lack of traffic at the reference desk do not speak to the value of libraries at community colleges. So, what will?

SURVIVAL SUPPORT

One source of support for the survival of libraries at community colleges lies within accreditation standards. Accreditation requires extensive preparation work for many people at the college (and for the visiting teams) and generates anxiety for the whole campus. While time-consuming and stressful, accreditation standards often support the value of libraries by calling out libraries and related support services as being necessary to the college. The standards vary across the country depending on which accrediting body holds sway,[7] and not all of them have as much language about the library in place as others. Just the

> While time-consuming and stressful, accreditation standards often support the value of the libraries by calling out libraries and related services as being necessary to the college.

Table 17.3 Other uses of library space, California community colleges, 2018-2020

Year	Writing Centers	Tutoring Centers	Faculty Offices	Learning Spaces	Other Departments and Services
2018-2019	23	32	29	34	33
2019-2020	19	30	27	34	66

Data derived from Council of California Community Colleges Chief Librarians (2022).

same, libraries are included in the accreditation standards. In California, the Accrediting Commission for Community and Junior Colleges (ACCJC) is the accrediting body for two-year institutions. In the current standards, the library is central to Standard II.B (Student Learning Programs and Support Services: Library and Learning Support Services).[8] This inclusion is significant because it means that colleges must provide library services sufficient in quantity and quality. Although each college may establish what constitutes sufficiency, there must be consideration of that. So long as accreditation requires library services and support, libraries will at least survive at community colleges.

MEANS TO THRIVE

Survival is the baseline, though, and thriving is the goal. Consider what my dean essentially asked of me in early 2023: What other things can the library do? How can it transform or add more value?

Change is not a new thing for libraries, but it may be an uncomfortable thing. Returning to the survey data in Table 17.3, we see that libraries have expanded the types of services and functions that they offer and house. For example, writing and tutoring centers have become common, as well as learning spaces and offices for non-library faculty. Of particular note is the leap from 2018-2019 to the following year in terms of other departments and services now being housed in the library. Among the examples given were uses that are more mundane and reflect a passive use of library space (i.e., ones that do not have an immediate connection to supporting students' achievements), such as administrative or faculty offices or conference rooms. But there were other, more offbeat, and interesting things worth noting, among them:

- campus archives,
- center for entrepreneurship and innovation,
- county genealogical society,
- marketing services,
- multicultural center, and
- reading center.

Of these, archives and a reading center seem to align with more familiar ideas of what a library can and should do. Genealogy, which is not uncommon at public libraries, is only slightly more of a stretch.

Look at the others, though. As libraries commit to equity, diversity, and inclusion efforts, hosting a multicultural center makes sense. A center for entrepreneurship and innovation, though? Two instances of marketing departments? These are not the skills or relationships that were commonly taught in library school a quarter century ago. Nonetheless, they are exciting because they demonstrate how the library can leverage its space, collections, and research staff experience to connect with units that might otherwise have been siloed elsewhere on campus. A strategy may be to actively court or acquiesce to providing these units space in our library buildings. As neighbors within the same facility, we can easily become mutual supporters and collaborators. And, further, as the library takes responsibility for new things beyond our familiarity, the library is in embracing challenges that lead toward a path to thriving.

CONCLUSION

When I reflect on the options I was asked to consider for the library space, I regret that I did not try to reach for some of the services that currently exist elsewhere. The special and digital collections options were fine but may not connect with innovation on campus all that effectively. It is okay: our library will survive.

I want more. I want my library to thrive. I want all our community college libraries to thrive. Remaining protective of our library space and becoming entrenched in the services and resources that are familiar is likely a path to survival. Moreover, we have the means and even the support to survive. However, my vision for a thriving library in 2035 is for community colleges to stop relying on a long-held presumption that libraries are simply a good thing to have. Instead, a thriving library of the future will adapt, change, and invite in other campus services that can be our partners or expand our libraries in new ways.

NOTES

1. S. Carlson (2022), *The Library of the Future: How the Heart of the Campus Is Transforming*, Chronicle of Higher Education.
2. Michael Burke, Daniel J. Willis, and Debbie Truong, "California community college enrollment plummets to 30-year low," *Los Angeles Times* (November 18, 2022), https://www.latimes.com/california/story/2022-11-18/california-community-college-enrollment-plunges.
3. Ibid.
4. Mark J. Drozdowski, "Looming enrollment cliff poses serious threat to colleges," Best Colleges, 2023, https://www.bestcolleges.com/news/analysis/looming-enrollment-cliff-poses-serious-threat-to-colleges/.

5. u capture, "How to Climb Higher Ed's Impending Demographic Cliff," March 17, 2022, https://www.capturehighered.com/how-to-climb-higher-eds-impending-demographic-cliff/.

6. Council of California Community Colleges Chief Librarians, 2022, "Annual Library Data Survey Master File 2005 to 2020," https://cclibrarians.org/sites/default/files/masterfilelibrarysurvey05_06to19withpivottablefordistrubtion.xlsx.

7. Accrediting Commission for Community and Junior College (ACCJC), "Eligibility requirements, accreditation standards, and commission policies," 2019, https://accjc.org/eligibility-requirements-standards-policies/#accreditation-standards. Higher Learning Commission (HLC), "Criteria for accreditation," 2019, https://www.hlcommission.org/Policies/criteria-and-core-components.html; New England Commission of Higher Education (NECHE), "Standards for accreditation," 2019, https://www.neche.org/standards-for-accreditation/; Northwest Commission on Colleges and Universities, "NWCCU 2020 STANDARDS," 2020, https://nwccu.org/accreditation/standards-policies/standards/.

8. ACCJC, "Eligibility requirements, accreditation standards, and commission policies."

18

New Jersey School Libraries 2035

Ewa Dziedzic-Elliott

The library of 2035 will collaborate with community leaders and policymakers to provide diverse collections of resources and safe spaces while also advocating for acceptance and tolerance.

The New Jersey Association of School Librarians (NJASL)[1] is a state organization made up of dedicated practicing, retired, and pre-service school librarian[2] members. In January 2023, NJASL made national headlines with the passage of NJ S588, which would require the creation of the Information Literacy (IL) Student Learning Standard. It took several years to achieve this goal. We learned a lot about ourselves, about our partners, and, most importantly, about the legislative process. As we look toward the library of 2035, these learnings could be useful to other library institutions across the country.

NEW JERSEY INFORMATION LITERACY BILL

BRIEF HISTORY

In 2016, the New Jersey Library Association (NJLA)[3] and NJASL released a report: "School Library Programs in New Jersey: Building Blocks for Realizing Student Potential with ESSA Legislation Opportunities."[4] The report was written after President Obama signed the 2015 Every Student Succeeds Act (ESSA), which recognized the role effective school library programs and school librarians play in student academic achievement and their literacy skills.[5] New Jersey librarians saw this as an opportunity to advocate for librarians by assessing the status of their library programs.

The NJASL and the NJLA created two tools to gather information: a census of certified librarians in New Jersey and a survey of the same group. Key findings from the census include:

- The number of school library media specialists declined 20 percent since 2007-2008.
- Only about 10 percent of charter schools had school librarians.
- Ninety-one of six hundred New Jersey school districts had no school librarians.
- Thirty-three of them had no librarians in elementary schools.[6]

The main results from the survey were as follows:

- School librarians performed non-library duties (e.g., monitoring lunchtimes, coordinating tests, and overseeing school technology).
- School librarians didn't have time to collaborate with teachers.
- School library budgets were flat or decreasing.
- Many districts didn't have Information Literacy Plans (40 percent).
- Librarians didn't have aids or assistants (70 percent).

Participants also voiced their concerns for diminishing school library positions and support for their programs.[7] The authors of the report recommended a list of stakeholders and suggested next steps, which included: statewide advocacy for public and school librarians and library programs, collaboration with the New Jersey Department of Education (DOE), and the creation of resolutions and regulations for well-funded school library programs.

The report was followed by several additional documents, statements, and articles.[8] Between 2017 and 2022, the NJASL leadership identified key stakeholders and reached out to several New Jersey decision-makers to find support for the bill. The organization also hired a legislative consultant, retired school librarian Mary Moyer Stubbs. In 2020, the NJASL enlisted the help of EveryLibrary,[9] which trained the NJASL leadership on coalition-building. What made this bill different from previous information literacy bills, such as the one originally drafted and promoted by the NJLA in 2016, was the pivot from curriculum to student learning standards.

PROCESS AND CONTENT

The legislation requires that:

- "The State Board of Education shall adopt New Jersey Student Learning Standards in information literacy,"[10] and
- "Each school district shall incorporate instruction on information literacy in an appropriate place in the curriculum of students in grades kindergarten

through 12 as part of the district's implementation of the New Jersey Student Learning Standards. The school library media specialist shall be included in the development of curriculum concerning information literacy whenever possible."[11]

New Jersey governor Phil Murphy signed the bill on January 4, 2023. The bill requires that the New Jersey Department of Education: "convene a committee of educators, the majority of which shall include certified school library media specialists, as well as teaching staff members across a broad spectrum of subject areas."[12] The DOE's work on the draft standard is slated to begin in the summer of 2023. After the draft is completed, public hearings will be held in 2024 to discuss the rigor, clarity, and reasonableness of the standards.[13] The expected release of the standard is Fall 2025. The bill describes the standard and offers the following definition of information literacy:

"Information literacy" means a set of skills that enables an individual to recognize when information is needed and to locate, evaluate, and use the needed information effectively. Information literacy includes, but is not limited to, digital, visual, media, textual, and technological literacy. The content of information literacy shall include, at a minimum:

1. the research process and how information is created and produced;
2. critical thinking and using information resources;
3. research methods, including the difference between primary and secondary sources;
4. the difference between facts, points of view, and opinions;
5. accessing peer-reviewed print and digital library resources;
6. the economic, legal, and social issues surrounding the use of information; and
7. the ethical production of information.[14]

NEED FOR EQUITY

Why did New Jersey librarians want to have their own standard? To be very honest, it all came down to equity. Here are some of the challenges librarians faced:

- The New Jersey education system is decentralized.
- The New Jersey DOE creates standards and oversees the processes of teaching in public and private schools, but many of the state-level requirements are recommendations that the department does not have a way to reinforce.
- The New Jersey Administrative Code and Statute[15] allows school districts to interpret the laws regarding school librarians instead of providing clear rules, which raises a number of questions: Are we supposed to have a

librarian in each building or one for the district? Is having a non-certified library worker or a "library consultant" enough to be compliant with the statute? Year after year, the NJASL closely follows our New Jersey School Performance Report.[16] Even though we know some school districts report non-certified school library staff as school librarians, the numbers keep going down. In 2016, the state ratio showed one librarian to 911 students. In 2022, there were 1,157 school librarians serving 1,400,737 students—a ratio of one librarian to 1,211 students.

Creating a state standard with clearer rules was a response to these issues.

THE VALUE OF NEW JERSEY HAVING THEIR OWN STATE STANDARD

The passage of the standard is a victory on its own, but library practitioners know it is not enough. The bill didn't require that the standard be taught by school library media specialists, the content taught be assessed through state testing, or financial support be provided to hire more school librarians, additional professional development, or resources. Introducing the standard and not supporting school librarians would be ineffective and cause further disconnection between the state standards and school practices. Therefore, the NJASL, in collaboration with the New Jersey State Library (NJSL),[17] is in the process of supporting school librarians through professional development opportunities, with the main focus on information literacy in our schools.

THE VISION

The NJASL, in collaboration with other stakeholders such as the DOE, school administrators, the NJSA, and the NJLA, hopes to:

- provide statewide in-person, virtual, and hybrid workshops for school librarians with hands-on practical learning opportunities;
- identify and hire instructors/IL specialists/consultants who can provide professional development for New Jersey educators and librarians;
- create digital guides on IL implementation in K-12 for educators and librarians; and
- make statewide resources available to *all* New Jersey students.

At the time this chapter was written (2023), New Jersey school librarians were waiting for the DOE to lead the work on drafting the standard. Therefore, we are currently unsure what will be in the standard, and we are unable to start training New Jersey librarians and educators or work on creating a model research or model curriculum.

ORGANIZATIONAL APPROACH

The NJASL is partnering with other associations across the state to support their members. The NJASL has identified two types of associations for further collaboration:

1. *Library-oriented institutions (e.g., NJSL, NJLA, and Library Link NJ).*[18] Each of these organizations has different resources, ways of connecting with library patrons, and ways they can support school librarians.
2. *Educational institutions, such as the DOE, school administrators, and teachers' organizations.* Successful application of the new standard depends on the buy-in of all stakeholders. If school administrators or content area teachers don't understand why librarians are the *information literacy specialists* who can teach, co-teach, and curate resources, the standard will not work.

The NJASL is also working on identifying key institutions that provide library undergraduate and graduate college programs. Having IL as a mandatory component of New Jersey state standards means that future librarians need to be prepared to teach it.

SCHOOL LIBRARIAN APPROACH

While waiting for the release of the standard, school librarians need to ask themselves: What does the creation of the standard really mean for them and their students? How can they make the best of it? How can they make the biggest impact? School library media specialists need to demonstrate how to be lifelong learners, how to pivot and learn new skills, and how to add new tools to their toolbox. They also need to overcome a number of challenges, including:

- *Staffing:* About 20 percent of our schools do not have certified librarians. According to the SLIDE study,[19] the number of New Jersey school librarians declined 27.5 percent between 2009-2010 and 2018-2019.[20]
- *Money:* School districts need money to retain and train current librarians, hire new ones, and create new positions in those districts that haven't had librarians in the most recent years or decades.
- *Time:* School librarians have to be very creative in finding opportunities to provide instructional services—often relying on personal and professional relationships with teachers, which creates inconsistency and a lack of equitable level of instruction for *all students.*
- *Resources:* The NJASL hopes that through state budget requests for education and libraries as well as access through NJSL resources, we will be able to provide equitable access to school library materials for all students in the state of New Jersey.

NEW JERSEY SCHOOL LIBRARIANS AS INFORMAL SCHOOL LEADERS

New Jersey school librarians are no longer "just librarians." They are informal school leaders who should have a seat at any table when conversations on the future of New Jersey schools happen. They support and advocate for everyone by equitably providing diverse collections of resources, offering safe spaces, and spreading acceptance and tolerance.

The NJASL has proven that their leadership on a state level is well-deserved. The NJASL's volunteers took a lead on successfully passing state legislation, and they continued their work on other ones, such as the Ratio Bill. The NJASL has developed close partnerships with multiple state and national organizations that support school and public libraries and library programs. The key to our success was preparation and the ability to explain our asks, show our value, and support our claims with data and specific examples of current state or district level policies, regulations, or codes.

> Building a strong library ecosystem is critical. Lack of school librarians and school library programs affects all library types, so we need to work together.

Below are some things we have learned in the process worth sharing.

1. School librarians need to demystify school principals/administrators as the only qualified decision-makers in school environments; school librarians should be recognized as equal partners. Our informal leadership matters. School librarians contribute information about new technology and tools, provide professional development opportunities for our colleagues, and create schoolwide programs for our faculty, staff, students, and administrators.
2. State board members and school boards do not necessarily understand how public-school systems or school libraries work and operate. School librarians need to educate them by providing a basic explanation of what information literacy is, why we need to teach research skills, and why it matters for our students to have equal access to resources.
3. We need to also demystify how school libraries work for state legislators. State legislators do not necessarily know how school libraries work, or even how public education works. For example, not all proposed bills make sense; some of them contradict current laws and highlight the lack of understanding of current regulations and the operations of the state and its governance.
4. Librarians need to stand united across all types of librarianship. A big part of the current success in New Jersey is the fact that each state-level library organization was included in the conversation about writing, supporting,

and advocating the bill to legislators. Building a strong library ecosystem is critical. Lack of school librarians and school library programs affects all library types, so we need to work together.

CONCLUSION

By 2035, New Jersey school library media specialists will have a school librarian in every school building in New Jersey, supported by statewide academic and nonacademic resources, as well as their own representative at the DOE who will advocate for the librarians and library programs the same way that is being done for other content areas, such as math, science, or social studies. We will also have liaison/representatives at the principals and school board associations. The NJASL will have a seat at the table with the main education associations that make decisions about New Jersey education. Most importantly, by 2035, we will have a very strong New Jersey library ecosystem that supports school, public, and academic librarians and library workers.

NOTES

1. New Jersey Association of School Libraries, "Home," accessed October 21, 2023, https://www.njasl.org/.
2. The official state certification uses the term *school library media specialist* for school librarians; I will be using these two terms interchangeably.
3. New Jersey Library Association, "Home," accessed October 21, 2023, https://www.njla.org/.
4. Maureen Donohue and James Keehbler, "School Library Programs in New Jersey: Building Blocks for Realizing Student Potential with ESSA Legislation Opportunities," NJASL (April 2016), https://njla.memberclicks.net/assets/docs/2016ESSAandNJSchoolLibraryPrograms.pdf.
5. Ibid.
6. Ibid.
7. Ibid.
8. Virtual Academic Library Environment, ACRL New Jersey Chapter, and New Jersey Library Association, "The Value and Importance of Highly Effective School Library Programs," accessed October 21, 2023, https://drive.google.com/file/d/0B2j6CyhsF01VY1NTY0F5bWYyVI9ESExpN3djeTBKanJVTDY0/view?resourcekey=0Q_Y2tPOS3MMOojTxYqffg; New Jersey Library Association, "A132—Information Literacy Skills for Students," accessed October 21, 2023, https://drive.google.com/file/d/16RjjvwOl7tDpz5lhtgWQxESRd_70cMLe/view; Cara Berg, Darby Malvey, and Maureen Donohue, "Without Foundations, We Can't Build: Information Literacy and the Need for Strong School Library Programs" (March 7, 2018), https://drive.google.com/file/d/18jEwqX_-B_TtW3d_Nx2Gfla4041Uzlr1/view.
9. EveryLibrary, "Home," accessed October 21, 2023, https://www.everylibrary.org/.
10. LegiScan, "Bill Text: NJ S588," Section C.18A:7F-4.4 1b (January 4, 2023), C.18A:7F-4.4 1b. https://legiscan.com/NJ/text/S588/2022.
11. Ibid., Section C.18A:7F-4.4 1c/.

12. Ibid., Section C.18A:7F-4.5.
13. Ibid., Section C.18A:7F-4.6.
14. Ibid., Section C.18A:7F-4.4.
15. Department of Education, "Administrative Code and Statute," State of New Jersey, accessed October 21, 2023, https://www.nj.gov/education/code/.
16. State of New Jersey, "NJ School Performance Report," accessed October 21, 2023, https://rc.doe.state.nj.us/.
17. New Jersey State Library, "Home," accessed October 21, 2023, https://www.njstatelib.org/.
18. LibraryLinkNJ, "Home," accessed October 21, 2023, https://librarylinknj.org/.
19. Debra E. Kachel and Keith Curry Lance, 2021, "State Contexts for School Librarian Employment. SLIDE: The School Librarian Investigation—Decline or Evolution?" *Grantee Submission*. Grantee Submission, https://search.ebscohost.com/login.aspx?direct=true&db=eric&AN=ED616794&site=ehost-live.
20. The Information Literacy Bill was not the only bill that was introduced in the 2017-2018 Legislative Session. New Jersey librarians created Bill S1903, called the Ratio Bill, that would require having a ratio of school librarians in every school building in New Jersey. New Jersey librarians understood that asking for two bills at the same time might be too much for our legislators and prioritized IL Bill above the Ratio Bill. However, we hope that New Jersey decision-makers will also support the pending Ratio Bill. See https://www.njleg.state.nj.us/bill-search/2022/S1903.

V
Library Workers

Part V: Library Workers focuses on the library's most essential resource: the people who work in libraries. The authors of chapters 19 through 21 emphasize the importance of investing in, retaining, and taking care of library workers, specifically noting that libraries will:

- require an understanding of the business of librarianship, prioritizing the management of the organization to an equal or greater degree than the management of the collection *(Dames and Zanders)*.
- uphold a strong commitment to adopting policies, practices, and environments that support wellness for library workers as well as the community *(Garcia-Febo)*.
- present several new kinds of job titles, some not yet imagined, that will be needed as libraries navigate the integration of new technologies for providing services and reliable, accurate, and relevant information *(Aldrich and Keller)*.

Dames and Zanders open Part V with chapter 19, highlighting the changed roles of the chief librarian in research libraries since the pandemic. They note how meeting user needs, providing appropriate technology and facilities, cultivating a customer-centered culture, and aligning priorities to the organizations' strategic goals have always been, and continue to be, key strategies of the chief librarian. However, decreased enrollments in higher education have placed growing pressures on library budgets. Talent management, including retaining staff, has become a key strategy that benefits the library as well as its operating budget.

When thinking about retention, Garcia-Febo notes throughout chapter 20 the critical need for strategies and policies that uphold the overall wellness of library workers. Wellness strategies may include a menu of options such as offering webinars and trainings, providing dedicated space for wellness, and troubleshooting workflows to combat fatigue and burnout. Wellness for library workers is not just the responsibility of the supervisor; instead, it should be a collaborative effort where libraries, library associations, and LIS programs work together to provide strategies and resources that support library workers' wellness goals.

In chapter 21, Aldrich and Keller discuss how changes in the library environment, such as the growth of technology like artificial intelligence and robots and the increasing importance of connecting users to truthful, reliable, and relevant information within the vast and highly virtual information landscape, will impact library job opportunities in the future. They specifically highlight four new job titles along with the skills needed to perform the job and examples of projects each position will likely undertake within these positions.

Archived webcasts of author interviews are available at: https://sites.google.com/sjsu.edu/library2035/home

19

The Library CEO

MONEY IN THE BANK, PEOPLE ON THE BUS

K. Matthew Dames and Tony Zanders

The library of 2035 will require an understanding of the business of librarianship, prioritizing the management of the organization to an equal or greater degree than the management of the collection.

Things seemed dire when the United States declared COVID-19 a pandemic on March 11, 2020. By then, most American colleges and universities—many of which had students on, leaving for, or returning from spring break—not only were actively discussing closure, but whether or not students should return to campus.

Provosts rarely call your personal mobile number unless a situation is urgent. We were members of Boston University Libraries' executive team when our provost called to ask the university librarian (K. Matthew Dames, co-author of this chapter) how long it would take to fully close the library—including shuttering the branches, evacuating staff, and moving all services and operations exclusively online for the foreseeable future. This call came at the midway point of co-author Tony Zanders's appointment as Boston University's (BU) inaugural entrepreneur in residence (EIR). In this role, Zanders served as a member of the libraries' executive team, helping craft the talent strategy to develop employees amidst a campus-wide hiring freeze. The overnight shift to remote work, coupled with the subsequent spending and hiring freezes, introduced constraints on existing roles that supported emerging tasks. This required library leadership to conceptualize the library as an organization, as opposed to the library as a collection, without much advance notice.

The pandemic solidified the reality that the chief librarian is, in reality, a chief executive officer of a dynamic information organization. This chapter explores how this evolution occurred, the role the COVID-19 pandemic played in accelerating this evolution, and what these changes mean for research libraries through 2035 and beyond.

TRADITIONAL NOTIONS OF LIBRARY MANAGEMENT

A contemporary chief librarian's worries are quite different from those of their predecessors. During the past quarter century, the academy welcomed new information-centric stakeholders across the institution. At minimum, the office of the chief information officer (CIO) and the office of research both have become central to the research enterprise, and in many cases, they are key partners to the library's operations. But these roles, while often symbiotic within the institution, pose new considerations for budget allocation, division of labor, space, services portfolio, and influence on the overall decision-making process.

This evolution in university administration requires library management to strategize beyond collections and services, and to focus more on strategic partnerships and alliances that will accentuate rather than dilute the library's value proposition. Developing capacity throughout the organizational ranks, such as in the areas of leadership, negotiation, public speaking, collaboration, branding, finance, and partnerships, has become a task that can no longer be outsourced to institutional HR, but instead must be prioritized by the chief librarian.

In some ways, the role of chief librarian used to be relatively simple. Rachel Singer Gordon aptly outlined some of the core functions of a chief librarian at the dawn of the twenty-first century: allocate resources, manage staff to best meet user needs, provide appropriate technology and facilities, cultivate a customer-centered culture, and set priorities to ensure the institution and library's goals are met.[1]

In addition to these core functions, curation of the library collections has always been considered a core function of the chief librarian within the academy. Furthermore, research collections have long been a source of prestige for Carnegie-classified doctoral universities with very high research activity.[2]

The correlation between the size and prestige of research collections historically has been reinforced by the Association of Research Libraries (ARL).[3] For decades, the ARL used its Membership Criteria Index (the ARL Index) as its primary membership criteria for membership. The ARL Index leaned heavily upon quantitative measures about research collections, including number of volumes held, number of volumes added, and current serials.[4] Even when the ARL moved from the ARL Index to the Library Investment Index (LII), beginning with the collection of 2002-2003 data, LII remained highly correlated with historic investments in research collections.[5]

For these reasons, the job of the chief librarian in the academy historically has been tightly connected to his or her ability to curate a collection that brings the requisite level of academic prestige upon the library, and by extension, the sponsoring college or university. In other words, the paradigm has been [research] collections over everything: collections over services, collections over talent, even collections over space. Any chief librarian who has tried to move collections out of the main library to allow for additional patron space can attest to the strength and durability of this standard.

NEW EXPECTATIONS OF THE POST-PANDEMIC CHIEF LIBRARIAN

But so many things have changed.

Consider the usual suspects: systemic problems in scholarly publishing from continued steep price increases for much of the published scholarly record despite purportedly electronic lower production costs, which are accelerated by the consolidation of publishers across the sector; the "enrollment cliff," or the national demographic phenomenon that predicts substantially lower numbers of college-aged students during much of the next two decades (which, in turn, threatens to diminish tuition revenue);[6] and increasingly contentious conversations about the value of higher education.[7]

But there are several other factors that make the current moment exceedingly difficult to maintain the historic, collections-focused paradigm of library leadership. One is the massive generational leadership shift that is occurring within research libraries. According to a 2019 study, turnover in ARL chief librarian positions were stable, and those leaders remained in their jobs for decades. Only sixteen new chief librarians were hired in the 1970s. Since that time, however, the ARL has reported thirty-eight new chief librarians in the 1980s, and sixty-nine new chief librarians in the 1990s. Between 2013 and 2018, the ARL reported that its members filled eighty-seven chief librarian roles.[8] Much of this recent change has been due to demographics that predicted a mass exodus of chief librarians during the past decade.[9]

Another factor is new expectations about the chief librarian's role. In an April 2022 study, Ithaka S+R[10] teamed with the ARL and the Canadian Association of Research Libraries (CARL)[11] to consult with university leaders in Canada and the United States to identify their strategic priorities, gauge their expectations of research libraries in achieving them, and determine how research libraries can advance their institutions' strategic priorities.

The study revealed mixed perceptions about the research library. Some academic leaders have modest expectations for their research library; they hope the library system can retain the status quo—including its continued focus on collections. Other academic leaders feel the library could offer substantially more value to their institution than it does and are discouraged by the pace of change.

In instances where university leaders consider the library system as a partner in helping the institution achieve or advance its strategic priorities, university leaders reported that it no longer is enough for the chief librarian to be chief collections officer, or even chief manager of the library, but instead a university leader with responsibility for the library. Instead of looking for the chief librarian to focus on protecting the library or advancing its interests, university leaders indicated that they wanted chief librarians to focus deeply on understanding the university and working as part of the leadership team of the university to advance the university's interests. In addition, university leaders reported that they now expect the chief librarian to push the library beyond its traditional responsibilities to serve the current and emerging needs of the university, and to take responsibility for resource stewardship—especially personnel.[12]

MANAGING THE TALENT IS MANAGING THE MONEY

The contemporary chief librarian must now be a fully mature chief *executive* officer. A key component in evolving from chief collections officer to chief executive officer is developing the ability to recognize the importance of, and managing effectively, all aspects of talent. Talent management is anticipating the need for human capital and then setting out a plan to meet it,[13] and it is inextricably linked to the chief librarian's need to effectively manage an institution's financial resources.

Our experience is illustrative. Once we began working together formally at BU Libraries,[14] we soon realized it was imperative that we emphasize talent management given the leadership challenges we faced at the time. When we began developing and implementing what we then called the talent chain,[15] BU Libraries had been for decades absent from the national marketplace for executive academic library talent, including trailing significantly behind peer institutions in professional headcount. For example, some of our initial strategic planning benchmarking analyses showed that BU Libraries employed at least thirty-five fewer full-time employees (FTE) than the library system at the Massachusetts Institute of Technology (MIT) and at least one hundred fewer FTE than those at Columbia and New York University, all of which BU had identified as Association of American Universities peers.

> Talent management is anticipating the need for human capital and then setting out a plan to meet it, and it is inextricably linked to the chief librarian's need to effectively manage an institution's financial resources.

And then there was the geography. At BU, we were recruiting nationally for elite research library talent against the library systems at Harvard University and MIT. Our scenario assessment was simple and daunting: not only did the Harvard and MIT library systems have greater brand recognition and the ability to wield significantly greater financial resources for salary and professional development than we had, but both are located in our backyard across the Charles River. In other words, we had no shot whatsoever to recruit, pay, develop, or retain the sort of elite library talent that could help us emerge from the deficit that we were in by competing directly with Harvard and MIT. Instead, we had to devise a way to provide candidates a significantly greater total career value proposition. We had to shift the paradigm: focusing fully on talent management, via our talent chain process, helped us to do so.

Ironically, part of shifting that paradigm had as much to do with effective money management as it did talent. Regardless of sector or industry, talent is always going to be one of the most—if not the most—expensive line items in any organizational budget. In most library organizations, talent and collections usually are the two largest budgetary allocations, often constituting as much as 40 percent each of a total budget. The historic focus on collections over (or instead of) talent always has been questionable based upon sheer math: if a leader ignores 40 percent of her or his budget, she or he is being irresponsible. This was true even before the COVID-19 pandemic. But once you add the unique factors the COVID-19 introduced and has perpetuated—including dispersion of individuals and teams, remote work, culture building, social and political pressures that many workers increasingly feel demand official institutional responses, demographic and geographic shifts that exacerbate talent shortages or compensation surges[16]—continuing to prioritize collections over talent is tantamount to professional negligence.

In other words, focusing on the talent that gets and stays on the bus *is* addressing the money in the bank. Indeed, returning to that March 2020 call from the BU provost about closing the library, the first thing we addressed as an executive team was how to best transition our talent to remote work for the foreseeable future. From that point forward, we and so many of our colleagues talked about how to pivot from one paradigmatic normality to another. And most of those pivots, and the money associated with them, involved talent management. Given the wide operational, labor, and economic disruption of the "Great Resignation"[17] and continued concerns about the viability of librarianship as a career,[18] we conclusively forecast that full-spectrum talent management will continue to be a top executive priority for library leaders for the foreseeable future.

CONCLUSION

What if library leaders fail to take seriously the responsibilities of talent management? Several discouraging alternatives emerge, including the continued outsourcing of library administration to nonlibrarians. For example, in April 2020, the Consortium of Academic and Research Libraries in Illinois (CARLI) issued a letter to member institutions titled "The Importance of a Director in Charge of the Academic Library."[19] In the letter, board members argued the risks of university leaders deprioritizing the recruitment of library directors to replace incumbents after retirement. The board issued this letter after a December

2019 board meeting where at least seven academic libraries cited searches not being launched after a director's departure.

Since that letter, the challenges higher education faces (including aforementioned factors like declining enrollment, tuition discounting, and evaporating state support)[20] only have gotten worse. Further, more than three years of social, political, and economic change have forced many libraries to do more with even less. Ironically, many librarians reinforced this notion's plausibility by providing stellar access to scholarly resources during the pandemic outside the library building.

After such a showing, some university leaders who are pressed for post-pandemic money and space might look at the library system, with its headcount and thousands of square feet of space on some of the best real estate on campus, and mull an alternative future without a traditional library system or leader. This, too, is a reasonably plausible 2035 scenario for academic libraries. No matter the focus, we conclude that one of the few, enduring ways an academic library or library leader can survive to see 2035 is to execute its library's talent management plan with a strategic, precise focus.

NOTES

1. Rachel Singer Gordon, "The Accidental Library Manager," *Information Today* (2005): 10–11.
2. Carnegie Classification of Institutions of Higher Education, "Basic Classification," accessed October 21, 2023, https://carnegieclassifications.acenet.edu/carnegie-classification/classification-methodology/basic-classification/#doctoral-universities.
3. Association of Research Libraries, "List of ARL Members," accessed October 21, 2023, https://www.arl.org/list-of-arl-members/.
4. Bruce Thompson, "Some Alternative Quantitative Library Activity Descriptions/Statistics That Supplement the ARL Logarithmic Index," Association of Research Libraries (October 2006), https://www.arl.org/wp-content/uploads/2006/06/bruce-thompson-oct06.pdf.
5. Martha Kyrillidou, "Library Investment Index Summarizes Relative Size of ARL University Libraries for 2013-2014," Association of Research Libraries (August 20, 2015), https://www.arl.org/news/library-investment-index-summarizes-relative-size-of-arl-university-libraries-for-2013-2014/.
6. Kevin Carey, "The incredible shrinking future of college," *The Highlight by Vox*, last updated November 21, 2022, https://www.vox.com/the-highlight/23428166/college-enrollment-population-education-crash.
7. Pew Research Center, "The Growing Partisan Divide in Views of Higher Education," August 19, 2019, https://www.pewresearch.org/social-trends/2019/08/19/the-growing-partisan-divide-in-views-of-higher-education-2/.
8. Erla P. Heynes, Erin R.B. Eldermire, and Heather A Howard, "Unsubstantiated Conclusions: A Scoping Review on Generational Differences of Leadership in Academic Libraries," *Science Direct* 45, no. 5 (September 2019), https://www.sciencedirect.com/science/article/abs/pii/S0099133319301867.

9. Stanley Wilder, "Selected Demographic Trends in the ARL Professional Population," *Research Library Issues*, no. 295 (2018): 32–46.
10. ITHAKA-SR, "Collaborative strategies and research for higher education and the arts," accessed October 21, 2023, https://sr.ithaka.org/.
11. CARL ABRC, "Home," accessed October 21, 2023, https://www.carl-abrc.ca/.
12. Danielle Cooper, Catharine Bond Hill, and Roger C. Schonfeld, "Aligning the Research Library to Organizational Strategy" (April 12, 2022): 16–18, https://sr.ithaka.org/wp-content/uploads/2022/04/ARL-CARL-SR-Report-Aligning-the-Research-Library-to-Organizational-Strategy-04122022.pdf.
13. Peter Cappelli, "Talent Management for the Twenty-First Century," *Harvard Business Review* (March 2008), https://hbr.org/2008/03/talent-management-for-the-twenty-first-century.
14. BU Libraries, "Tony Zanders joins Boston University Libraries as Inaugural Entrepreneur in Residence," Accessed May 11, 2023, https://www.bu.edu/library/news/2019/04/01/tony-zanders-joins-boston-university-libraries-as-inaugural-entrepreneur-in-residence/.
15. Dames has evolved this concept into the Talent Continuum and has implemented a newer version of these talent management concepts in his current role at University of Notre Dame's Hesburgh Libraries.
16. Lance Pauker, "How the Pandemic Has Changed Talent Management," Pace University (July 11, 2022), https://www.pace.edu/news/how-pandemic-has-changed-talent-management.
17. Ben Casselman, "The 'Great Resignation' Is Over. Can Workers' Power Endure?" *New York Times* (July 6, 2023), https://www.nytimes.com/2023/07/06/business/economy/jobs-great-resignation.html.
18. Alejandro Marquez, "When Librarianship Becomes a Dead-End Job," ACRLog (May 23, 2023), https://acrlog.org/2023/05/23/when-librarianship-becomes-a-dead-end-job/.
19. See https://www.carli.illinois.edu/sites/files/files/CARLIStatementImportanceof-Dean-or Director.pdf.
20. Frank H. Wu, "The Crisis of American Higher Education," Organization of American Historians (n.d.), https://www.oah.org/tah/february-3/the-crisis-of-american-higher-educatio/.

20

Wellness for Librarians

INNOVATIVE SOLUTIONS TO FOSTER TRANSFORMATION

Loida Garcia-Febo

The library of 2035 will uphold a strong commitment to adopting policies, practices, and environments that support wellness for library workers as well as the community.

The 2021/2022 Human Development Report from the United Nations revealed that humans are living in uncertain times; this is causing unsettled lives.[1] These findings reflect the realities of many library workers today. Since 2018, librarians have increasingly become aware of the benefits of wellness and how anxiety, stress, and burnout affect their performance.

The lack of wellness support may affect the workforce in performing their everyday library work; it may also impact other important endeavors, such as advancing digital transformation in libraries, creating sustainable libraries, and engaging in library advocacy. The wellness of librarians is also impacted by expanding threats, ranging from book banning campaigns,[2] to low salaries that make it hard to make ends meet,[3] to anxiety and health concerns about COVID-19,[4] to work-life balance challenges.[5]

In my travels for work, I have heard about librarians unable to take time off or work a flexible schedule to take care of loved ones. Librarians are worried about finding stable housing situations, having transportation to their workplace, developing the experience they need to move up the job ladder, and overcoming broken hearts, discrimination, and racism. While some librarians may be able to deliver fully on all aspects of their library work responsibilities despite wellness concerns, they may pay the price in other ways, such as by experiencing severe burnout. This is not a sustainable approach.

These anecdotes and studies support statements from the Geneva Charter of Well-Being from the World Health Organization (WHO)[6] about the urgency to create sustainable well-being societies. The Charter also linked its commitment to the United Nations 2030 Agenda for Sustainable Development,[7] indicating that the response to this urgent situation must include "planetary, societal, community, and individual health and well-being, and changes in social structures which would support people to take control of their lives and health."[8] Furthermore, it indicated that principles of human rights, social and environmental justice, equity, solidarity, gender and intergenerational equity, and peace are part of the foundation of well-being.

IMPORTANCE OF WELLNESS AND WELL-BEING

To speak about wellness and well-being, we need to speak about health. In its Constitution, the WHO says that health is "a state of complete physical, mental, and social well-being and not merely the absence of disease or infirmity."[9] Rather than being presented as a separate component, well-being and health are part of a whole. The Centers for Disease Control and Prevention, the National Institutes for Health, and the American Library Association-Allied Professional Association (ALA-APA) agree that well-being and wellness include emotional, environmental, physical, and social aspects.[10]

In this same vein, Maslow's Hierarchy of Needs[11] suggests that an individual fulfills basic needs before reaching self-actualization. This theory supports a framework where to reach self-actualization, people seek to meet physiological, security, safety, social, and esteem needs. Based on this, someone with a need for shelter may be unable to experience wellness in the same way that someone without that need would. The strategies to support library workers need to be holistic, including aspects related to all areas of their lives. Therefore, with well-being linked to the global development landscape and considered in a holistic way, we need individuals and library workers who have an optimal state of wellness and who are able to contribute to the transformation of their own lives, families, libraries, societies, and the world.

> Since wellness is intrinsically linked to the physical, psychological, and social aspects of a person, it would be in the best interests of an institution to develop policies to support the well-being of its workforce.

SUPPORTING WELLNESS IN THE LIBRARY WORKPLACE

We have a significant opportunity to support the wellness of library workers who, as human beings, deserve to be treated with dignity and equity, and to receive fair opportunities and justice in the workplace. Since wellness is intrinsically linked to the physical, psychological, and social aspects of a person, it would be in the best interests of an institution to develop policies to support the well-being of its workforce.

A range of approaches is useful in helping to promote and support wellness in library workplaces. For example, instituting policies related to work schedules, workspaces, teleworking, caregiving, and salaries would benefit the employer and the employee. These types of workplace policies would also help to address emotional and invisible labor issues, such as fatigue and burnout. Coordination and planning in support of wellness must include everyone in the library. For example, when library administration supports wellness efforts, this encourages managers and library staff in general to support it, too. The participation of library workers in planning is a key ingredient in understanding the types of wellness support needed by staff members.

The hardest part of any initiative is to get started and then build on it. During my term as ALA president (2018-2019), together with my Presidential Advisory Board, we built on the ALA-APA Wellness[12] website Dr. Loriene Roy developed during her presidency.[13] We revamped that website—adding new information and one other dimension of wellness—to help library workers manage stress and anxiety.

So, how can the library profession move forward to better support the wellness of library workers in the future? The following examples and ideas of organizations today could be adapted to other libraries, library associations, and institutions for improved wellness in the library field in the future.

LIBRARIES:

- *Provide opportunities for employees to attend workshops speaking to librarians' needs.* Library 2.023 Worldwide Virtual Conference[14] on "Mental Health and Wellness: Library Workers Thriving in Uncertain Times"[15] presented by the San José State University School of Information[16] in partnership with me included topics such as burnout and fatigue prevention, and self-care strategies.
- *Dedicate a space to support the wellness of staff members.* The Henry Wittemore Library's RAM Renew Space[17] is available for staff members, faculty, and students who can reserve it online. The room includes a massage chair, light therapy lamp, lighting options, daylight lamp, Bluetooth speaker, white noise machine, puzzles, games, coloring books, and yoga mats. iPads and prayer rugs are available for borrowing at the front desk. A curated collection of books, magazines, and encyclopedias is available on the space's webpage as well as guided relaxation videos. As part of the wellness efforts, the library workers created a committee to recommend wellness strategies.
- *Create a newsletter.* During COVID-19, Queens Public Library created a newsletter to share articles and information about health, safety, and wellness with employees.[18]

- *Advocate and develop policies.* Richland Library advocated for and revised family and medical leave and paid-time-off policies to benefit library workers.[19]
- *Research resources to implement changes.* The Board of Westerville Public Library approved a new pay range based on consultation of pay ranges in similar local industries and the Massachusetts Institute of Technology's Living Wage Calculator.[20]

LIBRARY ASSOCIATIONS:

- *Create a website.* The ALA-APA Wellness website for library workers offers information regarding the eight dimensions of wellness: emotional, environmental, intellectual, occupational, physical, spiritual, social, and financial wellness.[21]
- *Provide free continuing professional education.* The ALA Committee on the Status of Women in Librarianship[22] has hosted webinars about "Women in Librarianship and Wellness," "Salary Equity," "How Employers Can Support Library Workers Who Are Caregivers during COVID-19" (includes a toolkit), and "Wellness in the Library Workplace."[23]
- *Create a newsletter.* New York Library Association's Sustainability Initiative[24] newsletter also includes advice about wellness for librarians. The ALA-APA's Library Worklife[25] newsletter is dedicated to sharing articles with recommendations for supporting the wellness of library workers.
- *Expand conference programming.* As ALA president, I hosted a cooking demonstration sharing nutritious recipes of vegetable juices and shrimp/veggie stir-fry on the Cooking Stage of the ALA Annual Conference Exhibits Floor. One of my presidential programs was about how to manage trauma with a doctor counselor providing tools helpful to manage all types of traumas. The New England Library Association's annual conference provided a "mindful labyrinth," which attendees walked through to calm their body and mind. ACRL-Oregon/Washington's joint conference included scheduled walks through the forest overlooking the beautiful Columbia River Gorge.[26]
- *Create dedicated spaces.* The ALA provides a conference meeting room for conference attendees to meditate, relax, practice yoga, or simply sit. Wellness mentors also carry a distinctive button on their conference badge for attendees to identify them.

LIBRARY AND INFORMATION SCIENCES PROGRAMS:

- *Support the program's community.* On March 2023, the San José State University School of Information introduced the innovative role of a health and wellness ambassador to support its community.[27]

- *Develop resources.* Blogs, videos, social media messaging, symposiums, and observance of special days are vehicles to support wellness.
- *Embed subject areas in the LIS curriculum.* Build a block of courses embedding wellness principles, try study groups and pilots, and find out what works and what does not.
- *Connect to the university.* Liaise with the university's mental health and wellness advisors to serve the LIS program, link to the university's wellness resources webpage, and dedicate webpages for wellness as part of the school's online resources.

CONCLUSION

To support the wellness of library workers, we need to include everyone in our planning, promote policy transformation, and support multi-sectoral alliances to bring efforts to fruition. As we move toward 2035, we should embrace this future where libraries, library associations, and LIS programs partner with organizations, academia, businesses, and local governments to implement strategies that make the well-being of librarians a reality. By doing so, not only will librarians benefit, but the well-being of societies will also improve.

NOTES

1. Pedro Conceicao, "Human Development Report 2021-22 Uncertain Times, Unsettled Lives: Shaping Our Future in a Transforming World," New York: United Nations Development Programme (2023), https://hdr.undp.org/system/files/documents/global-report-document/hdr2021-22pdf_1.pdf.
2. Xochitl Gonzalez, "The Librarians Are Not Okay," *Atlantic* (March 15, 2023), https://www.theatlantic.com/ideas/archive/2023/03/book-bans-censorship-librarian-challenges/673398/.
3. Loida Garcia-Febo, "Wellness for Library Workers," IFLA CPDWL (blog), August 26, 2019, https://blogs.ifla.org/cpdwl/2019/08/26/wellness-for-library-workers-by-loida-garcia-febo/.
4. Linda Salvesen and Cara Berg, "'Who says I am coping': The emotional affect of New Jersey academic librarians during the COVID-19 pandemic," *Journal of Academic Librarianship* 47, no. 5 (2021): 102422, https://doi.org/10.1016/j.acalib.2021.102422.
5. Tamara Townsend and Kimberley Bugg, "Perceptions of Work-Life Balance for Urban Academic Librarians: An Exploratory Study," *Journal of Library Administration* 60, no. 5: (2020): 493-511, https://doi.org/10.1080/01930826.2020.1729624.
6. "The Geneva Charter for Well-Being," World Health Organization (December 21, 2021), https://www.who.int/publications/m/item/the-geneva-charter-for-well-being.
7. Department of Economic and Social Affairs, "Transforming our world: the 2030 Agenda for Sustainable Development," United Nations, accessed October 21, 2023, https://sdgs.un.org/2030agenda.
8. World Health Organization, "The Geneva Charter for Well-Being."

9. World Health Organization, *Constitution of the World Health Organization* (1946): p. 1, https://apps.who.int/gb/bd/PDF/bd47/EN/constitution-en.pdf?ua=1.
10. Centres for Disease Control and Prevention, "Well-Being Concepts," 2019, https://www.cdc.gov/hrqol/wellbeing.htm#three; National Institutes of Health, "Your Healthiest Self: Wellness Toolkits," June 22, 2017, https://www.nih.gov/health-information/your-healthiest-self-wellness-toolkits; ALA-APA, "Helping to Support Overall Wellness for All Library Workers," accessed April 16, 2023, https://ala-apa.org/wellness/.
11. Abraham H. Maslow, "A Theory of Human Motivation," *Psychological Review* 50, no. 4 (1943): 370–96, https://doi.org/10.1037/h0054346.
12. ALA-APA Wellness, "8 Elements of Wellness," accessed October 21, 2023, https://ala-apa.org/wellness/.
13. M. Morales, "ALA President Unveils Enriched ALA-APA Workplace Wellness Website," News and Press Center (July 9, 2018), https://www.ala.org/news/press-releases/2018/07/ala-president-unveils-enriched-ala-apa-workplace-wellness-website.
14. SJSU School of Information, "Library 2.023 Worldwide Virtual Conference," accessed April 16, 2023, https://ischool.sjsu.edu/special-event/library-2023-worldwide-virtual-conference.
15. Library 2.0, "Mental Health and Wellness: Library Workers Thriving in Uncertain Times," accessed October 21, 2023, https://www.library20.com/mental-health-and-wellness.
16. SJSU School of Information, "Home," accessed October 21, 2023, https://ischool.sjsu.edu/.
17. Farmingham State University, "RAMS Renew Space," accessed April 16, 2023, https://libguides.framingham.edu/c.php?g=1188406&p=8705974.
18. D. Alderson, "SustainRT Awards the 2022 Citation for Wellness in the Workplace to Health and Safety Department at Queens Public Library," American Library Association News and Press Center (July 26, 2022), https://www.ala.org/news/press-releases/2022/07/sustainrt-awards-2022-citation-wellness-workplace-health-and-safety.
19. B. Calvin, "Richland Library First to Receive Presidential Citation for Wellness in the Workplace," American Library Association News and Press Center (June 7, 2019), https://www.ala.org/news/member-news/2019/06/richland-library-first-receive-presidential-citation-wellness-workplace.
20. D. Alderson, "Westerville Public Library to Receive 2021 SustainRT Citation for Wellness in the Workplace," American Library Association News and Press Center (May 25, 2021), https://www.ala.org/news/press-releases/2021/05/westerville-public-library-receive-2021-sustainrt-citation-wellness-workplace.
21. ALA-APA, "Helping to Support Overall Wellness for All Library Workers."
22. American Library Association, "Committee on the Status of Women in Librarianship (COSWL)," September 22, 2009, https://www.ala.org/aboutala/committees/ala/ala-coswl.
23. Loida Garcia-Febo, "Women in Librarianship and Wellness," American Library Association, accessed October 21, 2023, https://www.ala.org/aboutala/committees/ala/ala-coswl.

24. Sustainable Libraries Initiative, "Sustainability Library Certification Program," New York Library Association, accessed October 21 2023, https://www.nyla.org/4DCGI/cms/review.html?Action=CMS_Document&DocID=2251&MenuKey=si.

25. ALA-APA, "Library Worklife: HR E-News for Today's Leaders," accessed October 21, 2023, https://ala-apa.org/newsletter/.

26. Loida Garcia-Febo, "Immerse Yourself in Wellness Mindfulness Practices Have Intangible Benefits for Library Workers," *American Libraries* (January 2, 2019), https://americanlibrariesmagazine.org/2019/01/02/immerse-yourself-in-wellness/.

27. SJSU School of Information, "Health and Wellness," accessed April 16, 2023, https://ischool.sjsu.edu/health-and-wellness.

21

Future Library Job Descriptions 2035

Stacey A. Aldrich and Jarrid P. Keller

The library of 2035 will present new kinds of job titles, some not yet imagined, that will be needed as libraries navigate the integration of new technologies for providing services and reliable, accurate, and relevant information.

In 2013, we contributed a piece for *Library 2020: Today's Leading Visionaries Describe Tomorrow's Library*[1] that focused on library job descriptions of the future library. The job descriptions we created were based on five trends:

1. information everywhere,
2. increased use of mobile and embedded technology,
3. rise of social knowledge,
4. longer life expectancy and the emergence of lifestyle design, and
5. integration of robotics into the world.

At the time, we envisioned new jobs that would include librarians embedded in communities, collecting and packaging local content to make that content more accessible locally and globally. We also pictured librarians who would serve as formal *lifestyle designers* (public coaches who help individuals navigate learning, career transitions, health, and more). We further pictured a world of libraries equipped with robots performing public assistance and stack management, and even robotic maintenance engineers that would keep this new technology functioning and adding value. Ten years later, we see pieces of the jobs that were imagined, but some things are not quite there yet . . . like the proliferation of robots.

While we are still watching the evolution of our first set of trends, our world is full of new challenges and opportunities since the COVID-19 pandemic. We base our next group of future job descriptions on four trends that were identified through scouting the environment:

1. *Metaverse:* The emergence of parallel digital universes and economies.
2. *Divide and conquer with misinformation:* The continued use of misinformation to create division and distrust, which also creates a community of people who buy into the conspiracy.
3. *Bring it to me now:* The increased use of robots to deliver services on demand.
4. *Service with a pixel:* The use of AI and robots to provide services in a physical world.

We invite you to consider our next four job descriptions for the future and ask yourself the following questions:

1. What assumptions are being made about the future?
2. Do these jobs currently exist, or are there parts that library staff are doing now?
3. What would your library look like with these positions?
4. What is the same and what is different from today?

JOB DESCRIPTIONS

POSITION TITLE: TRUTHCLOUD LIBRARIAN

Position Description: This position is vital for the local, state, national, and global information ecosystem to ensure misinformation is identified, corrected, and cataloged with accurate information. TruthCloud librarians will serve as representatives from the library to the TruthCloud, where all researched and vetted information is securely stored and accessible.

Projects: In the first year, this position will ensure all local election information about candidates and data is accurate and vetted. They will also work with local scientists to verify the latest findings on water levels and climate change, and add validated information to social media platforms where information bots are spreading misinformation.

Skills: The position requires the ability to:

- Use artificial intelligence (AI) information bots effectively to identify inaccurate information.
- Do research outside traditional forms of information, but also in digital and physical formats.
- Identify deep fakes in words, images, and voice.
- Work with local, state, national, and global TruthCloud partners with openness and support.

- Use the latest TruthCloud cataloging and metadata standards.
- Challenge assumptions and ensure that information is fact-based and not biased.

POSITION TITLE: AUTOMATED SERVICE DELIVERY LIBRARIAN

Position Description: This position is responsible for managing the library's automated delivery services for the public, which deliver 24/7 to library patrons at their residences.

Projects: The first year for this position will be to evaluate the pilot program of three robot vehicles and two drones to identify pathways forward for full implementation.

Skills: The position requires the ability to:

- Manage one robot engineer and one logistics librarian and create an environment for learning and innovation.
- Understand the technology for automated delivery services and troubleshooting.
- Communicate with staff and stakeholders with clarity and curiosity.
- Manage budget and cost-effectiveness.
- Provide appropriate support for any issues or challenges within the community.
- Implement ongoing evaluations from patrons and community partners.

POSITION TITLE: SYNTHETIC CUSTOMER SERVICE PROGRAMMER AND WRANGLER

Position Description: This position is responsible for providing the logic and programming for human-robot collaboration for day-to-day interactions between the Customerbots and the public.

Projects: The first year of this position will focus on ensuring new AI programming is effectively implemented and introducing the public and staff to the Customerbot in a way that will create comfort.

Skills: The position requires the ability to:

- Manage a team of three Customerbot staff and create an environment for learning and innovation.
- Navigate human and machine relationships.
- Create and test logic models to ensure consistency in interactions with customers and staff.
- Implement and troubleshoot Customerbot AI programming.
- Train staff.
- Implement ongoing evaluation from patrons and staff.
- Challenge assumptions and ask good questions.

POSITION TITLE: LIBRARYVIRTUAL LIBRARIAN

Position Description: This position is responsible for planning, implementing, and maintaining the LibraryVirtual for metaverse inhabitants.

Projects: The first year of the position will focus on renovating the current LibraryVirtual landscape and services to better meet the needs of the metaverse inhabitants using metaverse design principles to construct a unique space that does not just replicate the physical library.

Skills: The position requires the ability to:

- Manage a metaverse team of five staff, which includes programmers, gamers, lifestyle designers, and human and AI staff for the LibraryVirtual.
- Use the appropriate programming language and evolving technology to maintain access and continue to grow metaverse services.
- Do rapid prototyping.
- Develop policies and procedures for the inclusion of services and objects into the library.
- Identify issues and troubleshoot challenges.
- Identify the linkages between the metaverse and physical services and programs, creating fluid integration.

After reading these job descriptions, do any of them interest you? Do you see these positions in your library in the future? What seems possible? Which positions seem far-fetched and why?

CONCLUSION

The future of our libraries in 2035 depends on all of us being intentional and creative about what kinds of work will need to be done to support our ever-changing communities, and what skills will be needed for us to continue to evolve. We encourage you to take time and look to the horizon and scan for the big and small changes happening around you. Which changes are affecting or will affect your community? Imagine the emerging services and/or programs the library could provide and create a few future job descriptions. You may be surprised that what you create may either help lay foundations for the future or be inspiration for action today. We would love to see what you build! Please share your future job descriptions with us by emailing stacey.aldrich@gmail.com or jarridpkeller@gmail.com.

> The future of our libraries in 2035 depends on all of us being intentional and creative about what kinds of work will need to be done to support our ever-changing communities, and what skills will be needed for us to continue to evolve.

NOTE

1. Joseph Janes, *Library 2020: Today's Leading Visionaries Describe Tomorrow's Library* (Scarecrow Press, 2013).

VI
Vision

Part VI: Vision focuses on envisioning and preparing for the future. The authors of chapters 22 through 25 highlight new strategies and considerations for leading their organizations forward to 2035, specifically noting that libraries will:

- use strategic foresight and futures thinking to design itself into existence *(Nichols)*.
- more easily navigate their varied futures by fostering communities committed to deep collaboration and openness to diverse ideas and perspectives *(Figueroa and Pelayo-Lozada)*.
- be influenced by new technologies, availability of funds, marketing to users, accessibility, and value-added services and need to think strategically in how to adapt to these changes *(Alman)*.
- be more resilient, responsive, collaborative, and essential to the success of its community *(Hirsh)*.

In chapter 22, Nichols presents several paradoxes—such as the paradox of library progress, the paradox of library access, the paradox of diversity, equity, inclusion, and belonging (DEIB), and the paradox of library neutrality—that emphasize the various dilemmas libraries face. He posits that libraries should incorporate strategies and methodologies, such as Natural Foresight, to overcome these dilemmas and to help them think about, innovate, and design a new future for their organizations, services, and community. He concludes with strategies that libraries could consider to offset some of today's challenges in library service and that could launch a new future for libraries. Similarly, Figueroa and Pelayo-Lozada encourage us to think beyond "predictions" and instead incorporate new strategies—such as foresight thinking and futures thinking—to envision a more dynamic future for libraries and communities. These strategies go beyond informing library staff about what the future will hold by including them in the dialogue and valuing the perspectives they bring from their own place in the library.

In chapter 24, Alman expands upon the theme of visioning the future and emphasizes the dynamic changes that technology and virtual services will have on that future. While we may not be able to predict what technologies will exist in 2035, we know libraries will continue to connect the community to the technologies they need (or want) to effectively learn, work, engage, create, and collaborate. She also encourages librarians to adopt foresight planning and technological preparedness strategies to prepare for the future.

Finally, in chapter 25, Hirsh summarizes the key themes throughout the book and echoes the focus that several authors placed on a future for libraries where they will be more resilient, responsive to, and collaborative with their communities. While the future will certainly present both opportunities and challenges, Hirsh notes that libraries that thrive in 2035 will have built a foundation of strategic insight, technological adaptability, community responsiveness, collaboration and partnerships, and the ability to consistently advocate their value.

Archived webcasts of author interviews are available at: https://sites.google.com/sjsu.edu/library2035/home

22

Come Back Yesterday

PARADOXES OF LIBRARY PROGRESS

Joel A. Nichols

The library of 2035 will use strategic foresight and futures thinking to design itself into existence.

Futures thinking and methodologies, particularly Natural Foresight,[1] offer a time-traveling and flexible operating system that can help libraries design themselves into the future. This chapter questions several core assumptions of library theory and practice, and demonstrates ways of thinking through, creating, and innovating the library of 2035.

There are the laws of library science and their modern application, and then there is the folk wisdom of the library: the transformative tales that shape library workers and institutional cultures. In my experiences (based in Philadelphia), we might call these transformative tales *urban legends*, which I mean both in their horror connotation as well as in their status as uncredible stories that are rooted more in passed-down work cultures than based upon fact. One of these early *legends* I learned was that once a book was deaccessioned (i.e., removed from the shelves for discard), a library user would surely come in the next day looking for it. In fact, this happened a few times to me. While it may not have been the very next day after a big weeding project, I noticed that sometimes people wanted something I had recently discarded, whether by title or by subject/genre—a phenomenon I refer to as "come back yesterday."

Consequently, this urban legend of library science impels some colleagues to under-weed severely; that is, they aim to keep every book on the shelf, no matter how tattered in form or repute, or how outdated in style or favor. Collection management demands constant assessment and eventual discards, but this "feeling" of the weeding paradox, a looming dread that you might not have something a patron wants, actively works against appropriate collection management.

So, why are these dilemmas so common among some library workers? Moreover, how can these dilemmas help us think about library progress, innovation, development, and impact over the next several years? This chapter considers how several different model paradoxes of library progress, facilitated by Natural Foresight methods, can guide current library workers and leaders to resilient and inclusive futures.

PARADOX OF LIBRARY PROGRESS

A foundational principle of Natural Foresight is understanding conscious and unconscious biases, their limits, and how to think "beyond" and outside them. This principle should act as a foundational law for serving library users in a community setting. The best public library worker must confront their own biases and learn to work against them. There is a tension between communities, in which librarians and library leaders often do not look, sound, or act like the communities that are seeking library services from them; I call this the Paradox of Library Progress.

THE PARADOX OF DEIB AS WINDOW DRESSING

Librarianship today remains white and femme-dominated, a place where cis straight white women are prevalent in most roles; numerous policies, statements, and initiatives aimed at diversifying the profession have not really moved the needle. Similarly, while some people are making direct efforts to address structural inequities in education, housing, and other institutions, many could do more than what appears to be just placating communities or staff stakeholders. Let us call this the Paradox of DEIB (diversity, equity, inclusion, and belonging) as Window Dressing, where a surface-level adjustment might rearrange a few deck chairs, but where efforts to make deep, structural changes come to no resolution, resulting in minimal progress. Consider a couple of other brief provocations as tangible ways out of this paradox:

- In order to increase the representation of people of color in library leadership positions, we need to make substantial changes to our institutional structures that continue to reinforce old patterns of white supremacy.
- We need to expand the institutional definition of and our textual notions of "librarian" to include "library worker." In fact, we may even want the term "library worker" to subsume "librarian" as the professional term to clarify that being a professional does not hinge on a master's degree from an iSchool.
- We need to embed the concept of the Ladder of Inference,[2] which is a method of foresight that enables participants to think beyond their assumptions and overcome the limits of their expertise. Confronting biases

and undoing systemic oppressions must be a fundamental part of any strategic design and planning.

PARADOX OF LIBRARY NEUTRALITY

Library Neutrality is the next Paradox of Library Progress. In a literature review and critique by Branum,[3] library neutrality is something persisting in the DNA of the profession, despite copious literature critiquing and questioning this concept, calling it "outdated discourse." It persists so much, it was finally the subject of a *New York Times* piece called, poignantly, "The Soul of the Library."[4] Yet this outdated model of neutrality remains firmly embedded in the culture of librarians and library institutions, and it often has the practical effect of frustrating, delaying, or blocking progress.[5]

Neutrality looks much more like a walled-off, distant observer than a public library worker participating in their work and life communities. My very existence as a queer person forces me not to be neutral unless I let myself be erased, for example, as do the lives of other marginalized people. So, what tools are available the next time you are trying to think through these tangled ideas with a team of staff or board members? There are other methods of foresight that can address the paradoxes above, as well as help library leaders prepare for the complex challenges any library of 2035 will face.

CAUSAL LAYERED ANALYSIS

Causal Layered Analysis (CLA) is a Strategic Foresight methodology that offers paths and solutions to problems that push past limited mental models. CLA identifies an issue—from surface-level assumptions through several other layers of meaning—to get at the deepest and most profound realities that cause, sustain, affect, and change the issue at hand. TSFX[6] makes this image an iceberg, an easy-to-see simile with a few peaks bobbing above the water on top of a much larger, denser, and more unknown, complex, and discoverable body lurking unseen.

Picture this stratigraphy. First, the surface-level layer in the Paradox of Library Neutrality is that library workers have to be neutral in order to provide equal and nonjudgmental access to information and resources to all seekers.

Second, the next layer down is the system, structures, and actors, that is, the material conditions under which we are working. We can only be as neutral as our structures are neutral, or as our workers are. So, if one of our structures (e.g., the internet filter used to be compliant with e-rate rates) is mostly neutral, except for blocking information about drug use and harm reduction or restricting access to all queer or trans content, then library users lose out. This results in valuable, useful, and relevant information getting blocked due to content that verges on unacceptable topics (sexuality or drugs, in this example).

Come Back Yesterday

Third, digging down to the next layer of our iceberg image, we uncover the values-level—the attitudes that govern our worldviews and cultural norms. In the case of Library Neutrality, Branum[7] demonstrates that this professional value arose, in part, to make library science less feminine/soft, to be taken more seriously, and to operate with the kind of masculine, scientific objectivity of other technical experts or scientists.[8]

Fourth, the deepest level that CLA reaches is where the ideas live in their most powerful and potentially transformative forms—the layer of *myth* and *metaphors*. While *myth* and *metaphors* sound like the previous layer, where cultural norms and values collide and reinforce each other, they rather contribute to the notion that myth and metaphors help us make sense of what is otherwise unexplainable. There is overlap here with neutrality as a principle that could make library science more objective and scientifically respectable. However, this layer runs even deeper—as a powerful and seductive belief. For example, as an individual librarian, the assumption is that I can tap into my holy "neutrality," meaning that I presumably know what is better for others. This deeply internalized neutrality can have negative consequences, such as stopping library workers from preventing bullying in the workplace and justifying panoplies of racist, ableist (the discrimination of and social prejudice against people with disabilities), and heterosexist micro and macro aggressions against coworkers and patrons, all according to one's own position along the norm.

The purpose is to explore the many truths and understandings at play in any given issue and to use the CLA to forge new paths and conceptions. It is a model to follow when you want a radical solution, as in, it reaches to understand and lay bare the fundamental, underlying structures at play and use them to chart new, and maybe speculative, paths.

THE PARADOX OF ACCESS

The Paradox of Access is that information wants to be free, but many libraries put up barriers, and our vendor interfaces make digital and electronic access more of a Borges labyrinth[9] than a utopian model of open, free, and accurate information on demand. On the one hand, we say, "All you need is a library card for all this stuff!" And then we say, "Oh, but you need a current ID, a utility bill, and you still have a book checked out from 2019." Fine forgiveness mitigates this barrier and has been an unqualified success at the Free Library of Philadelphia[10] and other libraries, which have also removed fines. As we design our way to 2035, let us consider multiple,

> As we design our way to 2035, let us consider multiple, simultaneous iterations of services, programs, policies, and practices that could try to undo the paradox of access.

simultaneous iterations of services, programs, policies, and practices that could try to undo the paradox of access.

The trend at play here is fine-free access, which libraries have started to implement over the last ten years, moving this policy change along a continuum from the edge of inception to more mainstream adoption. Trends are the present, and maybe even show the very recent past since they are already with us, and they do not point the way to the future or help you create one. You are already aware of trends—make sure they are not limiting your thinking and creating.

CONCLUSION

The future is coming as fast as it can, and Strategic Foresight offers a distinction between the push of the future (i.e., reacting to now, emergencies, and trends) and the pull of the future (i.e., planning for and creating the future). Here are additional scenarios that I hope will provoke further exploration into these methods:

- offer fee forgiveness, materials replacement amnesties, and fresh starts, especially to children,
- consider lost materials things you would have weeded anyway, and
- let folks start over again.

This is where many colleagues clutch for rules, payment in installments, agreements, and so on. I would urge the measured consideration of a truly transformative approach—maybe go for a straightforward and all-encompassing procedure of radical forgiveness for lost or damaged library materials that hold individuals harmless.

In closing, I propose another simultaneous path of possibility as we look toward the library of 2035. Specifically, I suggest that we abolish the library card altogether. Instead, let us figure out alternate ways of keeping track of our visitors and users, maybe with an email list or using their thumbprint? All this might be pipe-dreaming, but using these frameworks can open up a world of speculative and strategic design.

NOTES

1. TFSX, "WHAT IS NATURAL FORESIGHT?" (January 1, 2015), https://tfsx.com/2015/01/what-is-natural-foresight/; Natural Foresight by The Futures School is licensed under Attribution 4.0 International.
2. Marcel F. D'Eon, "The Ladder of Inference re-visited: 'Don't jump to conclusions!'" *Can Med Educ J.*, 13(5), (Sept. 1, 2022): 1-5. doi: 10.36834/cmej.76000. PMID: 36310912; PMCID: PMC9588189.
3. Candise Branum, "The myth of library neutrality," (2008), https://api.semanticscholar.org/CorpusID:158738938.

4. Stanley Kurtz, "The Battle for the Soul of the Library," *New York Times*, February 24, 2022.
5. Nicole A. Cooke et al., "Once More for Those in the Back: Libraries Are Not Neutral," *Publishers Weekly* (June 10, 2022).
6. The School for Excellence, "Home," accessed October 21, 2023, https://www.tsfx.edu.au/.
7. Candis Branum, "The myth of library neutrality."
8. D. McMenemy, "Librarians and Ethical Neutrality: Revisiting the Creed of a Librarian," *Library Review* 56.3 (2007): 177–81.
9. Wikipedia, "Labyrinths," accessed October 21, 2023, https://en.wikipedia.org/wiki/Labyrinths_(short_story_collection).
10. Free Library of Philadelphia, "Home," accessed October 21, 2023, https://www.freelibrary.org/.

23

Changing Our How, More Than Seeing Clearly Our What

Miguel Figueroa and Lessa Kananiʻopua Pelayo-Lozada

The library of 2035 will more easily navigate its varied futures by fostering communities committed to deep collaboration and openness to diverse ideas and perspectives.

As we imagine and realize our institutions' and communities' futures in 2035, we find inspiration in adrienne maree brown's vision for change through transformational emergent strategy: "My vision is changing our how, more than seeing clearly our what. I see a how where we are all much more comfortable with change, and with our personal power to change conditions.... I want a future where we are curious, interested, visionary, adaptive."[1]

Too often, our focus on the future is centered on predictions. But from those who have committed their work and study to futures and foresight thinking, there is a clear lesson that more than prediction, our focus should be on preparation. Marina Gorbis, executive director of the Institute for the Future (IFTF), shares five lessons from her over-twenty years at IFTF:

1. Forget about predictions.
2. Focus on signals.
3. Look back to see forward.
4. Uncover patterns.
5. Create a community.[2]

Similarly, Peter Bishop and Andy Hines, two of the leaders of the Graduate Program in Foresight Studies at the University of Houston, note, "The objective is not just to know what will happen but to be ready whatever does happen."[3]

That focus on being prepared for whatever future might happen seeds the tools and methods of futures thinking:

- framing (identifying and solving the right problems);
- scanning (mapping the landscape);
- forecasting (generating a range of possible futures);
- visioning (imaging preferred futures);
- planning (creating a path from the present to the future); and, ultimately,
- learning and acting.[4]

Almost all those efforts are vastly improved through deep collaboration with and openness to diverse ideas and perspectives.

But removing the focus on prediction is difficult. It forces us to forego specificity, loosen our sense of control, and reevaluate our belief in the expert, on a system of hierarchy that prioritizes singular leaders and extraordinary innovators. In place of prediction, true futures thinking and foresight requires an openness and humility that acknowledges the immensity of change happening in our world, the difficulty of assembling patterns from a rapid environment, and the inability for any one person to become expert in all the things we must understand.

That last lesson, then, from Marina Gorbis—"create a community"—is not just an appeal to inclusive practice; it is essential if we are serious in our desire to find a path forward for libraries in 2035.

STUDYING CHANGE AS INCLUSIVE COLLABORATION

In conversations with library staff following a presentation or other engagement related to visioning or futures thinking, we hear variations on some consistent themes:

- "I have two young children in our local school, but no one ever asks me about what is happening in education."
- "I am the only staff member in their twenties, but I work at the circulation desk, and no one ever asks me what people my age would be interested in."
- "I am a first-generation college graduate, but no one asks me about what is happening in higher education."
- "I am an avid reader, especially of news, but because I am not a manager, I am not involved in conversations about the future of the library or the community."

Two things become clear through these comments. First, people want to be asked; they have insights to share above and beyond the limits of their roles within the library. Second, and most concerning, is that they are not being asked about the changes they see, the possible and preferred futures they envision, and the planning, learning, and actions to which they could contribute.

Intentionally or unintentionally, many of our conversations about the future are shaped by hierarchical constraints that limit opportunities for participation based on age and tenure, position within the library, rank, or work role or function. We are too often stuck in cycles of "we have always done it this way" not only in our day-to-day operations, but also in our attempts to think about the future.

Library professionals advocate for more equitable access to information in our communities, but we sometimes fail to create equitable paths for library staff to contribute information to the futures thinking for our organizations. While futures thinking and foresight leverage specific tools and methods, there are accessible entry points to futures thinking that can be encouraged and developed across library staff. As Bishop and Hines note, "Foresight is fundamentally about the study of change."[5] Whether part-time or student workers, at the information or circulation desks, in public services or behind the scenes supporting library operations, nearly every staff member in a library has an opportunity to observe and report on changes in their library work. Yes, most futurists stress the importance of trends ("changes that occur through time") rather than individual events ("changes that occur very quickly and generally are less significant for understanding the future"),[6] but nearly every staff member can develop proficiency in identifying and differentiating sustained change rather than one-off anomalies.

Asking people what they are seeing and experiencing from their place in the library demonstrates interest in and respect for different perspectives. Some library staff will share information that we know—confirming changes that are on the horizon. Other library staff will share insights that create new and alternative futures. Still others will critique our assumptions, showing that some assumed futures for libraries may be less plausible.

And this has not yet even begun to explore the changes that library staff may experience in their lives outside the library. Introducing a practice to ask library staff to speak to the changes and trends they see in their lived experiences—as family members, members of communities, residents of a city and state—may take time, but it may also help build on the commitments our institutions have made to diversity, to the multiple and varied dimensions of personal experience that strengthen our organizations.

As part of a daily check-in or weekly meeting practice, asking about trends and changes begins to build staff capacity to identify what is new and different. It may also help foster collaboration as staff build on each other's contributions and find new connections across interests, concerns, and personal lived experiences. Ultimately, it also helps break down some of the gatekeeping that limits who is allowed to contribute. As an initial step toward more formalized trend scanning, encouraging the study and sharing of changes is a simple but inclusive step that generates a sense of community and contribution across staff.

FORECASTING AS INCLUSIVE COLLABORATION

From observing changes and trend scanning, we better position ourselves for forecasting and visioning possible and preferred futures for our libraries. While we acknowledge that we cannot predict everything that will come our way, by envisioning possible and preferred futures, we can challenge ourselves to consider the learnings and actions we must undertake to be successful whatever comes our way.

Forecasts and scenarios provide just one way of looking at the future. Based on the changes and trends observed in our day-to-day lives, we can begin to imagine possible and preferable futures. For a profession like ours that is constantly changing and evolving, we must hone in on the things we do well and prepare for the many possible futures we will encounter. As Edward Cornish, founder of the World Future Society, notes:

> One of the prime virtues of scenarios is that they provide a way to deal more effectively with almost any situation that is important but uncertain. We begin by admitting that we do not know what will happen, but instead of simply giving up and saying that we can do nothing but accept our ignorance, we try to identify things that might happen. As we identify these possibilities and create scenarios describing how they might actually happen and what their consequences might be, we are, in the most literal sense, analyzing our problem—that is, breaking it down into components and looking carefully at each.[7]

Forecasting also provides an opportunity for engagement across all staff. The reactions and interactions of people to the story that we tell about the future helps us understand possible solutions, tensions, concerns, and opportunities for the future. Many people will seek the path of stability (things stay the same), while others will pursue paths that get better or paths that get worse. Through each of these, individuals have an opportunity to ideate or innovate, to reveal their fears and concerns, or to express their optimism and interest. These are all opportunities to help make people more comfortable, confident, and, possibly, excited for future directions. If trend scanning provides the evidence for the next possible futures, then forecasting helps incorporate change management into our practice, forming the coalition, creating and communicating the vision, and addressing obstacles.

DIVERSITY AND THE FUTURE

As a profession, we have already seen the dangers in focusing on *the what* without changing *our how*. Librarianship has pursued and continues to pursue multiple diversity recruitment initiatives, always focused on changing the composition of the profession, with hardly any change in the racial and ethnic composition of the field as a whole. Too often in diversity work, we are more focused on the end goal of a more diverse workforce than on the deeper work of more inclusive workplaces for all people. Good effort has been expended on a vision for *what* our profession might look like, but without fundamental changes to *how* our profession operates internally, repairing and creating spaces for different dimensions of diversity to contribute to a new vision for our work.

As a profession in a society that is rooted in systemic oppression of historically marginalized voices, it is imperative that we change *the how* before we try to predict or create *the what*. In almost all areas of progress in diversity—race and ethnicity, ability, sexuality, and gender identity—we need to change our *how*, not just see clearly a desired *what*. Communities make progress in diversity when they engage in discourse, find strength in their collective leadership, and envision more equitable futures. To make real progress, societies also need to engage in an iterative practice of listening to the changes these communities are demanding, trusting their experiences, and learning and acting in ways that reflect these new understandings.

Futures thinking—an intentional focus on and openness to sustained changes in the library and in the lives of the library staff—could provide a path toward changing our *how*. We must make space for the whole human, recognizing differences and creating space for those differences. This sometimes requires more personal conversations. This includes identifying the areas that we do not fully understand and committing to learning from each other. Furthermore, it involves helping to connect the personal and the professional without falling into toxic behaviors that create overly familiar or dependent relationships.

Futures thinking and diversity thinking both begin with an openness to change—changes in our world and changes in the dimensions of identities in our organizations and communities. These are entwined pursuits. Identifying and building more productive futures requires development of organizations that live their commitments to diversity.

> As a profession in a society that is rooted in systemic oppression of historically marginalized voices, it is imperative that we change "the how" before we try to predict or create "the what." In almost all areas of progress in diversity—race and ethnicity, ability, sexuality, and gender identity—we need to change our "how," not just see clearly a desired "what."

CONCLUSION

The writer and activist Walidah Imarisha asserts, as does adrienne maree brown,[8] that all organizing is science fiction. Imarisha goes further to state:

> First you have to have that space to say "What do we want?" Beyond the boundaries of what we're told is possible or what is real. We must create those sort of visionary spaces, to have conversations with each other within institutions and within communities, so that we can be developing the vision we're moving towards.[9]

Changing how we do things is difficult. The ways that we do things are entrenched in policy, procedure, and culture. But there are ways that we can change our *how*—largely by adopting a more humane and inclusive practice for envisioning our future.

When we empower ourselves to lead from any position, and receive feedback from any position, we can create power for real change. Asking questions, being open to learning, acknowledging fears and concerns, harnessing interest and excitement, accepting vulnerability—these are all difficult, but they contribute to changing the ways we approach the future of libraries in 2035.

NOTES

1. adrienne maree brown, *Emergent Strategy: Shaping Change, Changing Worlds* (Chico: AK Press, 2017): 56.
2. Marina Gorbis, "Five Principles for Thinking Like a Futurist," *EDUCAUSE Review*, 54.1 (Winter 2019), https://er.educause.edu/articles/2019/3/five-principles-for-thinking-like-a-futurist.
3. Peter C. Bishop and Andy Hines, *Teaching About the Future* (New York: Palgrave Macmillan, 2012): 7.
4. Ibid., 55–59.
5. Ibid., 1.
6. Edward Cornish, *Futuring: The Exploration of the Future* (Bethesda: World Future Society, 2004): 78.
7. Ibid., 94.
8. adrienne maree brown, *Emergent Strategy*, 16.
9. Walidah Imarisha, "Science Fiction, Ancient Futures, and the Liberated Archive," in *What Future: The Year's Best Writing on What's Next for People, Technology, and the Planet*, eds. Meehan Crist and Rose Eveleth (Los Angeles: The Unnamed Press, 2018): 161.

24

Immersive and Virtual Technologies

THE FUTURE OF LIBRARIES

Susan W. Alman

The library of 2035 will be influenced by new technologies, availability of funds, marketing to users, accessibility, and value-added services and will need to think strategically in how to adapt to these changes.

"The best way to predict the future is to create it . . ." is imprinted on a desk plaque that was given to me during the development of a Massive Open Online Course in 2014: "The Emerging Future: Technology Issues and Trends."[1] At that time, the discipline of *foresight* was new to me. Since then, I have developed and taught a foresight course, and I have become a proponent of using these methods for determining what technologies will be needed in libraries in the future.

Librarians must continue to be proactive in preparing their organizations for the services and resources that will best serve their communities. Library leaders should plan strategically to understand and market to their communities, assess new technologies, forge partnerships, and secure the funding necessary for brick-and-mortar or virtual experiences.

SKILLS AND ISSUES IN LIBRARIES

The library in 2035 *might* be unrecognizable from the 2023 status quo; however, I suspect in the foreseeable future, libraries will remain individualistic depending on their proactive planning methods or reactive circumstances, their local community demands for technology-based resources and services, and their financial support. All types of library organizations (e.g., public, school, academic, special, and archival) will be on a continuum ranging from traditional Carnegie libraries residing in their original buildings to facilities that embrace the newest technologies in either a futuristic physical or virtual space.

Libraries in 2023 require librarians to master a number of important skills, specifically environmental scanning; planning; budgeting; equity, diversity, and inclusion; soft skills; and grant writing. These skills are also likely to be required for librarians in 2035. While today's libraries are grappling with a number of critical issues, such as security of systems, privacy, big data, access to information, and connectivity (i.e., technological, interpersonal/emotional, political/global, socioeconomic, and economic), we can't predict what major issues libraries in 2035 will face. For example: Will there be ways to secure all technologies so users and data are not compromised? Will there be free, equal, and unlimited access to everyone regardless of political restrictions, socioeconomic barriers, and cost of technologies? Will libraries offer physical and virtual spaces for individuals to interact in meaningful ways to fulfill their emotional needs? There may be new ways to handle or resolve some of these issues by 2035.

PACE OF TECHNOLOGICAL CHANGE AND IMPACT ON LIBRARIES

The pace of technological change is explosive. For example, Open AI's ChatGPT hit one hundred million users only two months after its introduction in late 2022,[2] making it history's fastest-growing platform. The technology and issues surrounding generative AI (artificial intelligence) are complex; legal, ethical, copyright, and privacy concerns must be considered and addressed.

Similarly, other technologies and applications now used on a regular basis had previously been unheard of in the past. For example:

- E-books gained popularity in the late 1990s and are now readily available for both virtual and in-person users in secondary and higher education, public libraries, archives, and other organizations.
- The technology for 3D printing was developed in the early 1980s and became mainstream with 3D makerspaces in libraries in the early 2010s.
- Social media began in the early 2000s. While it has been implemented in many types of libraries, it still does not have universal application standards.
- Smartphones were introduced in the mid-1990s and are now the device of choice for many library users.
- Zoom was widely adopted during the COVID-19 pandemic, becoming a household word and an integrative component of our lives.

More than ever, libraries provide unique new services that are both technology- and user-based. For example, immersive and virtual technologies (e.g., augmented reality [AR], virtual reality [VR], extended reality [XR], AI, and robotics) are increasing in libraries. At the time of this writing, there were several pocket examples of successful virtual libraries, such as Community Virtual Library[3] and Digital Public Library of America,[4] as well as numerous digital collections. These examples provide a window into the possibilities for the ultimate 2035 goal to attain universal information access and interactivity among a global community.

The librarian's role is to understand the new technologies and the community of users and non-users. User design, library resources, and new technologies need to be suited to each community; consequently, librarians must reach out to their communities to understand the needs and provide the necessary information and digital literacy training.

As a library and information science educator involved with updates to the curriculum, I observe the addition of courses designed to prepare our graduates for the emerging technological future. These courses address not only specific technologies, but also the ethics involved in their use. In the classroom, faculty and students engage in discussions about the future of information intermediation, programming, and services. Librarians in 2035 must possess an array of technical and interpersonal competencies to effectively interact with their constituencies and provide the necessary resources and services.

FUTURE TECHNOLOGY SCENARIOS AND CONSIDERATIONS FOR LIBRARIES IN 2035

New and even existing technologies have the potential to significantly impact the way libraries deliver their services and programs in the future. It is important for libraries to plan for these future scenarios.

EXISTING TECHNOLOGIES

Understanding library user needs in 2035 will be key to providing the right resources and services to the varying communities in both brick-and-mortar and virtual libraries. While virtual libraries can serve a global audience, few statistics track what percentage of users take advantage of them. The Digital Library of America, Internet Archive, Community Virtual Library,[5] and other virtual reference services are examples of services and resources that are freely available, but underutilized. Widespread usage may be limited due to a lack of promotion, information literacy skills, or access to technology or connectivity. Will communities of potential library users in 2035 be better equipped to use the applications that are available now and the ones that have yet to be invented?

REFERENCE SERVICES

Some libraries have used chatbots to answer directional and often-asked questions on a 24/7 basis for several years. However, the rapid ascent of an AI-powered chatbot, such as ChatGPT, using software that replicates human

> Understanding library user needs in 2035 will be key to providing the right resources and services to the varying communities in both brick-and-mortar and virtual libraries.

conversation and can create original material from simple or complex prompts is a potential game-changer for school, academic, and public librarians, as well as educators and the general public. The power and trustworthiness of this application, along with ethical concerns, the widening of the digital divide, and the loss of traditional library reference services, will take time to settle. Even more advanced AI chatbots will likely be developed and implemented in libraries of the future. Another reason to plan with a purpose.

PROGRAMMING

Virtual library programs increased during the COVID-19 pandemic, but there is a healthy revival of in-person events in academic, school, and public libraries and other information centers. The need for community gatherings and *library-as-place* supports traditional and innovative programs. Libraries of the future will continue to host naturalization ceremonies, job fairs, financial literacy seminars, jazz concerts, cooking classes, and film screenings. If prepared, librarians will offer state-of-the art training in using new technologies. Virtual events will also be offered to those who prefer to participate from their devices or who are unable to travel to the physical space of the library. In 2035, holography may be more common—allowing people to attend library events as their virtual selves.

INFORMATION AND DIGITAL LITERACY TRAINING

Today, some libraries provide TV, radio, video and podcast studios, heavy equipment simulators, and libraries of things (unique collections of items) and lend items such as smartphones, laptops, and Wi-Fi hotspots. Librarians should be engaged in expanding information and digital literacy training and providing opportunities for users to engage with the latest technologies, which currently includes VR/XR/AR apps, robots, and AI for complex research. Some current game-changing technologies that may be widely adopted in 2035 include self-sovereign identity (SSI),6 digital wallets, AI apps,[7] and digital libraries.

OTHER CONSIDERATIONS: ADDRESSING THE DIGITAL DIVIDE

While these new technologies have become widely popular and are used globally by hundreds of millions of people, there is still a significant digital divide. In 2021, Pew Research[8] reported that 7 percent of Americans (approximately twenty-three million people) did not use the internet and 23 percent did not have access to a broadband connection at home. A similar report by McKinsey and Co.[9] in 2020 indicated that approximately 40 percent of Black American households—as opposed to 28 percent of White American households—did not have high-speed, fixed broadband. These numbers are significant. Efforts must be made to close the digital divide and implement equity, diversity, and inclusion (EDI) measures in all our activities as we move toward 2035.

PLANNING FOR TECHNOLOGY CHANGES IN LIBRARIES IN 2035

There is no way to know with accuracy what technologies will be developed in the next decade, but it is safe to assume that libraries will be faced with decisions on what to adopt for their communities. The task of analyzing and synthesizing technologies is a critical component of the planning process.

Libraries of 2035 that have adopted new technologies and services resulting from a conscious planning effort may take on a variety of appearances. Here is one vision of a library in the future as described in *Cloud Cuckoo Land*,[10] a novel by Anthony Doerr:

> She stands in a vast atrium. Three tiers of bookshelves, each fifteen feet tall, served by hundreds of ladders, run for what appear to be miles down either side. Above the third tier, twin arcades of marble columns support a barrel-vaulted ceiling cut through its center by a rectangular aperture, above which puffy clouds float through a cobalt sky.
>
> Here and there in front of her, figures stand at tables or sit in armchairs. On the tiers above, others peruse shelves or lean on railings or climb or descend the ladders. And through the air, for as far as she can see, books—some as small as her hand, some as big as the mattress on which she sleeps—are flying, lifting off shelves, returning to them, some flitting like songbirds, some lumbering along like big ungainly storks.

While the scenario described above may not be a realistic goal for 2035, it is incumbent on librarians to start planning now for a realistic vision of the future.

It has been more than four decades since F. W. Lancaster outlined his prediction for a paperless society in the transformative publication *Toward Paperless Information Systems*.[11] While society has access to an abundance of electronic materials, the worldwide production of paper and paperboard has increased from 213.7 million metric tons in 1987 to 417.3 million metric tons in 2021.[12] Although ubiquitous cardboard is included in this statistic, it cannot be denied that paper is used widely for written communication and the dissemination of information. The point is that Lancaster's prediction did not turn out to be the anticipated overwhelming change agent because, in part, society was not willing to abandon print, nor was there a concerted effort to plan for its demise.

FORESIGHT PLANNING STRATEGIES

The vision for libraries in 2035 can be attained through the use of foresight planning methods and advocacy. Without a crystal ball, library and information professionals must employ these strategies to lead them to the future.

Forming a plan is the organization's road map to get from point A to point B. There must be a clear notion of what point B looks like and what route(s) will transport you to reach your destination. There are multiple publications to guide information professionals through the strategic planning process, but foresight analysts select the method or methods that enable them to make better-informed decisions leading to a path toward the future. The European Foresight Platform (EFP)[13] website provides a wealth of strategies for anyone endeavoring DIY foresight training. The EFP defines *foresight* as:

> a systematic, participatory, future-intelligence-gathering and medium-to-long-term vision-building process aimed at enabling present-day decisions and mobilizing joint actions. It can be envisaged as a triangle combining "Thinking the Future," "Debating the Future," and "Shaping the Future." Foresight is neither prophecy nor prediction. It does not aim to predict the future—to unveil it as if it were predetermined—but to help us build it. It invites us to consider the future as something that we can create or shape, rather than as something already decided.[14]

There are many forecast methodologies in use in organizations, and those involved in strategic planning may already employ these techniques without knowing that they are formal strategies. A novice can locate details about how to use these methods through self-study, and more in-depth concepts can be mastered through courses and certificate programs offered by educational institutions and professional foresight associations.

Some of the more recognizable foresight methods include scenario planning, Delphi technique, mind mapping, and back casting. Librarians would be well-served by exploring ways to include these methods continuously. Individually, librarians should be vigilant in scanning the global environment and keeping up-to-date with new technologies by identifying the people to watch, the publications to read, and the organizations to join. By 2035, this landscape will change, but start today to create a personalized list of the influencing sources you need to stay current. My list is in constant flux, but these resources provide an example of what you might select.

- Publications: *Popular Mechanics*, *Smithsonian*, *MIT Technology Review*
- Events: SXSW Festival, Consumer Electronics Show (CES)
- People: Paul Saffo, Ray Kurzweil, Cecily Sommers

CONCLUSION

Creating the future as an information professional will require a proactive, adaptive, and collaborative approach. By combining foresight strategies with technological preparedness, ethical considerations, and a commitment to innovation, we can contribute to shaping a positive and impactful future for the LIS field. Ultimately, many situations—world events, societal changes, environmental decline, and technological innovations—will dictate the shape of libraries in 2035.

NOTES

1. "The Emerging Future: Technology Issues and Trend MOOCs," SJSU School of Information, accessed October 21, 2023, https://ischool.sjsu.edu/post/emerging-future-technology-issues-and-trends-moocs.
2. Danny D'Cruze, "Open IS's ChatGPT hits 100 million users, makes history as fastest growing platform: Report," *Business Today* (February 3, 2023), https://www.businesstoday.in/technology/news/story/open-ais-chatgpt-hits-100-million-users-makes-history-as-fastest-growing-app-368753-2023-02-03.
3. Community Virtual Library, "Home," accessed February 13, 2023, https://communityvirtuallibrary.org/; V. Hill, "Libraries in the Metaverse—Metaliteracy for Digital Citizens," YouTube, accessed February 13, 2023, https://www.youtube.com/watch?v=ougyXBmf_z0.
4. Digital Public Library of America, "Home," accessed February 13, 2023, https://dp.la/.
5. Ibid.
6. Wikipedia, "Self-sovereign identity," accessed October 21, 2023, https://en.wikipedia.org/wiki/Self-sovereign_identity.
7. Souvick Ghosh, "Future of AI in Libraries," SJSU School of Information (March 14, 2023), https://ischool.sjsu.edu/ciri-blog/future-ai-libraries.
8. Andrew Perrin and Sara Ataske, "7% of Americans don't use the internet. Who are they?" Pew Research Center (April 2, 2021), https://www.pewresearch.org/fact-tank/2021/04/02/7-of-americans-dont-use-the-internet-who-are-they/.
9. McKinsey & Company, "Closing the digital divide in Black America," January 18, 2023, https://www.mckinsey.com/industries/public-and-social-sector/our-insights/closing-the-digital-divide-in-black-america.
10. Anthony Doer, *Cloud Cuckoo Land* (Simon & Schuster, 2022), https://www.simonandschuster.com/books/Cloud-Cuckoo-Land/Anthony-Doerr/9781982168445.
11. F. Wilfrid Lancaster, *Toward paperless information systems*, (Academic Press, 1978).
12. Statista Research Department, "Global production of paper and paperboard 1961–2021," *Statista* (January 25, 2023), https://www.statista.com/statistics/270314/global-paper-and-cardboard-production/.
13. Foresight, "ForLearn," accessed February 13, 2023, http://foresight-platform.eu/community/forlearn/.
14. Foresight, "What Is Foresight," accessed February 13, 2023, http://foresight-platform.eu/community/forlearn/what-is-foresight.

25

The Way Forward for Libraries

Sandra Hirsh

The library of 2035 will be more resilient, responsive, collaborative, and essential to the success of its community.

When *Library 2020: Today's Leading Visionaries Describe Tomorrow's Library*[1] was published in May 2013, who could have envisioned what would actually happen in 2020 in terms of our health and safety, our political system, and the pivotal role libraries would play in responding to these scenarios? Honestly, it was hard to imagine the devastation the world would experience in 2020. "The trauma of the COVID-19 pandemic and issues surrounding racial injustice, for example, have placed new pressures, opportunities, and challenges that will impact and change how information professionals do their work and serve their communities in the future."[2] Given all these uncertainties, how can we plan for the future of libraries in 2035?

RESILIENCY: LESSONS FROM THE REDWOODS

As the world was still reeling from the COVID-19 global pandemic lockdown, California experienced one of its worst wildfire seasons. Unfortunately, the Big Basin Redwood State Park[3] (California's oldest state park) became one of the severely affected wildfire victims, with around 97 percent of the park burning in August 2020.[4] I remember many happy summers visiting this park with my family and camping underneath the dense redwood forest canopy, so I was particularly saddened by what I heard and saw on the news about how the wildfire impacted the park.

In August 2023, I returned to the park for the first time since the fire expecting to see a completely devastated park. Instead, I was amazed by what I saw.

While still showing its burn scars and, of course, providing a much thinned-out canopy, there was also tremendous growth and vitality. Walking through the forest, I noticed a surprising amount of regrowth on the trees—just three years after the forest was almost completely destroyed. The amount of regeneration inspired me; it gave me hope.

It turns out redwood trees have a "superpower"—namely, they are fire resistant and can regenerate after fires. This superpower, combined with other important traits like their thick bark and shallow widespread root system that intertwines with the roots of nearby trees, prepares redwood trees to overcome many natural disasters and threats, like fire, insects, and fungi. In other words, redwood trees are highly resilient—just like our libraries.

As we look forward to the library of 2035, libraries can adopt similar strategies as those used by the redwood trees for protecting against threats, regenerating after disasters, supporting and caring for each other in the community, and preparing for a resilient future. Libraries can look forward to a resilient future because they are built upon solid library and information science foundational principles, such as a commitment to take care of their community, being innovative and adaptive to the environment, and continually advocating for the value of their services and resources. However, just like redwood trees, to be ready to meet future challenges and threats, libraries also need to prepare to embrace new opportunities.

CHALLENGES AND OPPORTUNITIES AHEAD FOR THE LIBRARY OF 2035

Contributors to this book discussed many real societal, economic, health, political, and environmental challenges that libraries must overcome to thrive and succeed, as well as opportunities for libraries to pursue. Some of the challenges were specific to different types of libraries (i.e., school, academic, community colleges, and public libraries); concerns included increasing book bans and intellectual freedom challenges, decreasing library funding, increasing barriers and costs in publishing and purchasing threatening the library's ability to grow its collections, waning appreciation for the value of libraries, and growing technology threats.

Several general themes also arose. For example, libraries need to support the needs of individuals who face real concerns about their own future (e.g., job stability and security, economic outlook, impact from governmental policies, and environmental sustainability) and their community's future too. Libraries must also be prepared to support communities through increased natural disasters, ongoing social inequities and unrest, and rising challenges to the rights we historically have fought hard to attain. Other considerations that will transform the work of libraries in 2035 include:

- *Globalization:* Technology is helping to speed up the rate of global connectivity. These globalization forces are changing the ways that people

work, collaborate, and share information, but they raise privacy and safety concerns as our personal devices, information, networks, and information become exposed to increased threats.
- *Technological Innovation:* "Throughout history, forces such as globalization have reshaped most employees' jobs. Technology, including AI, stands to revolutionize those positions even more."[5] In fact, AI and ChatGPT were referenced several times in this book as key influencers in the future. These technologies will bring opportunities to the library environment, such as streamlining the process of creating catalog records and metadata[6] and "assisting users with formulating research questions and selecting topics."[7] AI also brings possible threats, such as to job security and information accuracy, and raises concerns about its possible use in political warfare.
- *Information Literacy:* Ensuring that people develop strong information and digital literacy skills will continue to be a challenge, particularly given growing distrust due to fake news and concerns over AI. The "ability of citizens to sort fact from fiction [and] understand the difference between science and opinion"[8] is, and will continue to be, a critical need throughout all societies. Librarians in 2035 will uphold their critical role in advocating for these literacies as well as teaching information seekers how to ethically engage with the new technologies that connect them to the information resources they need.
- *Equity of access, diversity, and inclusion (EDI):* Libraries must remain committed to their EDI efforts. All community members have the right to access the resources they need regardless of their "age, race, ethnicity, sexuality, religion, disability status, or socioeconomic status."[9] Communities also desire programming that accurately represents their cultural customs and family values; libraries that connect to their diverse communities will thrive in 2035. Inclusion is needed "to ensure that those who have historically been marginalized are invited to the table."[10]
- *Fostering connections and culture-sharing:* The success of libraries will be contingent on their ability to establish strong partnerships and collaborations with educational partners, community leaders, innovation centers, and most importantly, the library's patrons. Without these partnerships, libraries will not only lack resources, but they may also come up short on providing services and programming that foster culture-sharing, participation, and understanding.

THE WAY FORWARD FOR THE LIBRARY OF 2035

Is there a way forward for the library of 2035? Yes! Libraries and librarians have repeatedly demonstrated their resiliency, innovation, transformative nature, and value. To sustain their impact on the communities they serve, the library of 2035 will need to adapt to the changing needs of their communities and advocate their value and resiliency.

THE LIBRARY OF 2035 WILL EVOLVE AND THRIVE

I believe in the library of the future—even though the road to the library of 2035 will likely be bumpy. While libraries will continue to exist and serve their communities in 2035 and beyond, they will do so in different ways as they adapt to the surrounding environment and evolve to meet changing user needs. The library of 2035 will:

- Be highly responsive to the continuing shifts in how society works, communicates, plays, and engages with others, such as adapting to an increasingly digitized information landscape and new technologies like AI.
- Be trusted partners that provide support, relief, and resources which build a safety net and take care of its community members.
- Serve as community liaisons and change agents that will "envision a brighter future, manage and lead change, and participate with their like-minded colleagues in building a better future—not just for their organizations (and themselves) but for all information users."[11]

THE LIBRARY OF 2035 ADAPTS TO THE CHANGING NEEDS OF ITS COMMUNITY

While the onslaught of COVID-19 and the global shutdown may have been a once-in-a-lifetime occurrence, the library's role in the crisis was not. In fact, many developments beyond COVID-19 have forever changed the role libraries play in their communities. Every nation has witnessed increased threats due to global warming, climate issues, and the frequency of natural disasters (e.g., wildfires, earthquakes, hurricanes, and drought). Consequently, libraries worldwide have taken on critical new roles as first responders and community connectors, which have helped libraries demonstrate their value. "Wide-scale natural and manmade emergencies throughout the country have demonstrated to local and regional emergency management and elected officials the versatile role information organizations can play in disaster response serving as a welcoming refuge for the community."[12]

Safety and caretaking are not limited to natural disasters or other crises. The need for people to safely access viable information will only increase, placing an even higher call to action on libraries and librarians. To help address this need, libraries are connecting to worldwide initiatives (such as the United Nations Sustainable Development Goals),[13] increasing partnerships and collaborations across national and international borders, and collectively advocating for policies and procedures that protect user information privacy. While these strategies have helped us endure the challenges of the past decade, they also help set the course for the library of 2035.

Key competencies that librarians in 2035 will need to remain adaptive and responsive to the community's needs include:

- Providing community members safe and efficient access to the global network of information.
- Building and strengthening partnerships across all sectors—particularly funding agencies, governing agencies, and educational systems—and across city, county, state, and even national borders.
- Elevating the library's presence as a first responder and safe harbor and building community partnerships that support the community's needs during crises and economic recovery.

THE LIBRARY OF 2035 ADVOCATES ITS VALUE AND RESILIENCY

Sometimes organizations and resources can become irrelevant or at risk, even when they bring tremendous value to our environment and society. For example, while the redwoods bring tremendous value to the environment and ecosystem, only 5 percent of the original redwood trees along the Pacific Coast remain due to their value for commercial use.[14] There are now groups advocating for the preservation of the redwoods.

Similarly, advocacy has always been a critical strategy for libraries and librarians. Recent events, such as the resurgence of challenges on library books, resources, and programming only prove the criticalness of ongoing and effective communication and advocacy strategies. A lack of effective advocacy can result in less funding, decreased public trust, and at its worst, elimination of the library altogether. Advocacy requires demonstrating the library's value and building effective partnerships in the community—as well as across the organizational and political structures that serve that community. Advocacy will remain a critical role of the library of 2035. Librarians must develop skills in advocating for their organizations, their services, and most importantly, their patrons' rights. Challenges to books, materials, and services; demands for censoring user behaviors; and increased scrutiny of programming will continue, especially while political, safety and security, and social systems are under attack.

Key competencies that librarians in 2035 will need for advocating the library's value include:

- Demonstrating the library's relevance to community leaders, voters, and stakeholders to ensure the library remains a funding priority.
- Managing book and resource challenges, advocating for the user's right to free expression, and understanding how social, cultural, financial, and political power can limit intellectual freedom.

- Building effective community partnerships that expand information access (including materials and library services for marginalized populations)[15] and that focus on key literacies to help all community members access the resources they need to grow, find solutions, and improve their own lives.

CONCLUSION

While libraries will remain true to their core purpose of connecting users to the information they want and need, they will now do so in a much bigger, more complex, and vastly digital universe. Meanwhile, librarians must balance their day-to-day operations while also demonstrating value to all their stakeholders, advocating for support and funding, standing up to threats to not only their collections but also the community's right to information resources, and performing all the duties within these charges with a mindful focus on diversity, equity, and inclusion at every level. Furthermore, the threats beyond our control (e.g., pandemics, natural disasters, social injustices, and unstable economies and political systems) compromise libraries' operations while also elevating libraries' essential role as first responders, trustworthy community resources, and safe harbors for our communities.

> The library of 2035 will surely face its storms, threats, and crises; however, libraries and librarians who commit to innovation, stay ahead of emerging technologies, and strongly advocate their value will stand strong and tall with roots well-grounded as an essential community resource for learning, communicating, playing, and working.

"The redwood's ability to resprout or activate dormant buds beneath the bark and grow new stems, branches, and leaves, is an adaptation that enhances survival following fire."[16] Libraries, too, can renew, or "resprout," their environments; evolve, or "grow," their resources; and adapt their services to respond to technological innovations and changes in user behaviors, sustaining resiliency into the future. The library of 2035 will surely face its storms, threats, and crises; however, libraries and librarians who commit to innovation, stay ahead of emerging technologies, and strongly advocate their value will stand strong and tall with roots well-grounded as an essential community resource for learning, communicating, playing, and working.

NOTES

1. Joseph Janes, ed. (2013), "*Library 2020: Today's Leading Visionaries Describe Tomorrow's Library*," Scarecrow Press, Inc.

2. Sandra Hirsh (2022), "What It Means to Be an Information Professional Today," In Sandra Hirsh, ed, *Information Services Today: An Introduction*, 3rd ed., Rowman & Littlefield, p. 6.
3. See http://www.parks.ca.gov/?page_id=540.
4. Sempervirens Fund, "Top 10 Facts That Make Redwoods Magnificent," accessed October 7, 2023, https://sempervirens.org/learn/redwood-facts/#fact-list.
5. John Hall, "Why Upskilling and Reskilling Are Essential in 2023," *Forbes*, February 24, 2023. https://www.forbes.com/sites/johnhall/2023/02/24/why-upskilling-and-reskilling-are-essential-in-2023/?sh=33e1325e4088.
6. Almuth Gastinger, Rajen Munoo, Leo S. Lo, and Ray Pun, "ChatGPT in Libraries? A Discussion," IFLA, accessed September, 3, 2023, https://blogs.ifla.org/cpdwl/2023/05/14/chatgpt-in-libraries-a-discussion/.
7. Ibid.
8. Rebekkah Smith Aldrich and Michele Pavone Stricker, "Community Resilience," in Sandra Hirsh, ed., *Information Services Today: An Introduction*, 3rd ed., Rowman & Littlefield, 2022, p. 287.
9. Kawanna Bright (2022), "Equity of Access, Diversity, and Inclusion," in Sandra Hirsh, ed., *Information Services Today: An Introduction*, 3rd ed., Rowman & Littlefield.
10. Ibid.
11. Stephen Abram (2022), "The Transformative Information Landscape," in Sandra Hirsh, ed., *Information Services Today: An Introduction*, 3rd ed., Rowman & Littlefield, p. 36.
12. Aldrich and Stricker, "Community Resilience," 287.
13. Department of Economic and Social Affairs, "MAKE THE SDGS A REALITY," United Nations, accessed October 18, 2023, https://sdgs.un.org/.
14. "Top 10 Facts That Make Redwoods Magnificent."
15. Deborah Caldwell (2022), "Intellectual Freedom," in Sandra Hirsh, ed., *Information Services Today: An Introduction*, 3rd ed., Rowman & Littlefield.
16. Northern Arizona University, "The remarkable resilience of fire-scarred coast redwood trees," accessed October 7, 2023, https://ecoinfo.nau.edu/index.php/news/the-remarkable-resilience-of-fire-scarred-coast-redwood-trees/.

Bibliography

Abram, Stephen. "The Transformative Information Landscape." In Sandra Hirsh, ed., *Information Services Today: An Introduction*, 3rd ed., Rowman & Littlefield. 2022: 36.

Accrediting Commission for Community and Junior Colleges (ACCJC). "Eligibility Requirements, Accreditation Standards, Institutional Policies, and Operational Policies." 2022. https://accjc.org/eligibility-requirements-standards-policies/.

ACRL Research Planning and Review Committee. "Top trends in academic libraries: A review of the trends and issues." *Association of College and Research Libraries* 82, no. 6 (2022). https://crln.acrl.org/index.php/crlnews/article/view/25483/33379.

ALA-APA. "Helping to Support Overall Wellness for All Library Workers." Accessed April 16, 2023. https://ala-apa.org/wellness/.

———. "Library Worklife." Accessed April 16, 2023. https://ala-apa.org/newsletter/.

ALA-APA Wellness. "8 Elements of Wellness." Accessed October 21, 2023. https://ala-apa.org/wellness/.

Alderson, D. "SustainRT Awards the 2022 Citation for Wellness in the Workplace to Health and Safety Department at Queens Public Library." American Library Association News and Press Center. July 26, 2022. https://www.ala.org/news/press-releases/2022/07/sustainrt-awards-2022-citation-wellness-workplace-health-and-safety.

———. "Westerville Public Library to Receive 2021 SustainRT Citation for Wellness in the Workplace." American Library Association News and Press Center. May 25, 2021. https://www.ala.org/news/press-releases/2021/05/westerville-public-library-receive-2021-sustainrt-citation-wellness-workplace.

Aldrich, Rebekkah Smith, and Michele Pavone Stricker. "Community Resilience." In Sandra Hirsh, ed., *Information Services Today: An Introduction*, 3rd ed., Rowman & Littlefield. 2022: 287.

Alter, A., and E. Harris. "Attempts to Ban Books Are Accelerating and Becoming More Divisive." *New York Times*. September 15, 2022. https://www.nytimes.com/2022/09/16/books/book-bans.html.

American Libraries. "Are Libraries Neutral? Highlights from the Midwinter President's Program." 2018. https://americanlibrariesmagazine.org/2018/06/01/are-libraries-neutral/.

American Library Association. "2022 Book Ban Data." March 20, 2023. http://www.ala.org/advocacy/bbooks/book-ban-data.

———. "Committee on the Status of Women in Librarianship (COSWL)." September 22, 2009. https://www.ala.org/aboutala/committees/ala/ala-coswl.

———. "RESOLUTION FOR THE ADOPTION OF SUSTAINABILITY AS A CORE VALUE OF LIBRARIANSHIP." Accessed August 6, 2023. https://www.ala.org/aboutala/sites/ala.org.aboutala/files/content/governance/council/council_documents/2019_ms_council_docs/ALA%20CD%2037%20RESOLUTION%20FOR%20THE%20ADOPTION%20OF%20SUSTAINABILITY%20AS%20A%20CORE%20VALUE%20OF%20LIBRARIANSHIP_Final1182019.pdf.

Antonelli, Monika, Rene Tanner, Rebekkah Smith Aldrich, and Adrian K. Ho. "Libraries in the Doughnut Economy." Rollins College. 2022. https://scholarship.rollins.edu/cgi/viewcontent.cgi?article=1372&context=as_facpub.

Anyosha, Rochwell. "The History of Artificial Intelligence." *Science in the News* blog. *Harvard University Graduate School of Arts and Sciences*. August 28, 2017. https://sitn.hms.harvard.edu/flash/2017/history-artificial-intelligence/.

Ashiq, Murtaza, Farhat Jabeen, and Khalid Mahmood. "Transformation of libraries during Covid-19 pandemic: A systematic review." *Journal of Academic Librarianship* 48, no. 4 (2022): 1–12.

Ashmore, Beth, Kelly Farrell, Megan Kilb, Virginia Martin, and Abigail Wickes. "TRLN Guide to Negotiating Accessibility in E-Resource Licenses." Triangle Research Library Network. Last modified December 14, 2022. http://bit.ly/trln-a11y-eresource-license.

Aspen Institute. "Rising to the Challenge: Re-Envisioning Public Libraries." 2017. https://www.aspeninstitute.org/wp-content/uploads/2014/10/Aspen-LibrariesReport-2017-FINAL.pdf.

Association of Research Libraries. "List of ARL Members." Accessed October 21, 2023. https://www.arl.org/list-of-arl-members/.

Baldwin, Davarian L. *In the Shadow of the Ivory Tower: How Universities Are Plundering Our Cities*. Bold Type Books. 2021.

Bauld, Andrew. "Boston's Revolutionary Pledge: A School Library for Every Student by 2026." *School Library Journal*. December 20, 2022. https://www.slj.com/story/bostons-evolutionary-pledge-a-school-library-for-every-student-by-2026.

Berg, Cara, Darby Malvey, and Maureen Donohue. "WITHOUT FOUNDATIONS, WE CAN'T BUILD: INFORMATION LITERACY AND THE NEED FOR STRONG SCHOOL LIBRARY PROGRAMS." *The Library with the Lead Pipe*. March 7, 2018. http://www.inthelibrarywiththeleadpipe.org/2018/Strong-School-Library-Programs/.

Bishop, Peter C., and Andy Hines. *Teaching About the Future* (New York: Palgrave Macmillan, 2012): 1, 7, 55–59.

Bittle, Jake. *The Great Displacement: Climate Change and the Next American Migration*. Simon & Schuster. 2023.

BlackPast. "Linda Johnson Rice (1958–)." Accessed April 23, 2023. https://www.blackpast.org/african-american-history/linda-johnson-rice-1958/.

Borges, Jorge. *The Library of Babel*. David R. Godine, 2000.

Bosch, Stephen, Barbara Albee, and Sion Romaine. "Are We There Yet? | Periodicals Price Survey 2022." *Library Journal*. April 14, 2022. https://www.libraryjournal.com/story/Are-We-There-Yet-Periodicals-Price-Survey-2022.

Boston Public Schools. "Library Services." Accessed October 20, 2023. https://www.bostonpublicschools.org/libraryservices.

Branum, Candise. "The myth of library neutrality." *Semantic Scholar*. 2008. https://api.semanticscholar.org/CorpusID:158738938.

Brawley-Barker, Tessa. "Integrating Library, Archives, and Museum Collections in an Open Source Information Management System: A Case Study at Glenstone." *Art Documentation: Journal of the Art Libraries Society of North America* 35, no. 1 (2016): 86–113.

Breeding, Marshall. "2022 Library Systems Report." *American Libraries*. May 2, 2022. https://americanlibrariesmagazine.org/2022/05/02/2022-library-systems-report.

Bright, Kawanna. "Equity of Access, Diversity, and Inclusion." In Sandra Hirsh, ed. *Information Services Today: An Introduction*, 3rd ed. Rowman & Littlefield. 2022.

brown, adrienne maree. *Emergent Strategy: Shaping Change, Changing Worlds* (Chico: AK Press, 2017): 56.

Bryne, Amelia, and Marijke Visser. "Keeping Communities Connected: Library Broadband Services During the COVID-19 Pandemic." *ALA Policy Perspectives* 9. March 2022. https://www.ala.org/advocacy/sites/ala.org.advocacy/files/content/telecom/broadband/Keeping_Communities_Connected_030722.pdf.

BU Libraries. "Tony Zanders Joins Boston University Libraries as Inaugural Entrepreneur in Residence." Last accessed May 11, 2023. https://www.bu.edu/library/news/2019/04/01/tony-zanders-joins-boston-university-libraries-as-inaugural-entrepreneur-in-residence/.

Bunch, William. "After the Ivory Tower Falls: How College Broke the American Dream and Blew Up Our Politics—and How to Fix It," 1st ed. (New York, NY: William Morrow, an imprint of HarperCollins, 2022).

Buncombe, Andrew. "Allied Forces Knew About Holocaust Two Years Before Discovery of Concentration Camps, Secret Documents Reveal." *Independent*. April 18, 2017. https://www.independent.co.uk/news/world/world-history/holocaust-allied-forces-knew-before-concentration-camp-discovery-us-uk-soviets-secret-documents-a7688036.html.

Burke, Michael, Daniel J. Willis, and Debbie Truong. "California community college enrollment plummets to 30-year low." *Los Angeles Times*. November 18, 2022. https://www.latimes.com/california/story/2022-11-18/california-community-college-enrollment-plunges.

Butler, Octavia. *Parable of the Sower* (Warner Books, 1993).

Buzzflash. "A Buzzflash Interview with Michael Moore, Filmmaker, TV Host, and Author of 'Stupid White Men.'" March 13, 2002. https://buzzflash.com/flashback/moore-2002.

Caldwell, Deborah. "Intellectual Freedom." In Sandra Hirsh, ed. *Information Services Today: An Introduction*, 3rd ed. (Rowman & Littlefield, 2022).

California Community Colleges Chancellor's Office. "Management Information Systems Data Mart." Accessed May 14, 2023. https://datamart.cccco.edu/.

California Humanities. "Library Innovation Lab: Exploring New Ways of Engaging California's Immigrant Communities." Accessed June 22, 2023. https://calhum.org/programs-initiatives/programs/library-innovation-lab/.

California State Library. "The Value of California's Public Libraries." August 2021. https://www.library.ca.gov/wp-content/uploads/2021/09/Value-of-Libraries.pdf.

Calvin, B. "Richland Library First to Receive Presidential Citation for Wellness in the Workplace." American Library Association News and Press Center. June 7, 2019. https://www.ala.org/news/member-news/2019/06/richland-library-first-receive-presidential-citation-wellness-workplace.

Cappelli, Peter. "Talent Management for the Twenty-First Century." *Harvard Business Review*. March 2008. https://hbr.org/2008/03/talent-management-for-the-twenty-first-century.

Carey, Kevin T. "The incredible shrinking future of college." *The Highlight by Vox*. November 21, 2022. https://www.vox.com/the-highlight/23428166/college-enrollment-population-education-crash.

Carlson, S. *The Library of the Future: How the Heart of the Campus Is Transforming* (Chronicle of Higher Education, 2022).

Carnegie Classification of Institutions of Higher Education. "Basic Classification." Accessed October 21, 2023. https://carnegieclassifications.acenet.edu/carnegie-classification/classification-methodology/basic-classification/#doctoral-universities.

Casselman, Ben. "The 'Great Resignation' Is Over. Can Workers' Power Endure?" *New York Times*. July 6, 2023. https://www.nytimes.com/2023/07/06/business/economy/jobs-great-resignation.html.

Centres for Disease Control and Prevention. "Well-Being Concepts." 2019. https://www.cdc.gov/hrqol/wellbeing.htm#three.

Chang, Andrea. "Poetry Foundation Selects Michelle T. Boone as Its President." *New York Times*. April 29, 2021. https://www.nytimes.com/2021/04/29/arts/michelle-t-boone-president-poetry-foundation.html.

ChatGPT, personal communication, April 12, 2023.

———. "What are the benefits of library consortia over a single library?" March 2023.

Chicago City Council. April 19, 2023. https://youtu.be/1jqbZPkNOLc?t=1510.

Chicago Public Library Foundation. "Coming to You Live from the Library!" Accessed October 18, 2023. https://cplfoundation.org/coming-to-you-live-from-the-library/.

Chicago Sun Times. "Obamas, Oprah on growing list of top names reading children's books for Chicago Public Library." May 13, 2020. https://chicago.suntimes.com/2020/5/13/21257776/obamas-oprah-growing-list-top-names-reading-childrens-books-chicago-public-library.

City Club of Chicago. "Defending Democracy: The Role of Libraries and Civic Leaders in the Fight Against Disinformation." Published on November 15, 2021. Video, 1:01:08. Accessed on April 23, 2023. https://www.cityclub-chicago.org/video/3572/defending-democracy-the-role-of-libraries-and-civic-leaders-in-the-fight-against.

Clemens, Colleen. "Ally or Accomplice? The Language of Activism." *Learning for Justice*. June 5, 2017. https://www.learningforjustice.org/magazine/ally-or-accomplice-the-language-of-activism.

Coalition for Diversity and Inclusion in Scholarly Communications. "Latest News I Upcoming Events." Last accessed May 28, 2023. https://c4disc.org.

Coles, Amanda. "Creative class politics: unions and the creative economy." *International Journal of Cultural Policy* 22, no. 3 (2016): 456–72.

Communities of Excellence 2026. Accessed April 9, 2023. https://communitiesofexcellence2026.org/.

Community Virtual Library. "Home." Accessed February 13, 2023. https://communityvirtuallibrary.org/; V. Hill

Conceicao, Pedro. "Human Development Report 2021-22 Uncertain Times, Unsettled Lives: Shaping Our Future in a Transforming World." United Nations Development Programme: New York. 2023. https://hdr.undp.org/system/files/documents/global-report-document/hdr2021-22pdf_1.pdf.

Connaway, Lynn Silipigni, ed. *The Library in the Life of the User: Engaging with People Where They Live and Learn* (Dublin, OH: OCLC Research, 2015). http://www.oclc.org/content/dam/research/publications/2015/oclcresearch-library-in-life-of-user.pdf.

Connaway, Lynn Silipigni. "Meeting the expectations of the community: The engagement-centered library." In *Library 2020: Today's Leading Visionaries Describe Tomorrow's Library*, edited by Joseph Janes (Lanham, MD: Scarecrow Press, 2013): 83-88.

Connaway, Lynn Silipigni et al. "The Library in the Life of the Community: Twenty Years of OCLC Research." *Library Trends* (forthcoming).

Connaway, Lynn Silipigni, Ixchel M. Faniel, Brittany Brannon, Joanne Cantrell, Christopher Cyr, Brooke Doyle, Peggy Gallagher, Kem Lang, Brian Lavoie, Janet Mason, and Tita van der Werf. "New Model Library: Pandemic Effects and Library Directions." Dublin, OH: OCLC Research. 2021. https://doi.org/10.25333/2d1r-f907.

Cooke, Nicole A. "Decolonizing Our Hearts and Our Minds." *Dismantling Constructs of Whiteness in Higher Education*. (Routledge, 2022): 224-34.

———. *Information Services to Diverse Populations: Developing Culturally Competent Library Professionals* (Bloomsbury Publishing USA, 2016).

———. "Librarians as Active Bystanders: Centering Social Justice in LIS Practice." *The Portable MLIS: Insights from the Experts*, 2nd ed. (Santa Barbara, CA: ABC-CLIO/Libraries Unlimited, 2017): 39-48.

———. "Reading Is Only a Step on the Path to Anti-Racism." *Publishers Weekly*. June 19, 2020. https://www.publishersweekly.com/pw/by-topic/industry-news/libraries/article/83626-reading-is-only-a-step-on-the-path-to-anti-racism.html.

Cooke, Nicole A. et al. "Once More for Those in the Back: Libraries Are Not Neutral." *Publishers Weekly.* June 10, 2022.

Cooper, Danielle, and Katherine Klosek. "Copyright and Streaming Audiovisual Content in the US Context." Ithaka S+R. Last modified January 5, 2023. https://doi.org/10.18665/sr.318118.

Cooper, Danielle, Catharine Bond Hill, and Roger C. Schonfeld. "Aligning the Research Library to Organizational Strategy" (April 12, 2022): 16–18. https://sr.ithaka.org/wp-content/uploads/2022/04/ARL-CARL-SR-Report-Aligning-the-Research-Library-to-Organizational-Strategy-04122022.pdf.

Cornell University. "arxiv." Accessed October 20, 2023, https://arxiv.org/.

Cornish, Edward. *Futuring: The Exploration of the Future* (Bethesda: World Future Society, 2004): 78, 94.

Council of California Community Colleges Chief Librarians. "Annual Library Data Survey Master File 2005 to 2020." 2022. https://cclibrarians.org/sites/default/files/masterfilelibrarysurvey05_06to19withpivottablefordistrubtion.xlsx.

Cox, Andrew M., Stephen Pinfield, and Sophie Rutter. "The intelligent library: Thought leaders' views on the likely impact of artificial intelligence on academic libraries." *Library Hi Tech* 37, no. 3 (2019): 418–35.

Crowley, Kate, Rowan Jackson, Siona O'Connell, Dulma Karunarthna, Esti Anantasari, Arry Retnowati, and Dominique Niemand. "Cultural heritage and risk assessments: Gaps, challenges, and future research directions for the inclusion of heritage within climate change adaptation and disaster management." *Climate Resilience and Sustainability* 1, no. 3 (2022): 1–12.

Davis, Angela. "Moe Lectureship in Women's Studies." Saint Peter, MN: Gustavus Adolphus College, Women's Studies Program. 2006.

D'Cruze, Danny. "Open IS's ChatGPT hits 100 million users, makes history as fastest growing platform: Report." *Business Today.* February 3, 2023. https://www.businesstoday.in/technology/news/story/open-ais-chatgpt-hits-100-million-users-makes-history-as-fastest-growing-app-368753-2023-02-03.

DC History Center. "About the Carnegie Library." Accessed October 20, 2023. https://dchistory.org/about/carnegielibrary/.

Delaware Libraries. "About DLC." Accessed October 20, 2023. https://lib.de.us/about-us/about-dlc/.

D'Eon, Marcel F. "The Ladder of Inference re-visited: 'Don't jump to conclusions!'" *Canadian Medical Education Journal,* 13, no. 5 (2022): 1-5. doi: 10.36834/cmej.76000. PMID: 36310912; PMCID: PMC9588189.

Department of Economic and Social Affairs. "MAKE THE SDGS A REALITY." United Nations. Accessed October 18, 2023. https://sdgs.un.org/.

———. "Transforming Our World: The 2030 Agenda for Sustainable Development." United Nations. Accessed October 21, 2023. https://sdgs.un.org/2030agenda.

Department of Education, "Administrative Code and Statute," State of New Jersey. Accessed October 21, 2023. https://www.nj.gov/education/code/.

Digital Public Library of America, "Home," accessed February 13, 2023, https://dpla/.

Diliberti, Melissa Kay, and Heather L. Schwartz. "Educator Turnover Has Markedly Increased, but Districts Have Taken Actions to Boost Teacher Ranks: Selected Findings from the Sixth American School District Panel Survey" (Santa Monica, CA: RAND Corporation, 2023). https://www.rand.org/pubs/research_reports/RRA956-14.html.

Doer, Anthony. *Cloud Cuckoo Land* (Simon & Schuster, 2022).

Donohue, Maureen, and James Keehbler. "School Library Programs in New Jersey: Building Blocks for Realizing Student Potential with ESSA Legislation Opportunities." NJASL (April 2016), https://njla.memberclicks.net/assets/docs/2016ESSAandNJSchoolLibraryPrograms.pdf.

Drozdowski, Mark J. *"Looming enrollment cliff poses serious threat to colleges."* Best Colleges. 2023. https://www.bestcolleges.com/news/analysis/looming-enrollment-cliff-poses-serious-threat-to-colleges/.

Dytrt, Zdenek. "Leadership—Management Superstructure." *Economics World* 5, no. 4 (2017): 354-61.

ESS Open Archive. "Home." Accessed October 20, 2023. https://essopenarchive.org/

EveryLibrary. "Home." Accessed October 21, 2023. https://www.everylibrary.org/.

Food Secure Canada. "Our Work." Accessed October 18, 2023. https://foodsecurecanada.org/who-we-are/what-food-sovereignty.

Foresight. "ForLearn." Accessed February 13, 2023. http://foresight-platform.eu/community/forlearn/.

———. "What Is Foresight?" Last accessed February 13, 2023. http://foresight-platform.eu/community/forlearn/what-is-foresight/.

Framingham State University. "RAMS Renew Space." Accessed April 16, 2023. https://libguides.framingham.edu/c.php?g=1188406&p=8705974.

Free Library of Philadelphia. "Home." Accessed October 21, 2023. https://www.freelibrary.org/.

Frei, Frances X., and Anne Morriss. "Begin with Trust." *Harvard Business Review*. May–June 2020A. https://hbr.org/2020/05/begin-with-trust#:~:text=In%20our%20

Freire, Paulo. *Pedagogy of the Oppressed*. New York: Seabury Press, 1970.

Gaidhani, Shilpa, Lokesh Arora, and Bhuvanesh Kumar Sharma. "Understanding the attitude of generation Z towards workplace." *International Journal of Management, Technology and Engineering* 9, no. 1 (2019): 2804–12.

Gaiman, Neil. *The Sandman Vol. 4: Season of Mists* (Vertigo, 2011).

Garcia-Febo, Loida. "Immerse Yourself in Wellness Mindfulness Practices Have Intangible Benefits for Library Workers." *American Libraries*. January 2, 2019. https://americanlibrariesmagazine.org/2019/01/02/immerse-yourself-in-wellness/.

———. "Wellness for Library Workers. IFLA CPDWL" (blog). August 26, 2019. https://blogs.ifla.org/cpdwl/2019/08/26/wellness-for-library-workers-by-loida-garcia-febo/.

———. "Women in Librarianship and Wellness." American Library Association. Accessed October 21, 2023. https://www.ala.org/aboutala/committees/ala/ala-coswl.

Gastinger, Almuth, Rajen Munoo, Leo S. Lo, and Ray Pun. "ChatGPT in Libraries? A Discussion." IFLA. Accessed September 3, 2023. https://blogs.ifla.org/cpdwl/2023/05/14/chatgpt-in-libraries-a-discussion/.

Georgia Library Association. "About." Accessed October 20, 2023. https://gla.georgialibraries.org/about/.

Ghosh, Souvick. "Future of AI in Libraries." SJSU School of Information. March 14, 2023. https://ischool.sjsu.edu/ciri-blog/future-ai-libraries.

Giannoulias, Alexi. "First-in-the-Nation Legislation to Prevent Book Bans Approved by General Assembly: House Bill 2789 passes Senate today." May 3, 2023. https://www.ilsos.gov/news/2023/may/230503d1.pdf.

Global Climate Change. "The Effects of Climate Change." Updated July 26, 2023. https://climate.nasa.gov/effects/.

Gonzalez, Xochitl. "The Librarians Are Not Okay." *Atlantic.* March 15, 2023. https://www.theatlantic.com/ideas/archive/2023/03/book-bans-censorship-librarian-challenges/673398/.

Gorbis, Marina. "Five Principles for Thinking Like a Futurist." *EDUCAUSE Review* 54, no. 1 (Winter 2019). https://er.educause.edu/articles/2019/3/five-principles-for-thinking-like-a-futurist.

Gordon, Rachel Singer. "The Accidental Library Manager." *Information Today* (2005): 10–11.

Gorner, Jeremy. "Illinois House OKs measure to allow the state to deny grants to libraries that ban books." *Chicago Tribune.* March 22, 2023. https://www.everand.com/article/633178336/Illinois-House-O-Ks-Measure-To-Allow-The-State-To-Deny-Grants-To-Libraries-That-Ban-Books.

Grabnick, Colleen. (2021, September 28). "A School Librarian Is a 'Jack of All Trades.' Now Every DCPS Student Has Access to One." NPR/WAMU 88.5.

Guillermo-Wann, Chelsea, and Marc P. Johnston-Guerrero. "Contextualizing multiraciality in campus climate: Key considerations for transformative diversity, equity, and inclusion," in *Multiracial Experiences in Higher Education* (Routledge, 2021): 141–60.

Hall, John. (2023). "Why Upskilling and Reskilling Are Essential in 2023." *Forbes*. February 24, 2023. https://www.forbes.com/sites/johnhall/2023/02/24/why-upskilling-and-reskilling-are-essential-in-2023/?sh=33e1325e4088.

HBCU Library Alliance. "Home." Last accessed May 28, 2023. https://hbculibraries.org.

———. "A Call for Cooperation among HBCU Libraries." Last accessed May 28, 2023. https://www.hbculibraries.org/cooperation.html.

Heath, Chip, and Dan Heath. "Storytelling That Moves People." *Harvard Business Review* 81, no. 6 (June 2003): 51–55.

Heynes, Erla P., Erin R.B. Eldermire, and Heather A. Howard. "Unsubstantiated Conclusions: A Scoping Review on Generational Differences of Leadership in Academic Libraries." *Science Direct* 45, no. 4 (September 2019). https://www.sciencedirect.com/science/article/abs/pii/S0099133319301867.

Higher Learning Commission (HLC). *Criteria for Accreditation*. 2019. https://www.hlcommission.org/Policies/criteria-and-core-components.html.

Hill, V. "Libraries in the Metaverse—Metaliteracy for Digital Citizens." YouTube. Accessed February 13, 2023. https://www.youtube.com/watch?v=ougyXBmf_z0.

Hirsh, Sandra. "What It Means to Be an Information Professional Today," in Sandra Hirsh, ed., *Information Services Today: An Introduction*, 3rd ed. (Rowman & Littlefield, 2022): 6.

History, Art, & Archives. "The Sedition Act of 1798." Accessed January 24, 2024. https://history.house.gov/Historical-Highlights/1700s/The-Sedition-Act-of-1798/

hooks, bell. *Teaching to Transgress*. Routledge, 2014.

Imarisha, Walidah. "Science Fiction, Ancient Futures, and the Liberated Archive," in Meehan Crist and Rose Eveleth, eds. *What Future: The Year's Best Writing on What's Next for People, Technology, & the Planet* (Los Angeles: The Unnamed Press, 2018): 161.

ippc. "AR6 Synthesis Report: Climate Change 2023." Accessed August 6, 2023. https://www.ipcc.ch/report/sixth-assessment-report-cycle/.

Ishuzuka, Kathy. "About our February Cover I From the Editor." *Library Journal*. February 4, 2021. https://www.slj.com/story/about-our-february-cover-from-the-editor.

ITHAKA-SR. "Collaborative strategies and research for higher education and the arts." Accessed October 21, 2023. https://sr.ithaka.org/.

Jacobson, Trudi E., and Thomas P. Mackey. "Proposing a Metaliteracy Model to Redefine Information Literacy." *Communications in Information Literacy* 7, no. 2 (2013): 84–91. https://doi.org/10.15760/comminfolit.2013.7.2.138.

Janes, Joseph, ed. *Library 2020: Today's Leading Visionaries Describe Tomorrow's Library* (Scarecrow Press, Inc., 2013).

Jones, Barbara M. "Librarians Shushed No More: The USA PATRIOT Act, the 'Connecticut Four,' and Professional Ethics." IFLA. 2009. https://www.ifla.org/past-wlic/2009/117-jones-en.pdf.

Juarez, Adriane Herrick. "103. Dealing with Book Banning with Tracie D. Hall." *Library Leadership Podcast.* April 28, 2022. https://libraryleadershippodcast.com/103-dealing-with-book-banning-with-tracie-d-hall/.

Kachel, Debra E., and Keith Curry Lance. "Contexts of School Librarian Employment." *SLIDE: The School Librarian Investigation—Decline or Evolution?* (January 26, 2021): 9. https://libslide.org/pubs/contexts.pdf.

Kang, Cecelia. "Parking Lots Have Become a Digital Lifeline." March 5, 2020. https://www.nytimes.com/2020/05/05/technology/parking-lots-wifi-coronavirus.html.

Khasnabish, Alex, and Max Haiven. *The Radical Imagination: Social Movement Research in the Age of Austerity* (London: Zed Books, 2014). https://www.opendemocracy.net/en/transformation/why-social-movements-need-radical-imagination/.

Kurtz, Stanley. "The Battle for the Soul of the Library." *New York Times*. February 24, 2022.

Kyrillidou, Martha. "Library Investment Index Summarizes Relative Size of ARL University Libraries for 2013-2014." Association of Research Libraries (August 20, 2015), https://www.arl.org/news/library-investment-index-summarizes-relative-size-of-arl-university-libraries-for-2013-2014/.

Lancaster, F. Wilfrid. *Toward Paperless Information Systems*. Academic Press, 1978.

Lance, Keith C. Email. May 19, 2023.

Lance, Keith Curry, and Bill Schwarz. "How Pennsylvania School Libraries Pay Off: Investments in Student Achievement and Academic Standards. PA School Library Project." *HSLC*, Oct. 2012. Web (June 1, 2013). http://paschoollibraryproject.org/research.

Lance, Keith Curry, and Debra E. Kachel. "Perspectives on School Librarian Employment in the United States, 2009-10 to 2018-19. SLIDE: The School Librarian Investigation—Decline or Evolution?" July 2021. https://libslide.org/publications/perspectives/.

———. "Why School Librarians Matter: What Years of Research Tell Us." *Phi Delta Kappan* 99, no. 7 (2018): 15-20. https://doi.org/10.1177/0031721718767854.

Lance, Keith Curry, Debra E. Kachel, and Caitlin Gerrity. "The School Librarian Equity Gap: Inequities Associated with Race and Ethnicity Compounded by Poverty, Locale, and Enrollment." *Peabody Journal of Education* 98, no. 1 (2023): 85-99. https://doi.org/10.1080/0161956x.2023.2160112.

Lankes, R. David. "Exploring the Innovative Community Libraries of Korea." *Publishers Weekly*. January 12, 2023. https://www.publishersweekly.com/pw/by-topic/industry-news/libraries/article/91274-exploring-the-innovative-community-libraries-of-korea.html.

———. *Forged in War: How a Century of War Created Today's Information Society* (Lanham: Rowman & Littlefield, 2021).

———. *The New Librarianship Field Guide* (Cambridge: MIT Press, 2016).

Leff, Laurel. *Buried by the Times: The Holocaust and America's Most Important Newspaper* (Cambridge: Cambridge University Press, 2006).

Legal Information Institute. "right to privacy." Cornell Law School. Accessed October 18, 2023. https://foodsecurecanada.org/our-work/.

LegiScan. "New Jersey S588. Regular Session." January 4, 2023. https://legiscan.com/NJ/text/S588/2022.

Lepore, Jill. "The Data Delusion." *New Yorker*. April 3, 2023. https://www.newyorker.com/magazine/2023/04/03/the-data-delusion.

Library 2.0. "Mental Health and Wellness: Library Workers Thriving in Uncertain Times." Accessed October 21, 2023, https://www.library20.com/mental-health-and-wellness.

Library Accessibility Alliance. "Home." Last accessed May 28, 2023. https://www.libraryaccessibility.org.

LibraryLinkNJ. "Home." Accessed October 21, 2023. https://librarylinknj.org/.

Longley Arthur, Paul, and Lydia Hearn. "Toward open research: A narrative review of the challenges and opportunities for open humanities." *Journal of Communication* 71, no. 5 (2021): 827–53.

Mabalon, Dawn. *Little Manila Is in the Heart* (Duke University Press, 2013).

Mackey, Thomas P., and Trudi E. Jacobson. *Metaliteracy: Reinventing Information Literacy to Empower Learners* (Chicago, IL: ALA Neal-Schuman, 2014).

Mackey, Thomas P., and Trudi E. Jacobson. "Reframing Information Literacy as a Metaliteracy." College and Research Libraries 76, no. 1 (2011): 62-78.

Marquez, Alejandro. "When Librarianship Becomes a Dead-End Job." ACRL.org. May 23, 2023. https://acrlog.org/2023/05/23/when-librarianship-becomes-a-dead-end-job/.

Maslow, Abraham H. "A Theory of Human Motivation." *Psychological Review* 50, no. 4 (1943): 370–96. https://doi.org/10.1037/h0054346.

Matthews, Brian. "Think Like a Startup: A White Paper to Inspire Library Entrepreneurialism." Published April 4, 2012. http://chronicle.com/blognetwork/theubiquitouslibrarian/2012/04/04/think-like-a-startup-a-white-paper/.

McKinsey & Company. "Closing the digital divide in Black America." January 18, 2023. https://www.mckinsey.com/industries/public-and-social-sector/our-insights/closing-the-digital-divide-in-black-america.

McMenemy, D. "Librarians and Ethical Neutrality: Revisiting the Creed of a Librarian." *Library Review* 56, no. 3 (2007): 177–81.

Media Literacy Now. "Putting Media Literacy on the Public Policy Agenda." Accessed October 20, 2023. https://medialiteracynow.org/impact/current-policy/.

Menkart, Deborah J. "Deepening the Meaning of Heritage Months." *ascd*. April 1, 1999. https://www.ascd.org/el/articles/deepening-the-meaning-of-heritage-months.

Merriam-Webster Dictionary. "Story." Accessed May 1, 2023. https://www.merriam-webster.com/dictionary/story.

Metro Nashville Public Schools. "Limitless Libraries." Accessed May 21, 2023. https://www.mnps.org/learn/academics/library-services/limitless_libraries.

Monmouth University. "Protestors' Anger Justified Even If Actions May Not Be." June 2, 2020. https://www.monmouth.edu/polling-institute/reports/monmouthpoll_us_060220/.

Morales, M. "ALA President Unveils Enriched ALA-APA Workplace Wellness Website." *News and Press Center*. July 9, 2018. https://www.ala.org/news/press-releases/2018/07/ala-president-unveils-enriched-ala-apa-workplace-wellness-website.

Moss, Joseph. "The AAU Brings Greater Value to a U Degree." *Daily Utah Chronicle*. December 4, 2019. https://dailyutahchronicle.com/2019/12/04/association-of-american-universities/.

National Education Association (NEA). *What You Need to Know about Florida's "Don't Say Gay" Law*. June 2022. https://www.nea.org/sites/default/files/2022-06/FL%20Dont%20Say%20Gay%20KYR%20-%20Updated2022.06.pdf.

National Institutes for Health. "Your Healthiest Self: Wellness Toolkits." June 22, 2017. https://www.nih.gov/health-information/your-healthiest-self-wellness-toolkits.

National Library of Medicine. "PubMed Central." Accessed October 20, 2023. https://www.ncbi.nlm.nih.gov/pmc/.

National Public Radio: Talk of the Nation, "The Science in Science Fiction." Interview with William Gibson [Quotation is spoken around 11:50]. 1999. https://www.npr.org/2018/10/22/1067220/the-science-in-science-fiction.

New England Commission of Higher Education (NECHE). *Standards for Accreditation.* 2021. https://www.neche.org/resources/standards-for-accreditation.

New Jersey Association of School Libraries. "Home." Accessed October 21, 2023. https://njasl.org/.

New Jersey Library Association. "A132 -Information Literacy Skills for Students." Accessed October 21, 2023. https://drive.google.com/file/d/16RjjvwOI7tD-pz5lhtgWQxESRd_70cMLe/view.

———. "Home." Accessed October 21, 2023. https://www.njla.org/.

New Jersey State Library. "Home." Accessed October 21, 2023. https://www.njstatelib.org/.

New Visions for Public Schools. "Teacher 2 Librarian Second Certificate Initiative." April 25, 2023. https://advance.newvisions.org/teacher-2-librarian/.

New York City School Library System: Connect, Create, Lead. "NYC School Librarian Guidebook." Accessed October 20, 2023. https://nycdoe.libguides.com/librarianguidebook/esifc.

NISO. "Unanticipated Metadata in the Age of the Net and the Age of AI." March 2023. https://www.niso.org/niso-io/2023/03/unanticipated-metadata-age-net-age-ai.

Noble, Safiya Umoja. *Algorithms of Oppression* (New York University Press, 2018).

Northern Arizona University. "The remarkable resilience of fire-scarred coast redwood trees." Accessed October 7, 2023. https://ecoinfo.nau.edu/index.php/news/the-remarkable-resilience-of-fire-scarred-coast-redwood-trees/.

Northwest Commission on Colleges and Universities (NECCU). "NWCCU 2020 STANDARDS." 2020. https://nwccu.org/accreditation/standards-policies/standards/.

OpenAI. "Creating Safe AGI that benefits all of humanity." Accessed October 18, 2023. https://openai.com/.

———. "Introducing ChatGPT." Accessed October 18, 2023. https://openai.com/blog/chatgpt.

Ortiz, Sabrina. "What is ChatGPT and why does it matter? Here's what you need to know." ZDNet. April 18, 2023. https://www.zdnet.com/article/what-is-chatgpt-and-why-does-it-matter-heres-everything-you-need-to-know/.

Padilla, Thomas. "Collections as Data: Implications for Enclosure." *College & Research Libraries News* [Online], 79, no. 6 (June 5, 2018). https://doi.org/10.5860/crln.79.6.296.

Parkside Realty. "Bob Wislow." Accessed on April 23, 2023. https://www.parkside-realty.com/bob-wislow.

Pauker, Lance. "How the Pandemic Has Changed Talent Management." Pace University. July 11, 2022. https://www.pace.edu/news/how-pandemic-has-changed-talent-management.

Perel, Maayan, and Niva Elkin-Koren. "Accountability in Algorithmic Copyright Enforcement." *Stanford Technology Law Review* 19 (2016): 473. https://law.stanford.edu/wp-content/uploads/2016/10/Accountability-in-Algorithmic-Copyright-Enforcement.pdf.

Perrin, Andrew, and Sara Ataske. "7% of Americans don't use the internet. Who are they?" *Pew Research Center*. April 2, 2021. https://www.pewresearch.org/fact-tank/2021/04/02/7-of-americans-dont-use-the-internet-who-are-they/.

Pew Research Center. "How Americans Value Public Libraries in their Communities." 2013. https://www.pewresearch.org/internet/2013/12/11/libraries-in-communities/.

———. "The Growing Partisan Divide in Views of Higher Education." August 19, 2019. https://www.pewresearch.org/social-trends/2019/08/19/the-growing-partisan-divide-in-views-of-higher-education-2/.

Pitchford, Veronda, Felicia Kelley, Bobbi Luster, Curita Tinker, and Denise Lopez. "Welcoming Immigrants through Cultural Programming: Lessons from the Field." *Infopeople*. February 24, 2022. https://infopeople.org/content/welcoming-immigrants-through-cultural-programming-lessons-field.

Pokorná, Lenka et al. "Silver Lining of the COVID-19 Crisis for Digital Libraries in Terms of Remote Access." *Digital Library Perspectives* 36, no. 4 (2020): 389–401.

Poverty Truth Network. "The Distinctives of Our Work." Accessed October 2, 2023. https://povertytruthnetwork.org/the-network/the-distinctives-of-our-work/.

"Public Statement of Library Copyright Specialists: Fair Use & Emergency Remote Teaching & Research." March 13, 2020. https://tinyurl.com/tvnty3a.

Ranganathan, Shiyali Ramamrita. *The Five Laws of Library Science* (London: Edward Goldston, Ltd., 1931).

Rieger, Oya Y. "Collaborative Collections Development: A New IMLS-Funded Partnership." Ithaka S+R. Last modified December 19, 2022. https://sr.ithaka.org/blog/collaborative-collection-development.

Rosenzweig, Robert M. *The Political University: Policy, Politics, and Presidential Leadership in the American Research University* (Baltimore: Johns Hopkins University Press, 2001): 20.

Rotter, J. B. "Interpersonal trust, trustworthiness and gullibility." *American Psychologist* 26 (1980): 1–7.

Salvesen, Linda, and Cara Berg. "'Who Says I Am Coping': The Emotional Affect of New Jersey Academic Librarians during the COVID-19 Pandemic." *Journal of Academic Librarianship* 47, no. 5 (2021): 102422. https://doi.org/10.1016/j.acalib.2021.102422.

San Matteo degli Armeni Library. "Home." Accessed October 20, 2023. https://turismo.comune.perugia.it/poi/san-matteo-degli-armeni-library.

Schmieding, Jane. "Why Native American Heritage Month can actually be a nightmare for Native people." *Hello Giggles*. November 22, 2018. https://hellogiggles.com/native-american-heritage-month-nightmare-for-native-people/.

Scott, D., and L. Saunders "Neutrality in public libraries: How are we defining one of our core values?" *Journal of Librarianship and Information Science* 53, no. 1 (2021): 153–66. https://doi.org/10.1177/0961000620935501.

Sempervirens Fund. "Top 10 Facts That Make Redwoods Magnificent." Accessed October 7, 2023. https://sempervirens.org/learn/redwood-facts/#fact-list.

SJSU School of Information. "Health and Wellness." Accessed April 16, 2023. https://ischool.sjsu.edu/health-and-wellness.

———. "Home." Accessed October 21, 2023. https://ischool.sjsu.edu/.

———. "Library 2.023 Worldwide Virtual Conference." Accessed April 16, 2023. https://ischool.sjsu.edu/special-event/library-2023-worldwide-virtual-conference.

———. "The Emerging Future: Technology Issues and Trend MOOCs." Accessed October 21, 2023, https://ischool.sjsu.edu/post/emerging-future-technology-issues-and-trends-moocs.

SoftBank Robotics. "For better business, just add Pepper." Accessed January 31, 2024. https://us.softbankrobotics.com/pepper.

Souli, Sarah. "Does America Need a Truth and Reconciliation Commission?" *Politico*. August 16, 2020. https://www.politico.com/news/magazine/2020/08/16/does-america-need-a-truth-and-reconciliation-commission-395332.

South Pasadena Public Library. "Equity, Diversity, and Inclusion." City of South Pasadena. April 17, 2023. https://www.southpasadenaca.gov/government/departments/library/about-the-library/equity-diversity-and-inclusion.

Stamberg, Susan. "How Andrew Carnegie Turned His Fortune into a Library Legacy." NPR. August 1, 2023. https://www.npr.org/2013/08/01/207272849/how-andrew-carnegie-turned-his-fortune-into-a-library-legacy.

Stanford Encyclopedia of Philosophy. "Thomas Kuhn." Accessed Jan. 12, 2024. https://plato.stanford.edu/entries/thomas-kuhn/.

Stanford University. "The 2019 AI Index Report." Human Centered Artificial Intelligence. Accessed July 27, 2023. https://hai.stanford.edu/sites/default/files/ai_index_2019_report.pdf.

State of New Jersey. "NJ School Performance Report." Accessed October 21, 2023. https://rc.doe.state.nj.us/.

State of New Jersey Governor Phil Murphy. "Governor Murphy Signs Bipartisan Legislation Establishing First in the Nation K-12 Information Literacy Education." January 4, 2023. https://www.nj.gov/governor/news/news/562022/20230104b.shtml.

Statista Research Department. "Global production of paper and paperboard 1961–2021." *Statista*. January 25, 2023. https://www.statista.com/statistics/270314/global-paper-and-cardboard-production/.

SUNY Library Services. "EBC eBook Lending Project." Last modified May 18, 2023. https://slcny.libguides.com/sls/ebc_lending.

Sustainable Libraries Initiative. "Home." Accessed October 18, 2023. https://sustainablelibrariesinitiative.org/.

Tardi, Carla. "What Is Moore's Law and Is It Still True?" *Investopedia*. March 22, 2023. https://www.investopedia.com/terms/m/mooreslaw.asp.

Tavernise, Sabrina, and Robert Gebeloff. "Census Shows Sharply Growing Numbers of Hispanics, Asians, and Multiracial Americans." *New York Times*. August 21, 2021. https://www.nytimes.com/2021/08/12/us/us-census-population-growth-diversity.html.

TFSX. "What is Natural Foresight." (January 1, 2015), https://tfsx.com/2015/01/what-is-natural-foresight/.

The Empathetic Museum. "Maturity Model." Accessed October 2, 2023. http://empatheticmuseum.weebly.com/maturity-model.html.

The New York Times. "RUSSION SPIES ON WATCH IN NEW YORK LIBRARIES; They Follow All Who Call for Books on Anarchy. FACT COMES OUT IN COURT Secret Service Agents Never Relax Their Vigilance in Reading Hours, Says Astor Library's Chief." June 23, 1906. https://www.nytimes.com/1906/06/23/archives/russian-spies-on-watch-in-new-york-libraries-they-follow-all-who.html.

The Repair Association. "The Repair Association: Moving the repair industry forward." Accessed October 18, 2023. https://www.repair.org/.

The School for Excellence. "Home." Accessed October 21, 2023. https://www.tsfx.edu.au/.

The White House. "OSTP Issues Guidance to Make Federally Funded Research Freely Available Without Delay." August 25, 2022. https://www.whitehouse.gov/ostp/news-updates/2022/08/25/ostp-issues-guidance-to-make-federally-funded-research-freely-available-without-delay.

Thompson, Bruce. "Some Alternative Quantitative Library Activity Descriptions/Statistics That Supplement the ARL Logarithmic Index." Association of Research Libraries. October 2006. https://www.arl.org/wp-content/uploads/2006/06/bruce-thompson-oct06.pdf.

Today in Civil Liberties History. "*New York Times* Exposes FBI Library Awareness Program." September 18, 1987. http://todayinclh.com/?event=new-york-times-exposes-fbi-library-awareness-program.

Torres, Gabes. "The Burden of Asian and Pacific Islander Month Under the White Gaze." *Yes!* May 25, 2022. https://www.yesmagazine.org/opinion/2022/05/26/asian-pacific-islander-month-white-gaze.

Townsend, Tamara, and Kimberley Bugg. "Perceptions of Work–Life Balance for Urban Academic Librarians: An Exploratory Study." *Journal of Library Administration* 60, no. 5 (2020): 493–511. https://doi.org/10.1080/01930826.2020.1729624.

Tutt, Paige. "Setting Up Libraries to Be the Best Space in School." *Edutopia*. August 8, 2023. https://www.edutopia.org/article/setting-up-libraries-to-be-the-best-space-in-school/.

u capture. "How to Climb Higher Ed's Impending Demographic Cliff." March 17, 2022. https://www.capturehighered.com/how-to-climb-higher-eds-impending-demographic-cliff/.

United Nations. "Shifting demographics." Accessed October 21, 2023. https://www.un.org/en/un75/shifting-demographics#:~:text=WE%20ARE%20GETTING%20OLDER,(ages%2015%20to%2024).

University of Illinois at Urbana-Champaign School of Information Sciences. "IS 410: Introduction to Data Science." Accessed April 23, 2023. https://ischool.illinois.edu/degrees-programs/courses/is410.

University of North Carolina at Chapel Hill School of Information and Library Science. "Courses." Accessed April 23, 2023. https://sils.unc.edu/courses#558.

University of Sydney. "University of Sydney and University of Melbourne Launch Virtual Reading Room." December 14, 2022. https://www.sydney.edu.au/news-opinion/news/2022/12/14/university-of-sydney-fisher-library-launch-virtual-reading-room.html.

University of Washington Information School. "LIS 561: Database Management." Accessed April 23, 2023. https://myplan.uw.edu/course/#/courses/LIS561.

Urban Dictionary. "Booty Call." Accessed October 2, 2023.

U.S. Department of Education. "Family Educational Rights and Privacy Act (FERPA)." Accessed January 24, 2024. https://www2.ed.gov/policy/gen/guid/fpco/ferpa/index.html.

Uslaner, E. M. *The Moral Foundations of Trust*. Cambridge: Cambridge University Press, 2022.

Valenza, J. K., H. Dalal, G. Mohamad, B. Boyer, C. Berg, L. Charles, R. Bushby, M. Dempsey, J. Dalrymple, and W. Dziedzic-Elliott. "First years' information literacy backpacks: What's already packed or not packed?" *Journal of Academic Librarianship* 48, no. 4 (2022): 102566. https://www.sciencedirect.com/science/article/abs/pii/S0099133322000829?via%3Dihub.

Vespa, Jonathan, Lauren Medina, and David M. Armstrong. "Demographic Turning Points for the United States: Population Projections for 2020 to 2060." Census.gov. February 2020. https://www.census.gov/content/dam/Census/library/publications/2020/demo/p25-1144.pdf.

Virtual Academic Library Environment, ACRL New Jersey Chapter, and New Jersey Library Association. "The Value and Importance of Highly Effective School Library Programs." Accessed October 21, 2023. https://drive.google.com/file/d/0B2j6CyhsF01VY1NTY0F5bWYyVl9ESExpN3djeTBKanJVTDY0/view?resourcekey=0-cQ_Y2tPOS3MMOojTxYqffg.

Wallace-Wells, David. "Beyond Catastrophe: A New Climate Reality Is Coming into View." *New York Times* magazine. October 26, 2022. https://www.nytimes.com/interactive/2022/10/26/magazine/climate-change-warming-world.html.

White, Rachel S. "Ceilings Made of Glass and Leaving En Masse? Examining Superintendent Gender Gaps and Turnover over Time across the United States." *Educational Researcher*. 2023. https://doi.org/10.3102/0013189x231163139.

Wikipedia. "Augusta Braxton Baker." Accessed October 20, 2023. https://en.wikipedia org/wiki/Augusta_Braxton_Baker.

———. "ChatGpt." Accessed October 18, 2023. https://en.wikipedia.org/wiki/ChatGPT.

———. "DALL-E." Accessed October 18, 2023. https://en.wikipedia.org/w/index.php?title=DALL-E&oldid=1150373107.

———. "Labyrinths," accessed October 21, 2023, https://en.wikipedia.org/wiki/Labyrinths_(short_story_collection)

———. "Library Awareness Program." Accessed October 18, 2023. https://en.wikipedia.org/wiki/Library_Awareness_Program

———. "Little Manila." Accessed October 18, 2023. https://en.wikipedia.org/wiki/Little_Manila.

———. "Midjourney." Accessed October 20, 2023. https://en.wikipedia.org/w/index.php?title=Midjourney&oldid=1150344616.

———. "Nothing, Forever." Accessed January 12, 2024. https://en.wikipedia.org/wiki/Nothing,_Forever.

———. "OpenAI_Codex." Accessed October 20, 2023. https://en.wikipedia.org/w/index.php?title=OpenAI_Codex&oldid=1149385669.

———. "Proud Boys." Accessed October 18, 2023. https://en.wikipedia.org/wiki/Proud_Boys.

———. "Self-sovereign identity." Accessed October 21, 2023. https://enwikipedia.org/wiki/Self-sovereign_identity.

———. "Stable Diffusion." Accessed October 18, 2023. https://en.wikipedia.org/w/index.php?title=Stable_Diffusion&oldid=1150723699.

———. "Truth Commission," accessed October 18, 2023, https://wnwikipedia.org/wiki/Truth_commission.

———. "What Is Koomey's law." Accessed January 12, 2024. https://en.wikipedia.org/wiki/Koomey%27s_law.

———. "White Gaze." Accessed October 2, 2023. https:/en.wikipedia.org/wiki/White_gaze.

Wilder, Stanley. "Selected Demographic Trends in the ARL Professional Population." *Research Library Issues*, no. 295 (2018): 32–46.

Williamson, Charles C. et al. "Training for Library Service; a Report Prepared for the Carnegie Corporation of New York." Ann Arbor, MI: University Microfilms, 1923.

WordsRated. "State of US Public Libraries—More popular & digital than ever." February 17, 2022. https://wordsrated.com/state-of-us-public-libraries/#:~:text=More%20registered%20borrowers%20than%20ever,37.39%25%20of%20all%20collection%20use.

World Health Organization "Constitution of the World Health Organization" (1946): 1. https://apps.who.int/gb/bd/PDF/bd47/EN/constitution-en.pdf?ua=1.

———. "Infodemic." Accessed October 18, 2023. https://www.who.int/health-topics/infodemic#tab=tab_1.

———. "The Geneva Charter for Well - Being." December 21, 2021. https://www.who.int/publications/m/item/the-geneva-charter-for-well-being.

Wu, Frank. "The Crisis of American Higher Education." Organization of American Historians. Accessed October 21, 2023. https://www.oah.org/tah/february-3/the-crisis-of-american-higher-education/.

Wyoming State Library. "WYLD Network." Accessed October 20, 2023. https://library.wyo.gov/services/wyld-network/.

About the Editor

Sandra Hirsh, PhD, is associate dean for academics in the College of Professional and Global Education at San José State University and previously served ten years as professor and director of the School of Information. She has an extensive and varied background as a library and information science educator, leader, researcher, and professional—both in library and other information environments.

After getting a PhD from UCLA and a MILS from the University of Michigan, she applied her library and information science skillset to work for more than a decade leading Silicon Valley companies in user experience developing and managing web, mobile, and TV consumer products resulting in five U.S. patents/applications, as well as in research and development. She also has worked in academic, public, and special libraries and has taught previously at the University of Arizona and the University of Washington.

Hirsh's research and professional activities span the globe. Her research interests focus on information-seeking behavior, online and global learning, and the changing role of the information professional; this work has been published in peer-reviewed journals and has appeared in international conference proceedings. She explored the possibility of using blockchain technology for library applications through an IMLS-funded grant; this research was published as a book in 2019 in ALA's Library Future Series, Book 3: *Blockchain*. The third edition of her foundational library and information science textbook, *Information Services Today: An Introduction*, was published by Rowman & Littlefield in 2022.

She has held leadership and committee roles in several associations. She served as president of the Association for Library and Information Science Education (ALISE) in 2021 and president of the Association for Information Science & Technology (ASIS&T) in 2015. She also serves on committees and is a leader in the American Library Association (ALA), for example as chair of the ALA Membership, Publishing, and Education committees, as a longtime member on the advisory board for the Center for the Future of Libraries, and as an active leader in the International Relations Roundtable. She also has participated in International Federation of Library Associations and Institutions (IFLA), as a standing committee member of the Section on Education and Training and of the Continuing Professional Development & Workplace Learning. Other global activities include serving as the co-chair of the global virtual Library 2.0

conference series, which she co-founded in 2011. She was a visiting scholar at Rikkyo University in Japan in 2017 and was a Salzburg Fellow in 2013.

Hirsh has also worked in her own local community, serving for many years on the Palo Alto's Library Advisory Commission and the Palo Alto Library Bond Oversight Committee to realize the long-term vision of exciting new library facilities for the city.

She was selected as an ASIS&T Distinguished Member for 2021–2026 in the inaugural class of awardees. She also received the UCLA Library and Information Studies Distinguished Alumni Award in 2019.

About the Contributing Authors

Rebekkah Smith Aldrich, MLS, LEED AP, is executive director of the Mid-Hudson Library System (NY) and cofounder of the Sustainable Libraries Initiative. Aldrich is author of such titles as *Sustainable Thinking: Ensuring Your Library's Future in an Uncertain World* and is sustainability columnist for *Library Journal*.

Stacey A. Aldrich, MLS, is state librarian of Hawaii and has thirty years of library experience. She has been the state librarian in three states, an academic librarian, and a futurist. Always curious and learning, she believes we all should have a little futurist in us so we can create our preferred futures.

Susan W. Alman, PhD, is lecturer in the San José State University School of Information where she teaches a course, "The Emerging Future: Technology Issues and Trends." She is excited about the rapid changes in technology and their impact on society, and she is looking forward to visiting the 2035 library!

Tarida Anantachai, MSLIS, is director, inclusion and talent management at the NC State University Libraries. She previously worked in a number of public service-oriented and leadership positions and in the academic publishing industry. Anantachai's research and professional interests include: equity, diversity, and inclusion; career development and mentoring; leadership; and outreach programming.

Erin Berman, MLIS, is Equitable Libraries Division director for the Alameda County Library in California. She is a fierce privacy advocate, formerly leading the American Library Association's Privacy Subcommittee. As innovations manager for San José Public Library, Berman published the book *Your Technology Outreach Adventure: Tools for Human-Centered Problem Solving*.

Chris Brown, MLIS, MPA, is library commissioner for the Chicago Public Library (CPL), one of the world's largest library systems. In this role, he has prioritized equity and expanded access, implementing Sunday hours at every CPL location, launching the Book Sanctuary movement, appointing CPL's first equity officers, and creating new mental health liaison positions.

Anthony Chow, PhD, MS, is professor and director of San José State University's School of Information. Chow has worked for the past twenty-three years teaching and conducting research in information-seeking behavior, usability and UX in digital spaces, leadership and management, instructional design and technology integration, and informatics and analytics.

Lynn Silipigni Connaway, PhD, is executive director, research at OCLC. She has numerous journal publications, is an international speaker, and is co-author of the fourth and fifth editions of *Basic Research Methods for Librarians* and the sixth and seventh editions of *Research Methods in Library and Information Science*. For more information, visit https://www.oclc.org/research/people/connaway-lynn_silipigni.html.

Nicole A. Cooke, PhD, MEd, MLS, is Augusta Baker endowed chair and professor at the University of South Carolina. Her research and teaching interests include human information behavior, critical cultural information literacy, and equity and social justice in librarianship. She is founding editor of ALA Editions/Neal-Schuman's *Critical Cultural Information Studies* series.

K. Matthew Dames, PhD, JD, MS, serves as Edward H. Arnold Dean, Hesburgh Libraries and University of Notre Dame Press at the University of Notre Dame. Dames served as the sixty-first president of the Association of Research Libraries (2021–2022).

Ewa Dziedzic-Elliott, MLIS, MA, is subject librarian in the School of Education at The College of New Jersey. She has previous experience as a K-12 librarian. Her research interests include research skills of high school and first-year college students, diversity and equity in collection management, and barriers to information. She is executive board member for New Jersey Association of School Librarians (NJASL) and NJASL past president.

Miguel Figueroa, MA, is president and CEO of Amigos Library Services. He previously held positions with the American Library Association (Center for the Future of Libraries, Office for Diversity & Spectrum Scholarship Program, Office for Literacy and Outreach Services), the American Theological Library Association, New York University Medical Center, and Neal-Schuman Publishers.

Loida Garcia-Febo, MLS, is a Puerto Rican American international library consultant expert in library services to diverse populations and human rights. She serves as San José State University School of Information's health and wellness ambassador. Garcia-Febo was president of the American Library Association (2018–2019) and currently serves as an IFLA Governing Board member.

Jason Griffey, MSILS, is director of strategic initiatives at NISO. Griffey was previously a technology consultant for libraries, an affiliate at metaLAB and a fellow and affiliate at the Berkman Klein Center for Internet & Society at Harvard University, and an academic librarian at the University of Tennessee at Chattanooga.

Peter Hepburn, EdD, MLIS, is head librarian at the College of the Canyons in Santa Clarita, California. He previously worked at the University of Illinois at Chicago. Hepburn is serving as ALA Treasurer (2022-2025).

Alexia Hudson-Ward, MLIS, is associate director of research, learning, and strategic partnerships of the Massachusetts Institute of Technology (MIT) Libraries. She is also editor-in-chief of *Toward Inclusive Excellence*—an award-nominated blog focused on diversity-centered research. Hudson-Ward is an American Antiquarian Society member, a trustee of the Corning Museum of Glass, and a trustee at *The Conversation* U.S. edition.

Joseph Janes, PhD, MLS, is associate professor at the University of Washington Information School, teaching and researching the evolution, history, impacts, and uses of information resources and forms. Janes is creator of the podcast "Documents That Changed the World" and the author of several books, including *Documents That Changed the Way We Live,* and *Library 2020: Today's Leading Visionaries Describe Tomorrow's Library.*

Debra Kachel, MLIS, is affiliate faculty for Antioch University Seattle, with thirty-plus years as a school librarian. Kachel is active in state and national school library advocacy. She earned AASL's Distinguished Service Award in 2014. She is project director of an IMLS-funded project, SLIDE: The School Librarian Investigation—Decline or Evolution?

Jarrid P. Keller is deputy director of support services at the Sacramento Public Library responsible for collection services, facilities, IT, and safety and security. Prior to joining the Sacramento Public Library in 2015, Keller was the chief information officer and acting deputy state librarian at the California State Library.

R. David Lankes, PhD, MS, is Virginia & Charles Bowden Professor of Librarianship at The University of Texas at Austin. He is recipient of RUSA's 2021 Isadore Gilbert Mudge Award for distinguished contribution to reference librarianship. Lankes is a passionate advocate for librarians and their essential role in today's society.

Joel A. Nichols, MSLIS, MA, is chief of neighborhood libraries at the Free Library of Philadelphia in Philadelphia, Pennsylvania. Nichols is author of *Out of* *this World Library Programming: Using Speculative Fiction to Promote Reading and Launch Learning* (2017) and *iPads in the Library* (2013); he also writes fiction.

Annie Norman, EdD, MSLIS, is state librarian of Delaware. Her dissertation, *Librarians' Leadership for Lifelong Learning*, received top honors. Norman has been inducted in the Hall of Fame of Delaware Women, and she was appointed by President Biden to the National Museum and Library Services Board.

Lessa Kananiʻopua Pelayo-Lozada, MLIS, is assistant director of Glendale Library, Arts & Culture. She previously served as adult services assistant manager at the Palos Verdes Library District in California. She was the American Library Association president (2022-2023) and the Asian/Pacific American Librarians Association president (2016-2017) and executive director (2019-2022).

Veronda J. Pitchford, MLIS, is assistant director for the Califa Group, a California-based public library consortium. In this role, she supports national grant projects and manages Infopeople. She serves on the American Library Association Business Advisory group, the Public Library Association Board, and the Center for the Future of Libraries Advisory Group. She is a die-hard library chick.

Raymond Pun, EdD, MLIS, MA, is academic and research librarian at the Alder Graduate School of Education. Pun previously worked at Stanford University, Fresno State, New York University Shanghai, and The New York Public Library. He is a past president of the Asian Pacific American Librarians Association (APALA) and past president of the Chinese American Librarians Association (CALA).

Joyce Kasman Valenza, PhD, MLIS, is associate teaching professor and coordinator of the school librarianship and LIS concentrations in the School of Communication & Information at Rutgers University. In this role, she prepares future librarians to lead cultures of literacy and engage communities. Previously, she enjoyed forty years of practice as a school, public and special librarian.

Kelvin Watson, MLS, MBA, is executive director of the Las Vegas–Clark County Library District, the largest library system in Nevada (25 branches, 650 employees, and spanning 8,000 square miles of Clark County). Under Watson's leadership, the Library District has won two consecutive Library of the Future Awards from ALA (2022 and 2023).

Patty Wong, MLS, is city librarian for Santa Clara City Library. She enjoys work in managing change, equity and diversity, youth development, collaborations between public libraries and community agencies, and fund-raising. Wong is past president of ALA. As a part-time faculty for San José State University School of Information, she teaches how to serve young people and write grants.

Tony Zanders, BA, is founder and chief executive officer of Skilltype, an American talent management and data company that enhances the performance of libraries and their workforce. Zanders served as Entrepreneur in Residence as part of the executive team, with coauthor Dames, at Boston University Libraries. Zanders previously served as a vice president at Ex Libris Group and EBSCO.

www.ingramcontent.com/pod-product-compliance
Lightning Source LLC
Chambersburg PA
CBHW021840220426
43663CB00005B/331